into the PROMISE

A JOURNEY THROUGH JOSHUA

DONNA GAINES

JEAN STOCKDALE

DAYNA STREET

ANGIE WILSON

ABBEY DANE

Into the Promise: A Journey Through Joshua

©2024 Bellevue Baptist Church

Cover and book design: Amanda Weaver

Photography: Jim Barnwell

Map design: Paige Warren

Editing: Dayna Street, Donita Barnwell, Melissa Bobo Hardee, Lauren Gooden, Paige Warren, Vera Sidhom, Caroline Segars

CONTENTS

HOW TO USE THIS STUDY

Welcome to *Into the Promise: A Journey Through Joshua*!

As the book of Joshua opens, centuries have passed since God promised to give Abraham and his family the land of Canaan. Now the time is finally here! At God's command and under Joshua's leadership, the nation of Israel stands ready to take possession of their promised inheritance. As they step into the land, they will face overwhelming odds. But God will miraculously move on behalf of His people: parting waters, demolishing fortified walls, bringing down giants, and making the sun stand still. This is an action-packed story of battle, faith, and victory.

Yet, it is so much more. Joshua is not just an ancient tale about the history of Israel; it is a story that echoes through the corridors of time, resonating with every believer who faces battles daily. It is a call for God's people today to rise up in faith and move forward with strength and courage, armed with the promises of God, believing He will fight for us. And we will win because He has already won!

This Bible study is designed to provide an opportunity for personal study throughout the week, leading up to small group discussion and large group teaching time once a week. Each weekly lesson is divided into five daily homework assignments centered on comprehending the text as well as personal application. We cannot do what we do not know. Throughout our study, we will keep four goals in mind:

Observation: What does the text say? (Who? What? Where? When? Why? How?)

Interpretation: What does the text mean?

Application: How should this change me?

Transformation: The goal! Did it change me?

On our journey through Joshua, we will see that war precedes possession. Joshua and the Israelites have to fight for the land before they can possess the land. The same is true for us. We have to know how to do war with the enemy so that we can possess all that the Lord has for us. Each week we are going to learn and apply a new spiritual warfare principle that will help us in the battle.

Friend, God's promises are as true today as they were for Joshua and the Israelites. In this ten-week study, you will be encouraged and strengthened as you learn to depend on God Who fights for you and leads the way to your victory – *Into the Promise*.

INTRODUCTION

Into the Promise

I wonder what kind of tale we've fallen into? [1]
~ J.R.R. Tolkien

When Frodo and Sam set out from the Shire, they are just two little hobbits, out to save the world, with absolutely no idea what lies ahead. By the time they reach the shadow of Mordor, their journey has been filled with more wonders, and replete with more dangers, than they could have ever conceived:

- The heroic battle on Weathertop where Frodo is wounded.
- Their flight to the ford where the Black Riders chasing after them are swallowed up and drowned by a sudden deluge of water.
- The splendor of Rivendell in the foothills of the Misty Mountains where they take refuge while Frodo recovers. The place where the Fellowship of the Ring is formed.
- The dark mines of Moria, where they are forced to go on without their beloved leader, Gandalf, after he falls into the abyss.

By the time Frodo and Sam reach Mordor, the Fellowship has fallen apart, their friends are far away on a different journey, and the two hobbits realize they are alone in their quest to destroy the Ring. It's at this point that Samwise Gamgee (Sam), Frodo's loyal gardener from the Shire, asks, "I wonder what kind of tale we've fallen into?" [2]

What a fitting question from the little hobbit! Sam's query of the unknown foreshadows the gravity of the mission ahead. Ultimately, their pilgrimage will lead them into a place of promise: a world freed from the shadow of Sauron and the Ring, where the forces of good can thrive once again. But first, the journey ahead will be marked by adventure, danger, sacrifice, battles, uncertainty, redemption, and hope – much like the biblical journey of the Israelites into the Promised Land.

The Israelites' Journey

You can never separate theology from geography. [3]
~ Eugene Peterson

Over and over, across the pages of the Old Testament, we find God's people connected to a place through their relationship to the Promised Land. The initial journey of the Hebrews into the land of promise is tied to three geographical locations: Egypt, the Wilderness, and Canaan.

Egypt: Their Deliverance

The Israelites' pilgrimage begins in Egypt. After 400 years of generational slavery under Pharaoh, God responds to the Israelites' cry for deliverance and raises up Moses to lead them out of bondage. **The promise of a land originally given to Abraham is about to be fulfilled**, as God's people receive the rescue they want in an indisputably supernatural fashion.

First, God sends ten plagues to break the resistance of Pharaoh. Then, He guides them by day in a pillar of cloud, and by night, in a pillar of fire. And if that isn't enough to convince the Hebrews of the faithfulness of God: He rips the Red Sea in two for them to escape, and then utterly wipes out the Egyptian army, who is giving them chase, when the sea crashes down on them.

After that, the Israelites are so overwhelmed by God's unfailing commitment to them that they march right into the Promised Land and live happily ever after. The End...Hang on! That's not what happens, is it? Nope!

The Israelites' journey out of Egypt begins as the ultimate, epic road trip – miracles galore, fresh food from Heaven, and shouts of joy, "I will sing to the Lord, for He is highly exalted" (Exodus 15:1). But then, there is a pit stop and a plot twist.

When the Israelites reach the Desert of Sinai, they camp out in front of the mountain. This is like pulling into a rest area that has an incredible view, but they aren't there for the scenery. They are there for Moses to meet with God and receive a new set of rules for the road, The Ten Commandments.

And then comes the plot twist. While Moses is up on Mount Sinai getting instructions from God, the Israelites grow impatient. Instead of trusting the plan, they pressure Aaron to create a golden calf and begin worshipping it. It's a trap the enemy sets, and like vacationers drawn to a gimmicky tourist attraction, they fall for his ploy hook, line, and sinker. When Moses comes down and sees the mess, he can hardly believe his eyes. In anger, he throws down the tablets and breaks them. Talk about hitting a deep valley following a mountaintop experience!

Scholars believe the trip from Egypt to Mount Sinai took the Israelites around two months. [4] God has delivered them from centuries of slavery in Egypt, but it only takes them 60 days to forget all that He has done for them and turn to idolatry and disobedience. Their act of rebellion has severe consequences: Moses melts the calf, grinds up the gold, throws it into the water, and makes the people drink it. Then, he calls up the Levites and commands them to go throughout the camp killing people. Three thousand men die as a result of their sin. After Moses intercedes with God on behalf of the people, their journey resumes, and things are back on track for awhile.

But then, there is more trouble in the camp, as the people begin to murmur and complain. They are sick of manna. They want meat! So, God sends them what they ask for, quail to satisfy their cravings, and along with it, a plague. Lots more funerals after this incident.

Just when you might think the Hebrews would have learned their lesson, things actually take a turn for the worse. As they finally arrive at the edge of the Promised Land, God tells Moses to send in 12 spies to scout the land. Ten of them come back with a mission impossible report:

> "We scouted out the land from one end to the other – it's a land that swallows people whole. Everybody we saw was huge. Why, we even saw the Nephilim giants (the Anak giants come from the Nephilim). Alongside them we felt like grasshoppers. And they looked down on us as if we were grasshoppers" (Numbers 13:32b-33, MSG).

Although Joshua and Caleb give a believing testimony, the people trust the majority report. This time, their rebellion and unbelief earn them a reroute from God – a 40-year detour through the wilderness. (Imagine Siri saying, "Recalculating, recalculating, recalculating" for 40 long years!)

The Wilderness: Their Detour and Delay

A direct route from Egypt to Canaan would have only taken them about 11 days, but God's judgment on the Israelites for their lack of faith and obedience nets them a generational delay:

> "You will not enter and occupy the land I swore to give you. The only exceptions will be Caleb son of Jephunneh and Joshua son of Nun. You said your children would be carried off as plunder. Well, I will bring them safely into the land, and they will enjoy what you have despised. But as for you, you will drop dead in this wilderness" (Numbers 14:30-32).

In essence, God puts the entire nation of Israel in time-out for 40 years – one year for every day the spies spent scouting out Canaan – while they wait for all those over the age of 20 to draw their final breaths. For 14,600 days, they eat the same food. (They only thought they were sick of manna after that first few months!) Throughout their extended detour, they walk around in circles, day after day, month after month, year after year. Same dirt, same rocks, same trees. Same old, same old, everything. Every day is monotonous and tedious. And then they get up the next day and do it all over again. The wilderness is like that never-ending stretch of flat highway with no rest stops, no landmarks, and kids whining, "Are we there yet?" for 40 long years. And to be fair, the adults also do their fair share of whining along the way!

How is it that the Israelites have plummeted to this point? It certainly isn't due to a lack of miracles. They have seen the power of God on display in high definition. And yet, they still don't believe. They can't seem to shake off the deep-rooted thoughts, habits, fears, and desires that have been shaped by centuries of bondage. In the wilderness, they repeatedly look back and long for the life they had back in Egypt. Physically, they have been set free. But spiritually, they are still slaves at heart. They are out of Egypt, but Egypt is not out of them. Egypt is not merely a place that has been left behind, it is a mindset that must be evicted from deep inside.

God will use the wilderness experience to break the Israelites free from the mental and spiritual chains that remained long after their physical liberation from Egypt. Along the way, He will teach them obedience and implant a deeper reliance on Him. Although the detour is long and difficult, it is not wasted. Each step they take has divine purpose as a new generation is prepared to enter the land of promise with faith and courage.

The Promised Land: Their Destination

As the book of Joshua opens, the longest and most challenging road trip imaginable is finally over. As Israel once again stands at the threshold of the Promised Land, their destination is in sight. This time, things will be different. This time, they will claim their inheritance.

Will it be easy? No. The land, rich in promise, will require effort and persistence as they navigate unfamiliar terrain and build new lives from the ground up.

Will there be difficult days? Yes. Israel will find out that their journey does not end with arrival. There will be battles to fight, enemies to conquer, and land to take. And not every day will end in success.

But, will the destination be worth the journey? A million times over...YES!

Our Spiritual Journey

As believers, Israel's journey mirrors our own spiritual quest. We too have traveled the itinerary from Egypt to the wilderness on our way to the land of promise.

Egypt: Our Deliverance

Egypt represents the type of life we lived before our salvation. Those days when we were in bondage to sin and separated from God. Our life before we experienced our very own Exodus, when we met our Deliverer, Jesus. Any time we lean into the flesh (money, power, clothes, position) for satisfaction and fulfillment, we are stepping back across the border into Egypt. And that can happen to any believer at any time. In Christ, we have been set free from our old life and offered a brand new life of promise, a life free from the control of sin and death, a life filled with abundance and purpose. It is the life of a heart set free!

The Wilderness: Our Detour and Delay

During the Israelites' time in the wilderness, progress was slow, and victories were scarce. And that is not unlike the delays in spiritual formation that can occur after we come to Christ. In the wilderness:

- The Israelites were saved, but not strong in their belief.
- They were redeemed, but not released from the bondage of their past.

Sadly, the wilderness describes the lives of many believers: Stuck. Bored. Enslaved. Defeated. Discouraged. Existing, but not flourishing. And that is right where the enemy would like to keep every one of us: Languishing on a detour route between Egypt and the Promised Land.

But just imagine what would happen if every believer on this planet, all 2.4 billion of us, said "no more" to the wilderness life? [5] **If every believer took possession of their inheritance in Christ and began to live the Promised Land life, the very atmosphere of the world would change.** Peace, love, and joy would fill the air. Marriages would be saved and enriched. Relationships would be restored. Wars would be prevented.

Poverty would be eradicated. We would need less orphanages and fewer jail cells. Life would be full of promise!

The Promised Land: Our Destination

For Christ followers, the Promised Land is not a physical destination, but it can become our spiritual reality. The Promised Land is the Promised Life that Christ offers to all. It is a life in which:

- "We are more than conquerors through [Christ] who loved us" (Romans 8:37, NKJV).
- "We do not lose heart" and "our inner man is being renewed day by day" (2 Corinthians 4:16).
- We are "anxious for nothing" (Philippians 4:6).
- "We can rejoice...when we run into problems and trials" (Romans 5:3, NLT).
- We have "everything pertaining to life and godliness, through the true knowledge of Him who called us by His own glory and excellence" (2 Peter 1:3).
- "[Christ's] love has the first and last word in everything we do" (2 Corinthians 5:14, MSG).

Sounds like a great way to live, doesn't it? All of this and more – life abundant (John 10:10) – can be yours right now. God invites you to live every day in Canaan. There is only one caveat: You must turn your back on the wilderness before you can cross over into the land of promise. **The deed to the Promised Life has been signed. You just need to possess what is already yours.**

As Israel crosses over into the Promised Land, they will go from manna to feasts, from desert land to green pastures, from a slavery mindset to unabashed freedom, from delay to action, from defeat to victory, and from scarcity to abundance, as they possess their inheritance:

> So the Lord gave to Israel all the land He had sworn to give their ancestors, and they took possession of it and settled there. And the Lord gave them rest on every side, just as He had solemnly promised their ancestors. None of their enemies could stand against them, for the Lord helped them conquer all their enemies. Not a single one of all the good promises the Lord had given to the family of Israel was left unfulfilled; everything He had spoken came true (Joshua 21:43-45, NLT).

This is life as God intends you to live as well. Take a moment, right now, to make this promise your own by writing your name in the blanks:

> So the Lord gave to _____ all the land He had sworn to give...and _____ took possession of it and settled there. And the Lord gave _____ rest on every side, just as He had solemnly promised....None of _____'s enemies could stand against [her], for the Lord helped _____ conquer all [her] enemies. Not a single one of all the good promises the Lord had given to _____ was left unfulfilled; everything He had spoken came true.

This is life on the other side of the Jordan: your Promised Land life. To be sure, there will be some battles along the way. The enemy will not give up without a fight. But expect forward progress. **In the Promised Land, God's promises outnumber problems; victory and abundance become a way of life.** Along the way, you may find that you "wonder what kind of tale [you've] fallen into." And the answer is: You have stepped *Into the Promise*.

I came that they may have life, and have it abundantly.
~ Jesus (John 10:10)

Are you ready for a change of address? Don't delay! March on in!

A Journey Through Joshua

Not a single one of all the good promises the Lord had given to the family
of Israel was left unfulfilled; everything He had spoken came true.
Joshua 21:45, NLT

As the book of Joshua opens, the Israelites are poised on the plains of Moab, east of the Jordan River, on the verge of claiming the promise God had made to Abraham centuries before: "I will give to you and to your descendants after you, the land of your sojournings, all the land of Canaan, for an everlasting possession; and I will be their God" (Genesis 17:8).

For Israel, this is the end of one era and the beginning of another. The previous four books of the Bible have been dominated by one towering human character, Moses. For 40 years, he has been the mediator for Israel, the one that God has spoken to "face to face, just as a man speaks to his friend" (Exodus 33:11). But now, Moses, Israel's beloved leader has died, and Joshua has assumed the leadership role of the nation.

Generations of Israelites have awaited this very moment. This is the reason God brought them out of 400 years of slavery in Egypt. This is what they have anticipated for 40 years as they wandered in the wilderness. God is about to fulfill His repeated promise to make Israel a great nation and give them a land of their own: The Promised Land.

The book of Joshua follows the Pentateuch, the first five books of the Bible. God's story has been moving in this direction since Genesis 12: "In the book of Genesis, Israel was born. In the book of Exodus, Israel was chosen. In the book of Numbers, the nation was proven. In the book of Leviticus, it was brought nigh by the blood. In Deuteronomy, it was instructed." [1]

In a sense, Joshua is part two of the story that began in the Pentateuch. In part one, God delivered Israel from slavery in Egypt and promised them a land. Now, after a 40 year delay due to their disobedience, the time has come for Israel to step *into the promise* and possess all that God has for them there.

The Author

Since the Bible does not name the writer of the book of Joshua, the author remains anonymous. Several scholars believe the most likely candidate for the authorship of most of the book is Joshua, the key eyewitness to the events documented. Joshua 24:26 refers to Joshua writing a portion of the book himself: "And Joshua wrote these words in the book of the law of God; and he took a large stone and set it up there under the oak that was by the sanctuary of the Lord." Some suggest that perhaps the high priest, Eleazar ,or his son, Phinehas, finished the book by adding some additional details and attaching the comments about Joshua's death (Joshua 24:29-33). Others propose that the book may have been written by a scribe who knew Joshua and had a front-row seat to his feats. Another possibility is that Samuel or another unknown historian may be the author.

Regardless of authorship, the book of Joshua is a true record of the events that take place after Israel's exodus and wilderness wanderings.

Date and Setting

Joshua is the first of the historical books in the Bible. These 12 books (Joshua through Esther) narrate the events of Israel's history, from the time of the nations' entry into the Promised Land until the time of the return from exile some 1,000 years later.

Detailing the Conquest Era, the book of Joshua begins right after the death of Moses and spans a short period of time, less than 30 years.

1446 B.C.	1406-1400 B.C.	1375 B.C.
Exodus from Egypt	Conquest of Canaan	Joshua Dies

When we allow for the 20 year gap between Chapters 22 and 23, the actual history recorded is around 7 years. Albert McShane observes:

> It would be difficult to find anywhere in history an account of so much accomplished in so short a time. For two or three million people to invade a fortified land, where the cities were surrounded by massive walls, defended by giants as well as ordinary soldiers; to conquer it, and to establish themselves in it, was an achievement second to none. [2]

In ancient world history, this period falls into the Late Bronze Age (1550-1200 B.C.). During this time, Egypt is still the dominant power broker in the Middle East. The Pharaohs are much like puppet masters, controlling the kings of the city-states in Canaan, making them subservient to their demands.

The book of Joshua contains several literary genres that are consistent with other Middle Eastern records of the Late Bronze Age: annals of military campaigns, vassal treaties, boundary descriptions, and land grants. [3]

Key Words

In the Bible, a key word (or phrase) is essential to the text and is usually repeated by the writer to convey his message to the reader. Some of the key words in Joshua are:

God	Achan	ark of the Lord (ark
Lord	Caleb	of the covenant)
Joshua	Israel	captured
Rahab	altar	circumcised

(circumcise, circumcising)	courageous	land
command (commanded)	fear	possess (possessed, possession)
commandment	fight (fought)	promised
covenant	firm	serve (served)
	heard	under the ban
	inheritance	

Themes

The book of Joshua is written to the descendants of those who conquered the Promised Land, as a historical record of how they came to settle there. It is the connecting narrative between the time of Moses and the period of the Judges, when the book was initially circulated.

Francis Schaeffer comments on the significance of Joshua:

> Joshua is an important book for many reasons – for the history it records and for its internal teaching. But what makes the book of Joshua overwhelmingly important is that it stands as a bridge, a link between the Pentateuch (the writings of Moses) and the rest of Scripture. It is crucial for understanding the unity the Pentateuch has with all that follows it, including the New Testament. [4]

Several themes run throughout the book of Joshua:

God's faithfulness

God's presence

God's sovereignty

The blessing of obedience and the consequences of disobedience

Holiness and separation

The significance of leadership

The role of God's people

The land as an inheritance

Victory comes through faith

The importance of choosing well

The typology of Christ in Joshua

The summary message of the book of Joshua is one of faith, obedience, and the faithfulness of God to fulfill His promises. Tracing the Israelites' conquest and settlement of the Promised Land, this sixth book of the Old Testament emphasizes that victory and success come through trusting in God, following His commands, and remaining faithful to His covenant. It concludes with the need to choose to serve God wholeheartedly.

Zooming Out

The unifying theme of Scripture, from Genesis to Revelation, is the glory of God through the advancement and expansion of His Kingdom.

The book of Joshua serves as a critical link in the broader narrative as it bridges the gap between the Exodus and the establishment of Israel as a nation in the Promised Land. In its pages, we will see God's redemptive plan marching forward toward the ultimate fulfillment of the all-encompassing promises of life in Christ.

Zooming In

As 21st century believers, the overarching lesson of Joshua is three-fold:

- **God is faithful to keep His promises.** God is a steadfast and unwavering promise keeper. As Joshua 21:45 proclaims, "Not a single one of all the good promises the Lord had given to the family of Israel was left unfulfilled; everything He had spoken came true" (NLT). The New Testament reaffirms this truth, "For all of God's promises have been fulfilled in Christ with a resounding 'Yes!' And through Christ, our 'Amen' (which means 'Yes') ascends to God for His glory" (2 Corinthians 1:20, NLT). In Jesus, God's Word is proven true. We can hold on to the assurance that God's promises are not dependent on our circumstances, but on His unchanging nature. God's promises bring hope, comfort, strength, and security, reminding us that no matter what we face, He is always faithful to fulfill His purposes in our lives.

- **Obedience is the prerequisite to victory.** In the book of Joshua, we will see that victory comes to faithful people who trust and obey God. This model of faith is lived out through the person of Joshua as he leads Israel. The Israelites (with just a few exceptions) follow his example and obey the orders they receive to take, occupy, and dwell in the land. Warren Wiersbe makes the application for us, "God's commandments are still God's enablements for those who obey Him by faith." [5] Obedience to God aligns our will with His purpose, enabling us to rise above circumstances and experience victory – not just in external success, but in internal transformation. By obeying God, we position ourselves to receive His blessings, protection, and favor, yielding a life that reflects His glory and a heart secure in His promises.

- **God's abiding presence is the foundation of life and the ultimate Source of strength, peace, and purpose.** Joshua's ability to lead the Israelites into the Promised Land is directly tied to the empowering presence of God. His words to Joshua are clear, "Just as I have been with Moses, I will be with you; I will not fail you or forsake you. Be strong and courageous, for you shall give this people possession of the land which I swore to their fathers to give them" (Joshua 1:5b-6). The same is true for us. On Jesus' last day on earth, right before He ascended to Heaven, He promised, "And lo, I am with you always, even to the end of the age" (Matthew 28:20). His presence is a transformative force that silences fear, lifts burdens, and makes hearts whole. In Him, we are fully known, unconditionally loved, and enabled to fulfill the calling He has placed on our lives.

A Journey Through Joshua

Throughout our study, we will discover that the book of Joshua tells:

> **The story of a man:** Joshua.

> **The story of a people:** the Israelites.

The story of us. **The Old Testament picture of the Promised Land is the New Testament equivalent of the Promised Life we have in Christ.** In this study, we will be challenged to wholeheartedly obey God and possess the life God has for us, the Spirit-filled life that Jesus promises to all who believe.

The story of God. Above all else, Joshua is His Story. He is the Commander in chief and ultimate hero on every page. He is revealed as the Faithful One Who makes and keeps His promises, and the Sovereign Lord Who rules over all creation, fulfilling His redemptive purposes.

LESSON ONE

Be strong and courageous

JOSHUA 1

God's Charge to Joshua

[1] Now it came about after the death of Moses the servant of the Lord, that the Lord spoke to Joshua the son of Nun, Moses' servant, saying, [2] "Moses My servant is dead; now therefore arise, cross this Jordan, you and all this people, to the land which I am giving to them, to the sons of Israel. [3] Every place on which the sole of your foot treads, I have given it to you, just as I spoke to Moses. [4] From the wilderness and this Lebanon, even as far as the great river, the river Euphrates, all the land of the Hittites, and as far as the Great Sea toward the setting of the sun will be your territory. [5] No man will be able to stand before you all the days of your life. Just as I have been with Moses, I will be with you; I will not fail you or forsake you. [6] Be strong and courageous, for you shall give this people possession of the land which I swore to their fathers to give them. [7] Only be strong and very courageous; be careful to do according to all the law which Moses My servant commanded you; do not turn from it to the right or to the left, so that you may have success wherever you go. [8] This book of the law shall not depart from your mouth, but you shall meditate on it day and night, so that you may be careful to do according to all that is written in it; for then you will make your way prosperous, and then you will have success. [9] Have I not commanded you? **Be strong and courageous!** Do not tremble or be dismayed, for the Lord your God is with you wherever you go."

Joshua Assumes Command

[10] Then Joshua commanded the officers of the people, saying, [11] "Pass through the midst of the camp and command the people, saying, 'Prepare provisions for yourselves, for within three days you are to cross this Jordan, to go in to possess the land which the Lord your God is giving you, to possess it.'" [12] To the Reubenites and to the Gadites and to the half-tribe of Manasseh, Joshua said, [13] "Remember the word which Moses the servant of the Lord commanded you, saying, 'The Lord your God gives you rest and will give you this land.' [14] Your wives, your little ones, and your cattle shall remain in the land which Moses gave you beyond the Jordan, but you shall cross before your brothers in battle array, all your valiant warriors, and shall help them, [15] until the Lord gives your brothers rest, as He gives you, and they also possess the land which the Lord your God is giving them. Then you shall return

to your own land, and possess that which Moses the servant of the Lord gave you beyond the Jordan toward the sunrise." [16] They answered Joshua, saying, "All that you have commanded us we will do, and wherever you send us we will go. [17] Just as we obeyed Moses in all things, so we will obey you; only may the Lord your God be with you as He was with Moses. [18] Anyone who rebels against your command and does not obey your words in all that you command him, shall be put to death; only be strong and courageous."

Be strong and courageous

I am no longer anxious about anything, as I realize that He is able to carry out His will for me. It does not matter where He places me, or how. That is for Him to consider, not me, for in the easiest positions He will give me grace, and in the most difficult ones, His grace is sufficient. [1]

~ Hudson Taylor

Every four years, the Olympic Games become the focus of media headlines, conversations at work, and television viewing. Everyone wants to see their country take home a gold medal. For the athletes competing, those weeks are the culmination of years of hard work and sacrifice.

Imagine the pressure of the moment for each athlete as they prepare to compete in stadiums full of cheering, flag-waving fans. That was the atmosphere at the 2004 Summer Olympics in Athens, Greece, when four of the fastest women in the world ran for the United States in 4x100 meter relay race. Everyone expected the USA to win the gold. They easily won the semi-finals. In the finals, the team quickly moved into the lead, and it appeared they were on the way to victory. But then, disaster struck. As Marion Jones approached Lauryn Williams for the baton handoff, they missed the pass, ruining the chance for the team to win a medal.

In Joshua 1, we will see what is perhaps the most important baton pass in the Bible: the transition of leadership from Moses to Joshua. For the first time since Exodus 1, Moses is not the leader of the Israelites. It will take someone strong to lead the rebellious and headstrong Israelites into the Promised Land. Someone with vision. Someone with courage. Someone faithful. Someone humble. Someone flawed, who will sometimes fail. Someone who seeks after God. Someone who will not bungle the baton pass. Someone like Joshua.

DAY ONE
Joshua 1:1-2

As you begin your study this week, read Joshua 1:1-18. Pay close attention to the details. Read these verses like you are reading them for the first time, like you don't know the rest of the story. Put yourself in Joshua's place. Imagine what this moment is like for him. Then, read the verses again from the perspective of the Israelites gathered on the banks of the Jordan. Think about what they must be feeling. Ask the Lord to open your heart to what He is saying through this passage, and to prepare your heart for how He wants to speak to you personally through His Word.

Let's create a brief snapshot of the chapter. Answering the following questions will provide you a general overview of Joshua 1.

Snapshot
of Joshua 1

Who are the main characters in Joshua 1?

What significant events take place in this chapter?

What does this passage say about the land that is promised?

Repetition clues us in to what the author is emphasizing. What are some of the recurring words, phrases, and ideas in Joshua 1?

Even though the book of Joshua is not primarily about the man Joshua, it is helpful to know some of his backstory up to this point.

Joshua was from the tribe of Ephraim. The firstborn son of Nun (Numbers 13:8), he was born into slavery in Egypt. His original name was Hoshea, which means "salvation." On the night of the Passover, Joshua was saved when the blood was applied to the house of Nun (Exodus 12:7, 13). Later, Moses changed his assistant's name from Hoshea to Joshua, from "salvation" to "The Lord is salvation" (Numbers 13:16), signifying that God alone brings salvation. Growing up in Egypt, Joshua saw firsthand the signs and wonders that God performed (Exodus 7-12). He was there when God opened up the Red Sea and then closed it back up, drowning the Egyptian army that was in pursuit (Exodus 14-15). Because he experienced the power of God in his younger years, Joshua had faith to believe that what God promised, He would perform.

> **Did you know?** The name Joshua is the Hebrew equivalent of Jesus. Joshua is an Old Testament type of Christ, someone who foreshadows Jesus. Joshua points to the saving work of Christ that not only redeems us, but also provides us with the power we need to enter into the promised life that is ours in Him.

Joshua's preparation to assume the mantle of leadership from Moses is a long and intentional road that takes about forty years. God will not simply clone Moses. Joshua's mission is going to be different from his predecessor and will require a different preparation.

God's Preparation of Joshua

- **He was a soldier.** Joshua first appears in the Bible as an army general with exceptional military and leadership skills. About two months after the Israelites' exodus from Egypt, he courageously fought against the Amalekites at Rephidim and led Israel to victory (Exodus 17:8-13).

- **He was an assistant to Moses.** Joshua accompanied Moses to Mount Sinai when he received the Ten Commandments. He was right beside Moses when he judged the people for making the golden calf (Exodus 32:17). Wiersbe observes, "It wasn't enough that Joshua be a good warrior; he also had to know the God of Israel and the holy laws God gave His people to obey." [2]

- **He was devoted to God.** After the whole golden calf incident and God's subsequent judgment, Moses moved the tent of meeting, the temporary tabernacle, outside of the camp. There, apart from the people, Moses sought after God. Whenever he entered the holy place, the cloudy pillar of God's presence would descend upon the entrance (Exodus 33:9-10). After Moses would meet with God, he would return to the camp, but not Joshua. The young man made the tabernacle his home (Exodus 33:11). His intentional decision to identify with God rather than his rebellious countrymen would set him apart and prepare him for what was to come.

- **He was selected to spy out the land.** Joshua was one of the 12 spies sent by Moses to scout out the land of Canaan (Numbers 13). Along with Caleb, he returned with a positive report, encouraging the Israelites to trust in God's promise and enter the land. Joshua's faith (along with Caleb's) stood in stark contrast to the other ten spies who failed to believe God's promise and gave a discouraging report.

- **He was chosen to succeed Moses.** Near the end of Moses' life, God appointed Joshua as his successor (Deuteronomy 31:14-23). This transition was marked by ceremony in which the high priest anointed him, and Moses laid hands upon him, symbolizing the transfer of leadership (Numbers 27:22-23).

1. Read Deuteronomy 34:9. After Moses laid hands upon Joshua, what happened to him?

2. What are some ways Joshua's early life prepared him to lead God's people into the Promised Land?

With Joshua, God has found a man who is surrendered to Him. Phillip Keller writes, "Because there are so few of us totally available to God's purposes...seldom does His Spirit indwell a man or woman in such stupendous measure to become a formidable force in the world."[3] Joshua is Spirit-filled, single-minded, and submitted to God. We will learn from him. We will also learn much as we follow the Israelites *into the promise.*

Read Joshua 1:1-2 once again.

3. What event opens the book of Joshua? (v. 1)

Imagine the shockwaves the news of Moses' death sends throughout the nation of Israel. Moses, their leader for 40 years, is dead. The man who had been their liberator, lawgiver, and mediator is gone. The grief felt across the camp is palpable. The uncertainty about the future is intense. What will happen now? The bigger question they face is: Can we trust a God we cannot see after our leader is gone?

The truth is: No leader will lead forever. Warren Wiersbe writes, "There comes a time in every ministry when God calls for a new beginning with a new generation and new leadership."[4] A ministry built upon God will stand; a ministry built upon a man is sure to crumble. As J. Oswald Sanders notes, "A work originated by God and conducted on spiritual principles will surmount the shock of a change of leadership and indeed will probably thrive better as a result."[5]

God's people need a new leader. To the Israelites' credit, although they mourn the death of their revered leader for 30 days (Deuteronomy 34:8), they do not memorialize him. Moses is not forgotten; however, Moses is not the focus. God's purpose does not change because leadership changes. What matters is not the servant, but the Lord. Jesus makes this clear in John 13:16, "Very truly I tell you, no servant is greater than his master, nor is a messenger greater than the one who sent him" (NIV). **God's purpose is never dependent upon men, but God's men are always dependent upon God's purpose.**

4. What term is used to describe Moses in verse 1?

In the terminology of the ancient Near East, a king's servant was a trusted, honored envoy. [6] This person was someone the king could count on to carry out his will. From a biblical perspective, the servant of the Lord fulfills God's will and is often someone chosen by God for a leadership position to accomplish a specific divine work.

5. What term is used to describe Joshua in verse 1?

As the book of Joshua opens, the job title on Joshua's resumé is "Moses' servant." His position up to this point has been as a faithful subordinate to Moses. However, over the next two decades, Joshua will earn a new title.

6. Turn over to Joshua 24:29. At the time of his death, what is Joshua called?

Throughout our study we will see this progression in Joshua's life. Joshua will not confine himself to his own comfort level. With every step of faith he will take, the foundation will be laid for the greater things God wants to do through him.

7. Who is speaking in Joshua 1:2?

8. What word follows God's announcement of the death of Moses? (v. 2)

The book of Joshua is connected to the book which comes before it by the word, "Now." In a very real sense, it is the continuation of the story at the close of Deuteronomy. The report of the death and burial of Moses recorded in Deuteronomy 34 is not a breaking news moment for Joshua, but it is information that is echoed in his ears by God. "Now" is a word of urgency. Robert Smith gives us helpful commentary:

> The children of Israel had spent four hundred years in bondage in Egypt followed by forty years of wilderness wandering and thirty days of mourning the death of Moses...*Now* is the appropriate word. *Now* is the time. Too much time has been wasted. In the spirit of the Latin concept, *carpe diem* – "seize the day" – the children of Israel needed to go beyond Canaan's edge and cross over into the Promised Land. [7]

What "now" are you facing today? Will you step out in courage and seize it?

9. Label God's instructions to Joshua in verse 2 in the order He gives them. (Label them 1-4.)

_____ Cross the Jordan.

_____ Arise.

_____ Take all the people with you.

_____ Go into the land I am giving the children of Israel.

Did you know? The original languages of the Old and New Testaments (Hebrew and Aramaic in the Old Testament and Greek in the New Testament) did not contain punctuation marks. There were no periods, commas, semi-colons, or question marks separating the text. There were only words. But if you look at our modern Bibles, punctuation has been added. In some English versions, a period follows the first clause in Joshua 1:2, "Moses My servant is dead." Certainly, the finality of a period seems like the most likely punctuation to use after the word "dead." However, God's work does not end when His workman dies. While a period implies termination, a semi-colon suggests continuation. Versions such as the NASB and KJV that add a semi-colon following "dead" are theologically correct. Moses is dead, but God is not through. When we face change, we can either live in the theology of the period (termination) or the theology of the semi-colon (continuation). Let's choose the theology of the semi-colon and wait in faith to see what God does next! [8]

Standing there on the banks of the Jordan River, the Israelites cast a wishful eye to the land of Canaan on the other side. Looking around, the absence of those who dared to complain at Kadesh-barnea (Numbers 14) keep them from voicing their doubts and fears aloud, but the question remains. What do we do now? We can't go back. No warm reception would await us in Egypt. We can't stay put. Forty years circling the wilderness has gotten us nowhere. We have no other choice. We must go forward. But how? Can we even attempt to move into the Promised Land without Moses?

Figuratively speaking, perhaps you are standing in a similar place as the Israelites at the edge of the Jordan. And if you aren't there today, you will be one day soon. Time does not stand still. Things change. Life is a river that continually moves onward. **Like the people of Israel – you can't go back. You can't stay put. You must go forward.**

10. What life change are you facing now or in the near future?

Here, on earth, you can count on it: Things change. Seasons change. People change. We change. Life changes. But you can also count on this: God does not change. As He said in Malachi 3:6, "I am the Lord, and I do not change" (NLT). In a time of change, God wants to be our constant. In a time of uncertainty, God is always certain. With Him, you can put one foot in front of the other and move ahead in faith one step at a time.

Father, help me to navigate this change in a way that pleases You.
When things grow dark or seem overwhelming, remind me that You are all I need.
When feelings of fear and uncertainty rush my mind, give me confidence in Your abiding presence.
Guide my path and heart. Attend to my anxious thoughts with Your peace. Keep me from allowing the
sense of loss over "what was" from disrupting the potential of the new thing You are doing.
May Your whisper speak to my soul as I sit with You and remind me that I can trust
You no matter what. You know and hold the future. Help me to rest in You.
Amen.

DAY TWO
Joshua 1:3-7

In 1946, the Mosad Le'Aliya Bet, an agency that helped Jewish refugees immigrate to Mandatory Palestine, obtained an old American ship, the *President Warfield*, to facilitate the Jewish return to their homeland. In July 1947, 4500 passengers, most of them Holocaust survivors who had been living in displaced person camps in Germany, boarded the ship in Marseilles, France for the voyage to British Mandatory Palestine. Once the ship reached open waters, its name was changed to *Exodus 1947*, connecting the struggle of Holocaust survivors to the Jewish people's biblical migration from Egyptian slavery to the Promised Land. [9]

The bestselling 1958 novel by Leon Uris, *Exodus,* is loosely based on the account of this voyage and the birth of the State of Israel. When the book was turned into an Academy Award-winning film, Pat Boone wrote the lyrics to Ernest Gold's stirring theme for the movie:

> *This land is mine, God gave this land to me*
> *This brave and ancient land to me*
> *And when the morning sun reveals her hills and plain*
> *Then I see a land where children can run free*
>
> *So take my hand and walk this land with me*
> *And walk this lovely land with me*
> *Though I am just a man, when you are by my side*
> *With the help of God, I know I can be strong*
>
> *To make this land our home*
> *If I must fight, I'll fight to make this land our own*
> *Until I die, this land is mine* [10]

The lyrics capture the significance of the Promised Land to the Jewish people as the fulfillment of God's covenantal promise to Abraham and his descendants. God first promised the land to Abraham in Genesis 12:1-3:

> Now the Lord said to Abram, "Go forth from your country, and from your relatives and from your father's house, to the land which I will show you; and I will make you a great nation, and I will bless you, and make your name great; and so you shall be a blessing; and I will bless those who bless you, and the one who curses you I will curse. And in you all the families of the earth will be blessed."

The covenant God made with Abraham had two parts: a spiritual promise and a national promise. First, and most importantly, all the world would be blessed through Abraham. This aspect was related to God's promise in Genesis 3:15 that Someone was coming who would crush the serpent's head. Eventually, Christ fulfilled this portion of the promise when He came to the whole human race. In the second part of the covenant, God promised, "I will make you a great nation." A blessing attached to the national blessing was the promise of the land. After Abraham went to Egypt and then returned to Shechem, God repeated the promise He had made to Abraham:

> "Now lift up your eyes and look from the place where you are, northward and southward and eastward and westward; for all the land which you see, I will give it to you and to your descendants forever. I will make your descendants as the dust of the earth, so that if anyone can number the dust of the earth, then your descendants can also be numbered. Arise, walk about the land through its length and breadth; for I will give it to you" (Genesis 13:14-17).

God later reiterated His promise, this time with the conditions that had to take place before the gift of the land would be fulfilled:

> God said to Abram, "Know for certain that your descendants will be strangers in a land that is not theirs, where they will be enslaved and oppressed four hundred years. But I will also judge the nation whom they will serve, and afterward they will come out with many possessions. As for you, you shall go to your fathers in peace; you will be buried at a good old age. Then in the fourth generation they will return here, for the iniquity of the Amorite is not yet complete" (Genesis 15:13-16).

1. What are the five conditions that must take place before the Israelites can enter into the Promised Land? (Genesis 15:13-16)

-
-
-
-
-

Let's see where things stand historically at the beginning of Joshua 1:

Has Israel been exiled in a foreign land where they were enslaved for 400 years? Check. ✓

> Remember Egypt? The Israelites endured significant hardship and oppression during the 430 years they spent in Egypt (Exodus 12:40-41). During that time, they went from being a favored family in Egypt (under Joseph) to a people enslaved and subjected to harsh rule.

Has God judged the nation that enslaved them? Check. ✔

God's judgment included ten plagues that escalated in direct response to Pharaoh's refusal to release the Israelites from bondage. Following the plagues which culminated with the death of the firstborn, Pharaoh relented and allowed the Israelites to leave Egypt. However, he later pursued them, leading to the miraculous parting of the Red Sea and the destruction of Pharaoh's army.

Has Abraham died? Check. ✔

It has now been somewhere around 500 years since the death of Abraham.

Have four generations passed? Check. ✔

Most scholars interpret the four generations as:

Generation 1: Abraham

Generation 2: Isaac

Generation 3: Jacob (Israel)

Generation 4: The Israelites' descendants who were enslaved and later freed under Moses.

Have the sins of the Amorites reached their full extent? Check. ✔

At the time God promised His people the land, he told Abraham that the Amorites' iniquity was not yet at the level that it was time to deal with it. But as time passed, their wickedness increased. In Deuteronomy 9:4-5, Moses tells the people that they are not getting the land because of their righteousness, but it is "because of the wickedness of these nations that the Lord your God is driving them out before you, in order to confirm the oath which the Lord swore to your fathers, to Abraham, Isaac and Jacob."

Now, all the requirements God had given to Abraham have been met, and with the death of Moses, it is time to take the land. (Due to the disobedience of Moses and Aaron at Meribah, God would not allow them to lead His people into the Promised Land.) [11] This is a pivotal moment in the history of Israel as the Israelites are on the brink of crossing the Jordan River. As God passes the command to Joshua, He commissions him to step out in faith and lead the people into the land.

Read Joshua 1:3-4.

2. What promise does God make to the Israelites in verse 3?

3. Read what God promised to Moses in Deuteronomy 11:24-28. What was the requirement for the Israelites to receive God's blessing and what would cause them to be cursed?

The land is not just a physical space. It is a symbol of the covenant between God and the Israelites. Possessing the land is both a blessing and a responsibility; it is accompanied by the expectation that the Israelites will adhere to God's commandments.

4. Fill in the following chart with the specific boundaries of the Promised Land. (Joshua 1:4)

The Boundaries of the Promised Land	
From	
As far as	
All	
As far as	
Toward	

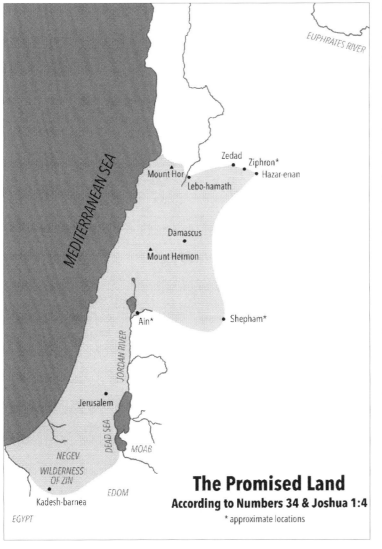

The Promised Land
According to Numbers 34 & Joshua 1:4
* approximate locations

These boundaries in Joshua 1:4 are the same territorial boundaries that God had given to Abraham over 500 years earlier. Robert Smith makes this observation, "Only an omniscient God who knows the end before the beginning begins could accomplish through His people what He had promised to His servant Abraham hundreds of years prior." [12]

The wilderness borders Israel on the South and East and includes the Negev, Edom, and the land east of Moab. "Hittites" is a reference to the native inhabitants of Canaan. The "Great Sea" is the Mediterranean Sea.

For us, the Promised Land is a picture of the promised life Jesus talked about in John 10:10, "I came that they may have life, and have it abundantly."

How much of the life, power, peace, and joy of Jesus are you actually possessing? Professing and possessing are not the same thing.

Read Joshua 1:5-7.

Because we are familiar with the story, we tend to overlook the magnitude of the task God has given to Joshua. He is facing one of the greatest challenges of his life. Questions must have flooded his mind: What if the children of Israel don't accept him as the successor to Moses? Or worse, what if they rebel... again? Or even worse than that, what if he fails? **Just because God has chosen and prepared Joshua doesn't mean that the task ahead is not daunting to him.** Neither does it mean that he will not feel the crushing weight of the responsibility.

Throughout Scripture, when God commands His people to do something difficult, He often gives promises to encourage those charged to carry out His instruction.

5. What three promises does God make to Joshua? (v. 5)

-

-

-

The Lord does more than reassure Joshua of His presence and power, He gives him specific commands. The first two are in Joshua 1:6-7. Each is preceded by God's instruction to be "strong and courageous." Courage is the strength that enables us to stand when we face difficult situations. The Hebrew word for "be strong" is *chazaq* and it means to "strengthen, prevail, harden, be strong, become strong, be courageous, be firm, grow firm, be resolute." [13] Courage is an attitude predicated upon a decision. It is the choice to keep pressing on, even in the face of danger and doubt. God will repeat these words to Joshua four times in this chapter. Clearly, courage will be a vital quality for Joshua as he leads the people into the land.

6. What specific instructions does God give to Joshua that will require him to be "strong and courageous"? (vv. 6-7)

Wiersbe observes, "Divine sovereignty is not a substitute for human responsibility. God's sovereign Word is an encouragement to God's servants to believe God and obey His commands." [14] God had promised Joshua victory, but that didn't mean he could just sit back and not do anything. God will fulfill His promises, but Joshua will have to exercise faith and "be strong and courageous."

7. What is the significance of God's instruction to obey the Law and not "turn from it"? (v. 7)

8. Identify two or three areas of your life where God is calling you to be strong and courageous. What are some specific promises from God's Word that you can stand upon in the face of these challenges?

Where I need to be "strong and courageous":	God's promises to me:

Write one or two of the promises from Scripture on a card or sticky note and put it someplace where you can see it often as a reminder of God's promise to you.

One of my favorite scenes from *The Chronicles of Narnia* takes place in *The Voyage of the Dawn Treader*. The ship and crew are headed into a mysterious darkness hovering over the sea. Lucy, feeling frightened and alone, calls out to Aslan (the lion who represents Jesus in the books) for help. "Aslan, Aslan, if ever you loved us at all, send us help now." [15] Suddenly, a stream of light appears and Lucy looks up to realize that an albatross is flying over the ship, singing a comforting song as it circles above. "No one except Lucy knew that as it circled the mast it had whispered to her, 'Courage, dear heart,' and the voice, she felt sure, was Aslan's, and with the voice a delicious smell breathed in her face." [16] And he led their ship to safety.

Whatever you are facing today, you are not alone. God's goodness and mercy are following you. He is with you. You can trust Him. Courage, dear heart.

DAY THREE
Joshua 1:8-9

At a critical point during World War II, Prime Minister Winston Churchill called a cabinet meeting to outline Britain's situation. France had just surrendered. The United States had not yet entered the war. The British Isles were literally standing alone against the Axis powers. As Churchill spoke, grim faces stared back at him in silence. Feelings of resignation and despair hung heavy in the room. As he finished his assessment, Churchill paused for a moment, lit a cigar, and with a hint of a smile said, "Gentlemen, I find it rather inspiring." Fear of failure never crossed his mind. No wonder people followed him! [17]

Did you know? The Hebrew word for "law" in Joshua 1:8 is *Torah*. The Torah contains all of God's revealed Word in Genesis through Deuteronomy: His self-revelation, His acts on behalf of the Israelites, and His covenant that includes commandments and principles for living.

Joshua is assuming the leadership of Israel, succeeding Moses, who had led the Israelites for more than 40 years. God has been clear to Joshua. He is God's man to lead Israel into Canaan. And, as will become increasingly evident, Joshua believes God. He believes that the nation of Israel will occupy the land of promise. He believes that God will deliver them from their enemies. He will not allow his faith to be tarnished by doubt. His allegiance to God will not waver. He will believe and obey.

Read Joshua 1:8-9.

Leading the people into the Promised Land is an immense responsibility, and God's continued encouragement will boost Joshua's confidence and resolve for the assignment ahead.

1. What three practices does God give Joshua to help him internalize the Word of God? (v. 8)

-
-
-

It is not enough for the priests to carry and guard the Torah. Joshua and the Israelites are to immerse themselves in God's Word.

Wiersbe shares an interesting insight about the word "meditate" in verse 8:

> The Hebrew word translated "meditate" means "to mutter." It was the practice of the Jews to read Scripture aloud (Acts 8:26-40) and talk about it to themselves and to one another (Deuteronomy 6:6-9). This explains why God warned Joshua that the book of the law was not to depart out of his mouth (Joshua 1:8). [18]

We cannot overexpose ourselves to the Word of God. It is not enough to just attend Bible study or follow a daily Bible reading plan. God's Word must become the core of our being. The pattern God gave to Joshua to engage with His Word is a simple three-step plan to follow: Say it. Think it. Do it.

> **Say it.** Read Scripture aloud. Memorize it. Pray it back to Him. Don't let God's Word depart from your mouth or mind.

> **Think it.** Ponder God's Word. Mull it over in your mind. Seek to allow His Word to be your first thought in the morning and your last thought at night.

> **Do it.** Obey God's Word. Apply it to your life and do what He says.

2. What two things does God promise if they will observe "the book of the law"? (v. 8b)

If Joshua and the Israelites comply with the commands and ordinances of God, they will prosper. God's laws were not weighty edicts meant to repress Israel. Rather, they were divine instructions meant for the flourishing and well-being of His people. The key to their success will come from their relationship with the God whose commandments and laws accompanied them wherever they went.

3. Read Psalm 1:1-3 and jot down the similarities in the passage to Joshua 1:8.

Both passages make it clear that ongoing engagement with God's Word leads to positive and fruitful outcomes, both spiritually and practically. In Psalm 1, the illustration used is a tree planted by water canals. Regardless of the weather or the condition of the soil, the tree's roots go down deep into the water and bring up life. As a result, it bears fruit when it is supposed to, and its leaves are always teeming with life. It is prosperous. The same is true for the person who is rooted in God through His law: "In whatever he does, he prospers" (Psalm 1:3); and "will have success" (Joshua 1:8). Success from God's perspective does not have a dollars and cents valuation. It is the life described in Jeremiah 29:11: "'For I know the plans I have for you,' says the Lord. 'They are plans for good and not for disaster, to give you a future and a hope'" (NLT).

4. What command does God give again in verse 9?

5. Why do you think God repeats His instruction to "be strong and courageous" so many times in Joshua 1?

Verse 9 concludes with the unparalleled promise of God's presence: "For the Lord your God is with you wherever you go." While preparation is important, it takes more than preparation to accomplish God's purposes. It takes the presence of God. Thomas Watson writes:

> The experience of Presence is the experience of peace, and the experience of peace is the experience not of inaction but of power, and the experience of power is the experience of a pursuing Love that loves its way untiringly to victory. He who knows the Presence knows peace, and he who knows peace knows power and walks in complete faith that the objective Power and Love which has overtaken him will overcome the world. [19]

Let's take a couple of moments and apply God's Word in Joshua 1:8-9 to our own lives.

6. What does it mean to you personally to "be strong and courageous" in your current circumstances?

7. How does the assurance that "the Lord your God is with you wherever you go" impact your understanding of God's presence in your daily life?

God's plans for you exceed any plans you have for yourself. There are no boundaries to His greatness. He delights to do great things in and through you – not because of you, but because He is a great God.

Great is the Lord, and highly to be praised, and His greatness is unsearchable.
Psalm 145:3

Close out your time in God's Word today by just being still in the Presence of God. Allow Him to overtake you with His peace, His love, His joy, and His power.

DAY FOUR
Joshua 1:10-18

In Joshua 1:1-9, God spoke directly to His chosen servant, Joshua. Now that Joshua has received his orders from God, it is time for him to speak to the officers leading the people. What has been conveyed to Joshua not only concerns himself, but it will also have a bearing upon the entire nation.

Read Joshua 1:10-11.

This is a critical juncture in the transition of leadership. Joshua takes the practical steps necessary to mobilize the people and set the stage for the journey ahead.

1. What are the people to prepare? (v. 11)

Notice that Joshua uses second person pronouns (you, yourselves) as he speaks to the people. Every person will need to be on board and do their part in the days ahead.

Did you know? In Scripture, the number three speaks to completeness. Moses was hidden from Pharaoh for three months. Jonah spent three days in the belly of the fish. After His crucifixion, Jesus rose from the dead on the third day. The most profound three is the triune nature of God, the Trinity: the Father, Son, and Holy Spirit.

Regarding Joshua's instructions to the people, Wiersbe writes:

> Instead of the command to prepare food, you would have expected Joshua to say, "Prepare boats so we can cross the Jordan River." Joshua didn't try to second-guess God and work things out for himself. He knew that the God who opened the Red Sea could also open the Jordan River. He and Caleb had been present when God delivered the nation from Egypt, and they had confidence that God would work on their behalf again. [20]

Wiersbe then explains that although Joshua trusts God to do the miraculous, he still has to prepare supplies needed for everyday life:

> In modern armies the Quartermaster Corps sees to it that the soldiers have food and other necessities of life, but Israel didn't have a Quartermaster Corps. Each family and clan had to provide its own food. The manna was still falling each morning (Exodus 16) and wouldn't stop until Israel was in their land (Joshua 5:11-12). But it was important that the people stayed strong because they were about to begin a series of battles for possession of their Promised Land." [21]

2. How long do the people have to get ready to cross the Jordan River? (v. 11)

3. Who is giving the people the land? (v. 11)

After 40 years of wilderness wanderings, it is soul-stirring news to hear that within three days, the entire nation will be standing in the Promised Land.

Read Joshua 1:12-15.

4. Who does Joshua address in these verses?

In Numbers 32:1-42 and Deuteronomy 3:12-22, we read the story of how these tribes chose to remain on the east side of the Jordan instead of seeking to settle in the Promised Land with the rest of Israel. The Reubenites, Gadites, and half-tribe of eastern Manasseh were attracted to this area because the open rangeland and semi-desert terrain were ideal conditions to raise sheep and cattle. Back when the two-and-a-half tribes approached Moses with their proposal, he bound them to a promise to participate in the battle on the west side to take the land. If they would not cross over the Jordan to help the other nine-and-a-half tribes take possession of the land, they would have no possessions among the rest of the people of God (Numbers 32:30). To fail to do so would be a sin; and Moses warned, "and be sure your sin will find you out" (Numbers 32:23).

Joshua now reminds them of their agreement with Moses.

5. What specific task is given to the two-and-a-half tribes? (v. 14)

These fighting men will form the advance guard for Israel. This is no small commitment for the men from the two-and-a-half tribes who will be away from their families for several years. Much like modern day military, soldiers in ancient times were often involved in combat in distant lands for long periods of time. Smith notes the significance of the word "until" in verse 15:

> They are to be faithful and active *until* the land is conquered. Upon carrying out their assignment and after Joshua has distributed lots to the nine-and-a-half tribes on the west side of the Jordan, then and only then will these two-and-a-half tribes be allowed to return to their families on the east side of the Jordan. [22]

6. What will they receive if they help the other tribes take the land? (vv. 13, 15)

In this context, "rest" is security from enemy attack on the land which has been given as an inheritance (Deuteronomy 12:9-10). Rest is a sign of God's presence (Exodus 33:14) and His provision (Joshua 1:13).

7. Look back over Joshua 1:10-15. Circle the words "possess" and "possession." How many times do these words occur?

Joshua uses the word "possess" intentionally. The Hebrew word for "possess," *yarash*, is found in Joshua fifteen times. *Yarash* means "to possess" or "to inherit." [23] The land is the Israelites' promised inheritance. Will they have to fight for the land? Yes. But they will not be the great conquerors. God will be. He will win. The Israelites' responsibility will be to trust Him and stay close to Him.

Read Joshua 1:16-18.

8. How does the statement from the Eastern tribes about obeying Joshua highlight their trust in God's plan and leadership? (vv. 16-17)

They are not only willing to obey Joshua's orders, but they are so zealous to follow him that they threaten to kill anyone who dares to disobey him. Then they affirm their full support for Joshua with the words, "only be strong and courageous" (v. 18). This is the fourth time in Joshua 1 that we have seen the words, "strong and courageous." Three times, God has spoken the words to Joshua. The fourth time, the two-and-a-half tribes echo God's words back to him.

To defeat the enemy and claim our inheritance in Christ, we must be "strong and courageous." As we saw in Joshua 1:8, there is a direct correlation between strength and courage and the Word of God. Joshua is to become so intimately familiar with God's Word that everything he thinks, feels, and does is filtered through Scripture. If he does that, then he will be "strong and courageous." Why? Because the Word of God shows us who God is and what He is like. Then, it helps us to see who we are in light of Who He is. And that is where courage originates. **We don't pull courage out of some inner reservoir; we find courage from knowing God.**

9. What have you learned about the character of God from Joshua 1?

10. How does what you have learned about God encourage you?

11. How can you encourage others with what you have learned about God?

Look! He has placed the land in front of you. Go and occupy it as the Lord, the God of your ancestors, has promised you. Don't be afraid! Don't be discouraged!
Deuteronomy 1:21 (NLT)

Be strong! Be courageous!

DAY FIVE
Joshua 1 | Be strong and courageous

The book of Joshua is full of practical lessons that will challenge us to live *into the promise,* to live the victorious Spirit-led and Spirit-filled life that Christ made possible for us through His death and resurrection. The key to these 24 chapters is given to us in 1 Corinthians 10:11, "Now these things happened to them as an example, and they were written for our instruction, upon whom the ends of the ages have come." Ray Stedman explains: "What the people of Israel went through in their actual historical experiences become patterns or metaphors, that we can apply to the spiritual battles in the spiritual pilgrimage in which we are engaged. These experiences have an exact and accurate application to us." [24]

Each week in our study, we will examine and apply a warfare principle from our Scripture passage. The warfare principle we see in Joshua 1 is:

> ## You have the DNA of a warrior.

Right now, in the realm of the unseen, a fierce battle is being waged. It is the clash between light and dark, good and evil, the spiritual and the natural. And in the middle of that cosmic battle is where each of us finds ourselves, as warriors called to fight in the spiritual realm. Joshua is a book of victory. Under the leadership of Joshua, Israel will encounter and defeat the enemy through the power of God. Likewise, through God's power, we must fight forces of wickedness in the spiritual realm for our inheritance. The principles we will learn from Joshua will help us stand against the attacks of the world, the flesh, and the devil, and lead us into the overcoming life that is available to us in Christ. From our study this week, we see three truths to stand upon in the battle.

The first battle truth is: **God is a Warrior**. Throughout Scripture, God is described as a valiant and victorious Warrior:

> The Lord is a warrior; The Lord is His name (Exodus 15:3).

> The Lord will go forth like a warrior, He will arouse His zeal like a man of war. He will utter a shout, yes, He will raise a war cry. He will prevail against His enemies (Isaiah 42:13).

> The Lord your God is with you, the Mighty Warrior who saves (Zephaniah 3:17, NIV).

Although Joshua was a boy during the exodus from Egypt, the remainder of his life was impacted by Moses' words as the Israelites stood on the banks of the Red Sea with the Egyptian army bearing down on them: "Do not fear! Stand by and see the salvation of the Lord which He will accomplish for you today; for the Egyptians whom you have seen today, you will never see them again forever. The Lord will fight for you while you keep silent" (Exodus 14:13-14). The victory God gave to the Israelites that day allowed

Joshua to experience God as a Warrior early in his life, and would have braced him with courage for the conquest ahead.

Perhaps Joshua had a flashback of the entire Egyptian army being swallowed up by the Red Sea when God promised Joshua victory over the giant Canaanites, "No man will be able to stand before you all the days of your life. Just as I have been with Moses, I will be with you; I will not fail you or forsake you" (Joshua 1:5). Later on, when he is faced with attacks from the enemy, this promise will be repeated to Joshua (10:8, 11:6) and that assurance will fortify his courage and faith.

Like Joshua, you can count on your Warrior God to not only fight the battle with you, but also to fight the battle for you. This side of eternity, there is no escaping the conflict of the spiritual battle we are in. But every conflict, every skirmish with the enemy, can be a victory. In Christ, there need not be any defeats.

1. Turn over to the New Testament and read John 16:33, 1 Corinthians 15:57, and 2 Corinthians 2:14. Summarize the message of these verses in one sentence.

2. Think on some of the Red Sea moments in your life, those times when God has given you victory over the enemy. What are some of the things you learned from those experiences?

3. When is a time when you have fought a battle in prayer for your family or a friend?

The second battle truth is: **You are a warrior.** You aren't a spectator in the battle. You are a participant. You are a warrior because your Father is a warrior. Because you are created in the likeness and image of God (*Imago Dei*), it is in your DNA to be a warrior. As Paul writes, "In all these things we overwhelmingly conquer through Him who loved us" (Romans 8:37).

4. Read 1 John 5:4. What is God's promise to believers in this verse?

In Joshua 1:2-3, God told Joshua, "Now therefore arise, cross this Jordan, you and all this people, to the land which I am giving to them, to the sons of Israel. Every place on which the sole of your foot treads, I have given it to you, just as I spoke to Moses." Although God has given the Promised Land to Israel, it still has to be possessed. Stedman notes, "Title to [the land] is the gift of God; possession of it is the result of an obedient walk." [25]

For believers, the land of Canaan is a picture of the Spirit-filled life, the way God intends for every one of us to live. As God told Joshua, you can have all the land that you want, "every place on which the sole of your foot treads" (v. 3). But He will never give you more than you are ready to possess. **The degree of your possession is in direct correlation to your degree of obedience** (Joshua 1:7b-8).

Obedience to God's Word is the prerequisite to possessing the promised life the Father has for you. It is only through the God-breathed Word that "you will know the truth and the truth will make you free" (John 8:32) to live in victory. An obedient heart results in the presence of the Holy Spirit: "For the Lord your God is with you wherever you go" (Joshua 1:9b). His Spirit empowers and enables us to live *Into the Promise!*

The third battle truth is: **Be ready for the battle.** No soldier goes to war without his armor and weapons. Archaeologists have found that soldiers in the Late Bronze Age (when Joshua lived) used weaponry such as bows and arrows, clubs, spears, slings, stones, shields, and helmets when they engaged in warfare. Most combat was hand-to-hand. It was up close and personal. Victory over the enemy required Joshua to "be strong and courageous" (Joshua 1:6, 7, 9, 18).

Battles fought in the spiritual realm also require us to be "strong and courageous," but call for us to use different weapons. In 2 Corinthians 10:4, Paul tells us that "the weapons of our warfare are not of the flesh." That means that our own strength offers us very little help in this war in which we are engaged. And that is great news! Because, in Christ, we can fight in God's strength and wear His armor. In Ephesians 6, Paul elaborates on what it means for us to be "strong and courageous" in the spiritual battles we face:

> Finally, be strong in the Lord and in the strength of His might. Put on the full armor of God, so that you will be able to stand firm against the schemes of the devil. For our struggle is not against flesh and blood, but against the rulers, against the powers, against the world forces of this darkness, against the spiritual forces of wickedness in the heavenly places. Therefore, take up the full armor of God, so that you will be able to resist in the evil day, and having done everything, to stand firm. Stand firm therefore, having girded your loins with truth, and having put on the breastplate of righteousness, and having shod your feet with the preparation of the gospel of peace; in addition to all, taking up the shield of faith with which

you will be able to extinguish all the flaming arrows of the evil one. And take the helmet of salvation, and the sword of the Spirit, which is the Word of God (vv. 10-17).

When spiritual forces come against you or your family, engage in the battle with the weapons God has provided for your victory. We have an enemy who is cruel and vicious. Based upon the instructions in Ephesians 6, you can stand strong and fight the battle against the enemy in prayer:

Father, I come to You in the name of Jesus, covered in His shed blood and robed
in His perfect righteousness. Today, I will stand firm in Your strength. Right now,
I put on the full armor of God. I put on the belt of truth so that I can discern lies from the truth.
I put on the breastplate of righteousness to guard my heart from the enemy's accusations.
I put on the shoes of the gospel of peace to equip me to stand firm and spread the good news of Christ.
I take up the shield of faith to extinguish the fiery darts of the enemy. I take up the helmet of salvation
to protect my mind against the enemy's attacks. And finally, I pick up the sword of the Spirit, the
Word of God, to stand strong against the enemy.

Thank You that Jesus is Lord and Satan is defeated. Fill me with Your indwelling Spirit.
Enable me to "be strong and courageous" today. Thank You that You will accomplish
exceedingly abundantly more than I can ask or think. I pray this in the strong and
victorious name of Jesus, refusing to doubt. Amen.

5. Ask the Holy Spirit to impress on your heart one lesson from Joshua 1 that you need to apply to your life. Then write out a specific goal.

With the help of God and the enablement of the Holy Spirit, I will:

Be strong. Be courageous. You are not alone. God is with you.

And lo, I am with you always, even to the end of the age.
Matthew 28:20

LESSON TWO

Tie this cord of scarlet thread

JOSHUA 2

Rahab Shelters Spies

¹ Then Joshua the son of Nun sent two men as spies secretly from Shittim, saying, "Go, view the land, especially Jericho." So they went and came into the house of a harlot whose name was Rahab, and lodged there. ² It was told the king of Jericho, saying, "Behold, men from the sons of Israel have come here tonight to search out the land." ³ And the king of Jericho sent word to Rahab, saying, "Bring out the men who have come to you, who have entered your house, for they have come to search out all the land." ⁴ But the woman had taken the two men and hidden them, and she said, "Yes, the men came to me, but I did not know where they were from. ⁵ It came about when it was time to shut the gate at dark, that the men went out; I do not know where the men went. Pursue them quickly, for you will overtake them." ⁶ But she had brought them up to the roof and hidden them in the stalks of flax which she had laid in order on the roof. ⁷ So the men pursued them on the road to the Jordan to the fords; and as soon as those who were pursuing them had gone out, they shut the gate. ⁸ Now before they lay down, she came up to them on the roof, ⁹ and said to the men, "I know that the Lord has given you the land, and that the terror of you has fallen on us, and that all the inhabitants of the land have melted away before you. ¹⁰ For we have heard how the Lord dried up the water of the Red Sea before you when you came out of Egypt, and what you did to the two kings of the Amorites who were beyond the Jordan, to Sihon and Og, whom you utterly destroyed. ¹¹ When we heard it, our hearts melted and no courage remained in any man any longer because of you; for the Lord your God, He is God in heaven above and on earth beneath. ¹² Now therefore, please swear to me by the Lord, since I have dealt kindly with you, that you also will deal kindly with my father's household, and give me a pledge of truth, ¹³ and spare my father and my mother and my brothers and my sisters, with all who belong to them, and deliver our lives from death." ¹⁴ So the men said to her, "Our life for yours if you do not tell this business of ours; and it shall come about when the Lord gives us the land that we will deal kindly and faithfully with you."

The Promise to Rahab

¹⁵ Then she let them down by a rope through the window, for her house was on the city wall, so that she was living on the wall. ¹⁶ She said to them, "Go to the hill

country, so that the pursuers will not happen upon you, and hide yourselves there for three days until the pursuers return. Then afterward you may go on your way." [17] The men said to her, "We shall be free from this oath to you which you have made us swear, [18] unless, when we come into the land, you **tie this cord of scarlet thread** in the window through which you let us down, and gather to yourself into the house your father and your mother and your brothers and all your father's household. [19] It shall come about that anyone who goes out of the doors of your house into the street, his blood shall be on his own head, and we shall be free; but anyone who is with you in the house, his blood shall be on our head if a hand is laid on him. [20] But if you tell this business of ours, then we shall be free from the oath which you have made us swear." [21] She said, "According to your words, so be it." So she sent them away, and they departed; and she tied the scarlet cord in the window.

[22] They departed and came to the hill country, and remained there for three days until the pursuers returned. Now the pursuers had sought them all along the road, but had not found them. [23] Then the two men returned and came down from the hill country and crossed over and came to Joshua the son of Nun, and they related to him all that had happened to them. [24] They said to Joshua, "Surely the Lord has given all the land into our hands; moreover, all the inhabitants of the land have melted away before us."

Joshua 2
Tie this cord of scarlet thread

True saving faith involves "the whole personality": the mind is instructed, the emotions are stirred, and the will then acts in obedience to God. [1]
~ Warren Wiersbe

August 2, 1776 stands as one of the most significant, but least celebrated days in American history. On that day, the 56 members of the Second Continental Congress began the process of signing the Declaration of Independence in Philadelphia. Officially, the Congress had declared its freedom from Great Britain on July 2, 1776, when it approved a resolution in a unanimous vote. Once that vote was taken, the group needed to write a document to explain their move to the public. The Committee of Five (John Adams, Roger Sherman, Robert Livingston, Benjamin Franklin, and Thomas Jefferson) had written the original draft, and following a two-day editing session, the Congress agreed on the final version of the Declaration of Independence on July 4, 1776.

The document was then sent to a printer, John Dunlap, who printed 200 copies (26 remain today). Finally, on August 2, 1776, the members of the Second Continental Congress began putting their signatures on the declaration. As president of the Congress, John Hancock signed first. The other congressional delegates signed by state delegation, beginning in the upper right column, and then continuing in five columns, ordered from the northern most state of New Hampshire to the southernmost state of Georgia. Risking their lives, 50 men from 13 states signed the document on August 2, 1776. The other six signed over the course of the next year and a half.

For the Founding Fathers of our nation, August 2, 1776 must have been surreal. From this point on, there would be no turning back. The battle had just begun. [2]

As we turn the page to Joshua 2, Joshua and the Israelites are at a similar crossroads. At this point, Israel is still on the opposite side of the Jordan from Canaan, based at Shittim (pronounced *sheh-TEEM*). Joshua has been commissioned by the Lord and given his instructions for possession of the Promised Land. The Lord told Joshua that "every place on which the sole of your foot treads, I have given it to you" (Joshua 1:3). He also promised that "No man will be able to stand before you all the days of your life. Just as I have been with Moses, I will be with you; I will not fail you or forsake you. Be strong and courageous" (1:5-6a).

But what God is telling Joshua and the Israelites in the Spirit realm does not match what they are seeing in the physical. Across the Jordan River is Jericho, a well-defended garrison with strong fortified walls, a custodial defense of Canaan standing in the way of Israel's move into the land.

In his first military move as Israel's new leader, Joshua does as Moses did and sends spies (two, not twelve) on a scouting mission to view the land, "especially Jericho" (Joshua 2:1). Little do the two men know, they are about to receive assistance from an unlikely source.

DAY ONE
Joshua 2:1-7

Before we dive into our passage for today, read the entire chapter of Joshua 2. Observe the specifics. Ask the Lord what He wants to say to you through these 24 verses. At times, we miss out on learning about something in Scripture because we are familiar with the passage and think we already know the details. This may be one of those times. As Robert Smith challenges:

> Is it possible for us to crawl up into the thoughts of Yahweh and stay there long enough until the common becomes uncommon, the familiar becomes unfamiliar, the mundane becomes magnificent, and the simple becomes stupendous?...Even those who have read this story many times can find that, like a diamond, it has many facets. As we turn to it anew, the new mercies we see daily can illuminate fresh revelation relevant to our current circumstances. We benefit most by assuming a childlike posture of second naivete in which we approach this story as if we are hearing it for the first time. [3]

After reading a chapter in Scripture, it is good idea to take a step back and recall what is going on in the passage. Answering the following questions will help you capture a snapshot of what you have just read.

Snapshot of Joshua 2

Who are the main characters in Joshua 2?

Where does the story take place?

What is the primary event that occurs in this chapter?

Which verse stood out the most to you as you were reading?

Now, let's focus on our passage for today.

Read Joshua 2:1-3.

Jericho is located on an oasis about five miles west of the Jordan River and six miles north of the Dead Sea. A fortified military outpost situated at the foot of the Judean mountains, it is positioned on a significant trade route and guards the passageway between the Jordan Valley and the hill country. Historians believe around 2000 people lived within the city walls. [4]

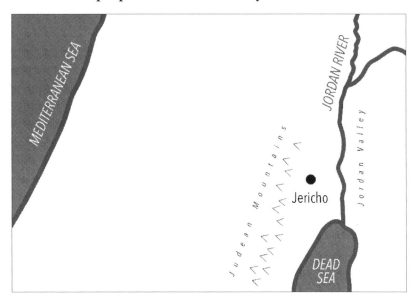

To make inroads into Canaan, Israel will first need to conquer Jericho before they can access the road, then, take the fortresses protecting the high ground at the top of the hills. From that point, they will be in a position to divide and conquer by launching military strikes to the north and the south.

1. Where is the first place the spies go when they arrive in Jericho? (v. 1)

2. Right off, what do we learn about Rahab? (v. 1)

The Hebrew word for "harlot" can also mean "inn keeper."

3. How is Rahab described in James 2:25-26?

Warren Wiersbe keeps us from trying to whitewash Rahab's profession, "If all we had was the Old Testament text, we could absolve Rahab of immorality and call her the 'proprietress of an inn.' But there is no escape, for in James 2:25 and Hebrews 11:31, the writers use the Greek word that definitely means a 'prostitute.'" [5]

4. What is said about Rahab in Hebrews 11:30-31?

There are only two women mentioned in the great Hall of Faith in Hebrews 11: Sarah and Rahab. What do these two women have in common? From the outside looking in, it appears they could not have been more different. Sarah was the wife of the Patriarch of the Jews. She gave birth to the promised heir. Rahab was a Gentile with a pagan background. The only thing that unites these women and places them in Hebrews 11 is their faith.

The story of Rahab is one of my favorite accounts recorded in Scripture. **Rahab is proof that the Lord will move Heaven and earth to get to the one who has turned her heart toward Him.** First, God moves in the heart of Joshua, the military leader, to send two spies in to check out the land and the city of Jericho. Then, the Lord sovereignly guides the spies to Rahab. We will look at her profession of faith tomorrow. But suffice it to say, she is a whole-hearted believer in what she has heard about the God of the Israelites. Nothing moves the heart of our God like faith!

5. Who finds out about the presence of the spies in Jericho? (v. 2)

As we reflect on the spies and their entrance into Jericho, we realize like the signers of the Declaration of Independence, these two men are risking their lives. Because the news about the arrival of the Israelites at the edge of the Jordan has already reached Jericho, the city would have been on high alert. The king has his watchmen guarding the city and surveilling everyone who enters and leaves through the city gates. Rahab's house is a public place on the outer wall that allows agents of the king to hear about the presence of the two Israelite spies.

6. What does the king of Jericho do when he learns there are spies in his city? (v. 3)

At this time, Canaan is not a unified nation. Instead, it is made up of lots of small kingdoms, each of which included a fortified city with small villages and farms surrounding it. Jericho is one of those small kingdoms with its own ruling king.

Read Joshua 2:4-7.

7. What is Rahab's response to the message from the king?

Rahab lies. Regarding her deception, David Jackman writes:

> Her lies are neither condemned, nor are they commended in the text. The narrative does not teach that lying is justifiable or that the end justifies the means. Rather Rahab seems to be trapped in a moral choice in which either option would involve sin. Either she could have disclosed the spies and almost certainly brought about their execution, or she could have

denied that she knew their whereabouts, which was clearly untrue...Probably it came quite naturally to her since, like us, she was a fallen human being living in a fallen world, as we need to remember before we are too eager to point the finger. [6]

Where else are people's lies recorded in Scripture? H.D.M. Spence points out several other instances:

Sisera requested Jael, as a matter of course, to do what Rahab did. Jonathan deceives his father to save David's life, and he is not blamed for doing so (1 Samuel 20:28, 29). David deceives Ahimelech the priest (1 Samuel 21:2). Even Elisha appears not to have adhered to strict truth in 2 Kings 6:19, and Gehazi is not punished so much for his lie as for his accepting a gift which his master had declined. Jeremiah, again, tells without hesitation the untruth Zedekiah asks him to tell (Jeremiah 38:24-27). [7]

8. Read Exodus 1:15-21. Note Pharaoh's order and the deception of the midwives.

When we read this passage carefully, we will see that the text does not reveal if the women lied to Pharaoh or delayed arriving to the births of the Israelite women. Either way, the Lord blessed them for protecting life. Pause and put yourself in the shoes of these two women. They had been called before the most powerful man on the earth at that time. They are slaves, and yet they defied the man with the power to order their death. Their faith in the God of Israel and their reverential fear of Him drove out the fear of man.

For Rahab, telling the lie is choosing the lesser of two evils. She risks her own life to save the spies. Richard Hess contends that the ethical dilemma of Rahab's lie is not the point of the narrative:

It stresses the deception, not in order to condemn Rahab but to magnify her personal risk in hiding the spies. After all, she could have said nothing and allowed the agents to search her house. By pointing in another direction, she risked being caught, but in the end she delivered her new-found friends. [8]

9. What does she encourage the king's envoys to do? (v. 5)

10. Under what does Rahab hide the spies? (v. 6)

Gathering flax is a tedious and laborious task. In the ancient world, women would spend hours gathering flax to make cloth. She has to have a large amount of flax gathered on the roof of her house for it to cover two adult men. Most scholars believe Rahab also has a clothing business.

11. Read Proverbs 31:13. What does it say about the virtuous woman?

In verse 7, after the king's men go out in search of spies, the gates are shut behind them. Think about the vulnerability of the spies at this point as well as how dependent they are upon Rahab for protection. Once the gates are shut, there is no other means of escape out of the town for them. We'll look at what happens next tomorrow.

As we close today's lesson, let's circle back around to Rahab. Think about her stained reputation. Her sin. And yet, she is not beyond the reach of God's grace. And friend, neither are you. Does your past sin make you feel unworthy? If so, I have good news for you! Only unworthy people go to Heaven! I'm pretty sure there is a smile spreading across your face as you think on that. Throughout this day, revel in the grace God has for you. He loves you and has amazing plans for you.

Did you know? Flax was a plant used to make linen cloth. Young plants were used to make high quality cloth, and ripe tougher plants made sturdier material such as rope. After flax was harvested, it would undergo a process called "retting" that involved soaking it in stagnant water to separate the fibers from the stems. (The stems would cause decay in the material if not removed.) The smell from the soggy stalks would have made hiding there an unpleasant experience.

Flax has stems that can cause decay in the material if it is not removed. The word for flax is also translated linen. The flax was a plant whose stalk and fibers were used for spinning and making cloth. This may have been a part of Rahab's daily life or she may have had a business making and selling cloth. [9]

DAY TWO
Joshua 2:8-11

Let's begin our lesson with a summary of what we know about Rahab at this point in the narrative:

- Rahab is a woman living in a world where women are not only considered "less than," but are also routinely victimized.

- Rahab is a Gentile. She is not a part of the covenant promise God made to Abraham and his descendants.

- Rahab is a pagan. She has been raised in an atmosphere of idolatry and gross immorality.

- Rahab is a harlot. She is part of what has been called the "world's oldest occupation."

All of those things might sound like they would disqualify her from the Hall of Faith in Hebrews 11. But right there on the list along with Abel, Enoch, Noah, Abraham, Sarah, Isaac, Jacob, Joseph, and Moses, is Rahab. Just like that, God rearranges all of our preconceived categories. If we were making the list, we would probably have all the men of faith on the good side of the ledger and put Rahab on the bad side, with a chasm in between. Can't let the men of faith get too close to a harlot! But that is not God's way. In just one moment of redemption, God can turn shame into glory. And that, in a nutshell, is Rahab's story.

Read Joshua 2:8-11.

In verse 8, we are reminded again that Rahab has hidden the men on the roof. Here, she will share with the spies her heart's belief and desire.

1. Summarize Rahab's statement of faith in verses 9-11.

Rahab's statement of faith is one of the longest, uninterrupted statements by a woman in Scripture. Her initial confession, "I know" (v. 9) is a direct contrast to the "I do not know" statement she makes to the agents the king of Jericho sent to her house in verse 5. Hess makes the observation that her "true confession would replace the former deceit." [10]

2. What specifically does Rahab "know"? (v. 9)

Matthew Henry gives us insightful commentary:

> But that which justifies her in this is that *she knew the Lord had given Israel this land* (v. 9), knew it by the incontestable miracles God had wrought for them, which confirmed that grant; and her obligations to God were higher than her obligations to any other." [11]

3. What miraculous feats of the God of Israel does Rahab include in her statement of faith? (v. 10)

4. What phrase does she use to describe the reaction of the people of the land to this news? (v. 11)

God uses Rahab's report to persuade "the spies that the Lord had defeated the land without them having to lift a sword." [12]

5. Read Deuteronomy 2:25 and 11:25. How does God fulfill these prophecies?

6. Why is Rahab's response different from the rest of the residents of Jericho? (v. 11)

7. What does she believe about God? (v. 11)

Let's not miss the fact that she not only confesses God as the God of Heaven, but also as the God of earth. What a testimony she gives to the sovereignty of God!

8. What does Hebrews 11:6 say that we must believe?

We must believe to see. Abraham was called by God to go to a place that God would show him. We too are called to follow Christ on a daily basis. We do not know what a day holds, but our great God does. We must believe to "see" and understand the spiritual truths that the Holy Spirit reveals. Without faith, we are locked into only what we can see in the natural.

It is only by faith that we are able to see as God sees.

As we have seen throughout the Lord's dealings with Moses and the Israelites, things are rarely as they seem in the natural. The ten plagues struck at every one of the Egyptian gods, proving the omnipotence of Yahweh. The parting of the Red Sea, manna raining down from Heaven, water coming from a rock, and the pillar of cloud and fire that led the Israelites all reveal an omnipotent God with Whom nothing is impossible!

We can't just believe whatever we want, we must believe God. We must know Him to believe Him!

When we read about the life of Jesus in the Gospels, we are granted spiritual insight. In John 6, Jesus feeds the 5000. Then, after hearing about John the Baptist's death, He sends the disciples away in a boat, but He goes up on the mountain to be alone with the Father. A storm arises on the Sea of Galilee, and Jesus is seen by the disciples walking on water. This happened during the fourth watch (between 3:00 a.m. and 6:00 a.m.).

This account is also recorded in Matthew 14:22-32 and Mark 6:45-52. It is from the account in Matthew that we read about Peter walking on water toward the Lord. The moment Peter looked at the wind and waves, he became frightened and began to sink. He cried out to the Lord, and Jesus "stretched out His hand and took hold of him and said to him, 'You of little faith, why did you doubt?'" (Matthew 14:31)

Did you know? Rahab is the first Gentile convert recorded in Scripture. In Rahab, God is fulfilling His promise to Abraham that "in you all the families of the earth will be blessed" (Genesis 12:3).

This same rebuke can be given to us when we look at the circumstances of our lives instead of looking to Jesus. If we are going to walk by faith, and thus please God, we must fix our eyes on Jesus (Hebrews 12:2). When we have an accurate and exalted view of Jesus, our problems will shrink in comparison to His majesty and glory.

John tells us that when Jesus and Peter got in the boat, they were immediately at the other side (John 6:21). The crowd came looking for Jesus. They had seen the disciples get in the boat after the miraculous feeding of the crowd without Jesus. They were confused and asked Him, "Rabbi, when did you get here?"

9. Read John 6:26-29. Why did Jesus say the people sought Him? (v. 26)

10. What did Jesus say was the "work of God"? (v. 29)

Our job is to believe! (John 6:29)

Because Rahab believes and places her trust in the God of the Israelites, she is saved. Her actions validate her professed faith.

DAY THREE
Joshua 2:12-21

Let's begin today by reading Joshua 2:12-14.

1. What request does Rahab make of the spies? (vv. 12-13)

Rahab is not just concerned about her own well-being. Wiersbe notes, "Once she had personally experienced the grace and mercy of God, she was burdened to rescue her family." [13]

2. What agreement do the two spies make with Rahab to guarantee her family's safety? (v. 14)

3. In the text, underline the two words that describe the way the spies pledge to deal with Rahab.

Woudstra explains that kindness and faithfulness is "the standard expression for acts done...in covenant agreements (Genesis 24:27, 49; 32:10). [14]

Read Joshua 2:15-22.

Rahab is a wise woman. She lets them down by a rope through a window in her home located on the city wall (v. 15), and gives the spies specific advice for evading their pursuers.

4. What advice does she give to the spies? (v. 16)

5. What are the conditions of the deal between Rahab and the two spies? (vv. 17-20)

6. What do the spies tell Rahab to tie in her window? (vv. 17-18)

Did you know? *Tiqvah*, the Hebrew word for "cord," is also translated "hope, things hoped for, outcome." [15]

7. After the spies depart, what does Rahab do? (v. 21)

The scarlet cord is a cord of hope. Rahab has placed her hope and faith in the God of Israel. She heard and believed. As Romans 10:17 tells us, "faith comes by hearing and hearing by the Word of God." In whom or what have you placed your faith? To whom are you listening? You cannot listen primarily to the voices of the world, whether it is the news or social media, and remain steadfast. You must listen to the Word of God.

Faith comes by hearing. We have so many resources available to us today. Select a few biblically faithful preachers and teachers, and strengthen your faith by listening to the Word!

Who you are listening to will be evident by your actions. Rahab believed what she heard about the God of Israel and her actions proved it. Your actions also give testimony to your belief. Are your actions proof of your belief and trust in God?

The scarlet, or red, cord is a reminder of the Passover blood in Exodus 12. Because the blood of the lamb was applied to the doorposts and lintel, the death angel passed over that house. Likewise, the scarlet cord marks Rahab's home. All who were within it when the Israelites conquered Jericho would be saved.

The red thread of salvation, often called the redemptive thread, can be traced throughout Scripture. It is a beautiful theme of God's provision through the shedding of the blood of the innocent on behalf of the guilty to cover sin. Let's take a few moments and do that.

8. Read the following verses and trace the evidence of the redemptive thread:

- Genesis 3:21 – What did God do to provide what is recorded?

    God establishes from the beginning that it will take the shedding of the blood of the innocent on behalf of the guilty to cover sin.

- Genesis 8:20-22 – What did Noah do?

    What did you notice about how the animals were designated? This is prior to the giving of the law under Moses when animals would be declared clean or unclean. There was obviously an understanding of the animals that were acceptable for a sacrifice to God.

- Genesis 22:1-18 – How do these verses foreshadow the cross?

- Exodus 12:1-13 – Describe how the Passover was to be observed.

- Exodus 25:1-9 – What was the purpose of the Tabernacle?

Leviticus 16 contains the laws for the Day of Atonement. Only the high priest could enter the Holy of Holies, and only on the Day of Atonement, or he would die. On that day, the high priest would offer a bull for a sin offering and a ram for a burnt offering for himself. Then he would choose two goats (or lambs) and cast lots for the scapegoat. One goat would be sacrificed, and its blood sprinkled on the mercy seat along with the blood of the bull. Then, the high priest would confess the sins of the people over the head of the scapegoat, and it would be led out into the wilderness by "the hand of a man who stands in readiness" (Leviticus 16:21). "But the bull of the sin offering and the goat of the sin offering, whose blood was brought in to make atonement in the holy place, shall be taken outside the camp, and they shall burn their hides, their flesh, and their refuse in the fire" (Leviticus 16:27).

- 1 Kings 8:1-11 – How did the Lord consecrate the temple?

- John 1:29 – What was John the Baptist's proclamation?

- Hebrews 10:10-18 – Why is there no more need for sacrifices?

- Hebrews 13:11-14 – Refer back to Leviticus 16:27. How did Christ fulfill the requirements of the sacrifice?

Once we are "in Christ," we are new creatures (2 Corinthians 5:17). We are no longer identified by our sin, but by our position "in Christ."

9. Read Matthew 1:5. How is Rahab listed in the genealogy?

Did you notice the descriptor that was omitted? Rahab became a new creation by believing!

Dear sister in Christ, you are no longer who you were! You have been bought with the precious blood of the Lamb. You are a new creation; all the old things have passed away. Any condemnation you now feel is due to the hiss of the serpent. He is the "accuser of the brethren" (Revelation 12:10). You refute his lies with the truth of God's Word (the sword of the Spirit, Ephesians 6:17).

We reviewed Ephesians 6 and the whole armor of God last week. We are called to be warriors, soldiers of Christ. Keep standing firm. Be strong. Be courageous!

DAY FOUR
Joshua 2:22-24

Rahab's faith in the God of Israel, and her knowledge of the actions of her city, are of great benefit to the spies.

Read Joshua 2:22-24.

1. How long do the men hide before returning to the Israelite camp? (v. 22)

2. In the text, underline the three verbs the writer uses to describe the way the spies return to Joshua. (v. 23a)

3. What do the spies tell Joshua? (v. 24)

This report is exactly what Joshua needs to hear the night before his forces will approach the flooding Jordan River. Phillip Keller insightfully comments that this report is "the magnificent provision arranged by God to fortify his faith on the eve of the great invasion." [16] The next morning, Israel will break camp for the last time after 40 years of wandering in the wilderness. They are about to enter *into the promise*!

As Joshua listened to the report of the spies, I can't help but wonder if he thought about the spy mission he and Caleb had been a part of four decades before.

4. Read Numbers 13:1-3. Who commanded Moses to send spies into the Promised Land?

5. Read Numbers 13:17-20. What was their assignment?

6. Read Numbers 13:25-33. Summarize the two different reports.

Because Joshua and Caleb entered the Promised Land with eyes of faith, it was obvious to them that the Lord was giving them the land. Their report sounds just like the faith report that Rahab gives to the two spies. It is evident to her that the God of Israel has given them the land (Joshua 2:9). Thus, the faith of the spies was boosted, and they were able to report to Joshua, "Surely the Lord has given all the land into our hands; moreover, all the inhabitants of the land have melted away before us" (Joshua 2:24).

When God speaks, His Word will always accomplish His purposes.

7. Read Isaiah 55:8-11. What do these verses tell us about God and His Word?

This promise is an excellent one to commit to memory!

In just a few chapters, the Israelite army will be given some very strange marching orders regarding the conquest of Jericho. I can only imagine that these soldiers will have to wonder about the strategy the Lord gives to Joshua. As we just read, God says, "'For My thoughts are not your thoughts, nor are your ways My ways,' declares the Lord. 'For as the heavens are higher than the earth, so are My ways higher than your ways and My thoughts than your thoughts'" (Isaiah 55:8-9).

Remember that the next time your flesh wants you to disregard or disobey the Word of the Lord.

8. Review Joshua 1:7-8. How can we apply these verses to our own lives?

> *Obedience to God's will is the secret of spiritual knowledge and insight.*
> *It is not willingness to know, but willingness to DO (obey) God's will*
> *that brings certainty.* [17]
> ~ Eric Liddell

DAY FIVE
Joshua 2 | Tie this cord of scarlet thread

Joshua 2 is just the beginning of Rahab's story. We will see her again in Lesson Four. But, spoiler alert, God has great things in store for Rahab. In due time, Rahab will be brought into the camp of Israel through her marriage to Salmon. You may be familiar with her son, Boaz, who later marries Ruth. Here is a look at Rahab's family tree:

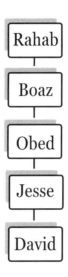

That's right! Rahab is David's great-great grandmother! The once harlot is in the royal line which ultimately leads to Christ. She is one of only four women (along with Tamar, Ruth, and Bathsheba) mentioned in the genealogy of Jesus in Matthew 1. Keller writes, "It was an act of obedient, living faith which transformed her from her past as a pagan prostitute, to an esteemed and cherished mother in Israel." [18] What made the difference? Rahab believed and obeyed.

Do you remember what Rahab told the spies in Joshua 2:10? "We have heard...." Rahab's fellow Canaanites had the same knowledge she did, but they did not acknowledge the God of Heaven. They had the same light that Rahab did, but did not believe. And because of their unbelief, they are heading for immediate destruction and eternal separation from God. Rahab, on the other hand, heard and believed as evidenced in her statement of faith in Joshua 2:9-11.

When the spies leave Jericho, they do not take Rahab back with them. She has to remain in the Canaanite city from the time she professed her faith in God until the time His judgment will fall.

1. What is the first thing Rahab does after the spies depart? (v. 21)

She immediately obeys, and make no mistake: Hers is a costly obedience. Francis Schaeffer writes:

> This woman Rahab stood alone in her faith against the total culture which surrounded her – something none of us today in the Western world has ever yet to do. For a period of time she stood for the unseen against the seen, standing in acute danger until Jericho fell. If the king had ever found out what she had done, he would have become her chief enemy and would have executed her. [19]

Scripture is clear that Rahab demonstrated her faith in God by her works, through her obedience. In the book of James, Rahab's faith stands alone in comparison to that of Abraham, "Was not Abraham our father justified by works when he offered up Isaac his son on the altar?...In the same way, was not Rahab the harlot also justified by works when she received the messengers and sent them out by another way?" (James 2:21, 25)

Rahab has a faith that has "teeth in it, structure to it, strength in it." [20] She is willing to risk her life to demonstrate her faith. Her faith in action leads us to the warfare principle in Joshua 2:

Obedience is a prerequisite to victory.

The Book of the Law given to Moses stressed God's blessings for obedience. The Lord also warned them of curses should they ignore God's commands and turn back to pagan idolatry.

2. Read Deuteronomy 28:1-14. Make a list of the blessings promised for obedience:

Scriptures	Blessings of Obedience
v. 1	
v. 3	
v. 4	
v. 5	
v. 7	
v. 8	
v. 9	
v. 10	
v. 11	

Scriptures	Blessings of Obedience
v. 12	
v. 13	

3. Read Deuteronomy 28:15-25. Make a list of the curses of disobedience.

Scriptures	Curses of Disobedience
v. 16	
v. 17	
v. 18	
v. 19	
v. 20	
v. 21	
v. 22	
v. 23	
v. 24	
v. 25	

The curses of disobedience paint a picture of widespread suffering, instability, and failure in every area of life: from the land, to the family, to the military. These curses are a sharp contrast with the blessings promised for obedience, serving as a warning of the severe consequences that disobedience to God can bring. The blessings and curses are all promises. God has promised to bless their obedience to the law of God and to curse their disobedience. We go against God's Word and His design to our own demise.

4. Read Deuteronomy 30:19-20. What choice did God give the Israelites?

When Jesus came, He told His followers that He did not come to abolish the law but to fulfill it (Matthew 5:17). Jesus fully obeyed the will of the Father. He is our example. Jesus told us our obedience is the proof of our love for Him.

A few months ago, the co-teacher for my high school girls class, Kristi Hall, made this statement, "Obedience is an invitation." I was immediately struck by that truth. **Obedience is an invitation into intimacy with God. Obedience says, "I believe God and will build my life on His Word."** God's invitation to obedience is open to all.

5. Look up the following verses and write down how God rewards obedience:

   • John 14:21

   • Joshua 2:11-14

   • Numbers 14:6-10

   • Joshua 14:11

Joshua and Caleb believed God. When everyone else in their generation perished, they not only survived, but Caleb was just as strong as he had been 40 years earlier (Joshua 14:11). They "saw" that God was giving them the land (Numbers 14:6-10). Now they would "see" it with their physical eyes!

We must remember that our disobedience does not just affect us. It also impacts our descendants. The unbelieving generation of Israelites all died. Their children were stuck wandering in the wilderness for 40 years until that generation passed away. Only then, were the children that they were so worried about (Numbers 14:31) able to go in and possess the land.

6. Joshua and Caleb are the only ones in their generation that were able to enter *into the promise*. Read Numbers 14:24. What blessing did the Lord pronounce over Caleb?

Because God's ways are not our ways and His thoughts are not our thoughts, we cannot assume we know His will. We must present ourselves as a living sacrifice (Romans 12:1) which is our service of worship. We must also choose not to be "conformed to this world, but to be transformed by the renewing of our minds, that we may prove what the will of God is, that which is good, acceptable and perfect" (Romans 12:2).

That's right – we must put our all on the altar. I must die to my will and way of life that I might come alive to Christ's life in me (Galatians 2:20). As I surrender to Him, He renews my mind and reveals His will.

His will is most often revealed in His Word. But there are also times that the Lord speaks through the promptings of His Spirit. Other times, He may confirm something He has been revealing to you by having someone else share a verse or pray for you and use the same words or verse that the Lord had given you. These moments, when the eternal pierces the temporal, are electrifying. It is in these moments that we know that we know: Our God is intimately acquainted with us and He still speaks!

Are you obeying the Lord in every area of your life? We do not get to pick and choose. Take a few minutes to sit quietly with the Lord. Ask Him to speak to you about any area of your life where you are not living in obedience.

Do you hear His invitation?

When Rahab "heard," she believed and obeyed. And as we will see soon, God blesses her obedience. Do you remember where Rahab's house was located? On the wall. And we all know what is going to happen to those walls. They are going to fall down. But what happens to Rahab's house when that occurs? There can only be one explanation: Left standing, for all to see is one small section, with one solitary house, a house with a scarlet cord hanging down from the window. God will honor her obedience with victory! And He will do the same for you.

Abba Father, thank You that You are good, and You only do good! Thank You that my name
is written in the Lamb's Book of Life. I thank You that You have invited me to obey You that I
might become more like Christ and be able join You in advancing
Your Kingdom on earth.

Father, help me to love You with my entire being and make my greatest desire obedience.
May I follow the example of Jesus and be able to say at the end of my life that I have accomplished
Your purpose and plan for my life. Thank You that You do it through me by Your Holy Spirit.
In Jesus' holy name,
Amen.

LESSON THREE
What do these stones mean?

JOSHUA 3

Israel Crosses the Jordan

[1] Then Joshua rose early in the morning; and he and all the sons of Israel set out from Shittim and came to the Jordan, and they lodged there before they crossed. [2] At the end of three days the officers went through the midst of the camp; [3] and they commanded the people, saying, "When you see the ark of the covenant of the Lord your God with the Levitical priests carrying it, then you shall set out from your place and go after it. [4] However, there shall be between you and it a distance of about 2,000 cubits by measure. Do not come near it, that you may know the way by which you shall go, for you have not passed this way before."

[5] Then Joshua said to the people, "Consecrate yourselves, for tomorrow the Lord will do wonders among you." [6] And Joshua spoke to the priests, saying, "Take up the ark of the covenant and cross over ahead of the people." So they took up the ark of the covenant and went ahead of the people.

[7] Now the Lord said to Joshua, "This day I will begin to exalt you in the sight of all Israel, that they may know that just as I have been with Moses, I will be with you. [8] You shall, moreover, command the priests who are carrying the ark of the covenant, saying, 'When you come to the edge of the waters of the Jordan, you shall stand still in the Jordan.'" [9] Then Joshua said to the sons of Israel, "Come here, and hear the words of the Lord your God." [10] Joshua said, "By this you shall know that the living God is among you, and that He will assuredly dispossess from before you the Canaanite, the Hittite, the Hivite, the Perizzite, the Girgashite, the Amorite, and the Jebusite. [11] Behold, the ark of the covenant of the Lord of all the earth is crossing over ahead of you into the Jordan. [12] Now then, take for yourselves twelve men from the tribes of Israel, one man for each tribe. [13] It shall come about when the soles of the feet of the priests who carry the ark of the Lord, the Lord of all the earth, rest in the waters of the Jordan, the waters of the Jordan will be cut off, and the waters which are flowing down from above will stand in one heap."

[14] So when the people set out from their tents to cross the Jordan with the priests carrying the ark of the covenant before the people, [15] and when those who carried the ark came into the Jordan, and the feet of the priests carrying the ark were dipped in the edge of the water (for the Jordan overflows all its banks all the days of harvest),

¹⁶ the waters which were flowing down from above stood and rose up in one heap, a great distance away at Adam, the city that is beside Zarethan; and those which were flowing down toward the sea of the Arabah, the Salt Sea, were completely cut off. So the people crossed opposite Jericho. ¹⁷ And the priests who carried the ark of the covenant of the Lord stood firm on dry ground in the middle of the Jordan while all Israel crossed on dry ground, until all the nation had finished crossing the Jordan.

JOSHUA 4

Memorial Stones from Jordan

¹ Now when all the nation had finished crossing the Jordan, the Lord spoke to Joshua, saying, ² "Take for yourselves twelve men from the people, one man from each tribe, ³ and command them, saying, 'Take up for yourselves twelve stones from here out of the middle of the Jordan, from the place where the priests' feet are standing firm, and carry them over with you and lay them down in the lodging place where you will lodge tonight.'" ⁴ So Joshua called the twelve men whom he had appointed from the sons of Israel, one man from each tribe; ⁵ and Joshua said to them, "Cross again to the ark of the Lord your God into the middle of the Jordan, and each of you take up a stone on his shoulder, according to the number of the tribes of the sons of Israel. ⁶ Let this be a sign among you, so that when your children ask later, saying, '**What do these stones mean** to you?' ⁷ then you shall say to them, 'Because the waters of the Jordan were cut off before the ark of the covenant of the Lord; when it crossed the Jordan, the waters of the Jordan were cut off.' So these stones shall become a memorial to the sons of Israel forever."

⁸ Thus the sons of Israel did as Joshua commanded, and took up twelve stones from the middle of the Jordan, just as the Lord spoke to Joshua, according to the number of the tribes of the sons of Israel; and they carried them over with them to the lodging place and put them down there. ⁹ Then Joshua set up twelve stones in the middle of the Jordan at the place where the feet of the priests who carried the ark of the covenant were standing, and they are there to this day. ¹⁰ For the priests who carried the ark were standing in the middle of the Jordan until everything was completed that the Lord had commanded Joshua to speak to the people, according to all that Moses had commanded

Joshua. And the people hurried and crossed; ¹¹ and when all the people had finished crossing, the ark of the Lord and the priests crossed before the people. ¹² The sons of Reuben and the sons of Gad and the half-tribe of Manasseh crossed over in battle array before the sons of Israel, just as Moses had spoken to them; ¹³ about 40,000 equipped for war, crossed for battle before the Lord to the desert plains of Jericho.

¹⁴ On that day the Lord exalted Joshua in the sight of all Israel; so that they revered him, just as they had revered Moses all the days of his life.

¹⁵ Now the Lord said to Joshua, ¹⁶ "Command the priests who carry the ark of the testimony that they come up from the Jordan." ¹⁷ So Joshua commanded the priests, saying, "Come up from the Jordan." ¹⁸ It came about when the priests who carried the ark of the covenant of the Lord had come up from the middle of the Jordan, and the soles of the priests' feet were lifted up to the dry ground, that the waters of the Jordan returned to their place, and went over all its banks as before.

¹⁹ Now the people came up from the Jordan on the tenth of the first month and camped at Gilgal on the eastern edge of Jericho. ²⁰ Those twelve stones which they had taken from the Jordan, Joshua set up at Gilgal. ²¹ He said to the sons of Israel, "When your children ask their fathers in time to come, saying, 'What are these stones?' ²² then you shall inform your children, saying, 'Israel crossed this Jordan on dry ground.' ²³ For the Lord your God dried up the waters of the Jordan before you until you had crossed, just as the Lord your God had done to the Red Sea, which He dried up before us until we had crossed; ²⁴ that all the peoples of the earth may know that the hand of the Lord is mighty, so that you may fear the Lord your God forever."

What do these stones mean?

Joshua 3-4

This was done, and recorded, in order to encourage God's people in all ages to trust Him in the greatest straits. What can't He do who did this? [1]

~ Matthew Henry

Let's begin this week's lesson by taking a look at the first phrase in Joshua 3: "Then Joshua rose early in the morning..." (Joshua 3:1). Most primary translations begin with this time stamp.

Joshua is a sequential, linear book that tells the story of what happens to the people of Israel as four decades of wandering in the wilderness finally come to an end.

Joshua 2 closed with words that bear repeating: "Surely the Lord has given all the land into our hands; moreover, all the inhabitants of the land have melted away before us" (Joshua 2:24). To summarize: The people of Israel finally believe that God is able.

This report is quite different from the report given by ten of the twelve spies back in Exodus. How wonderful this new report must have been in Joshua's ears – similar words to the report he and Caleb exclaimed to their countrymen 40 years prior. Words that, back then, fell on deaf ears. But not this time.

And this time, there is no time to waste.

So, "early the next morning," Joshua and his army prepare to cross the Jordan River.

The magnitude of this moment cannot be overstated. This is it. This is the promise. As Joshua stands at the edge of the Jordan, its waters brimming during flood stage, what must be going through his mind? At last, Israel is where he always knew they were meant to be, where God had promised them they would be. And this time, under his leadership, they will not miss the opportunity. He has seen too much. He knows too much. He believes what his God can do.

Under the guidance of the Lord, Joshua will lead the people not only into the land, but into a prophecy fulfilled. It will be a day to remember.

DAY ONE
Joshua 3:1-6

Our passage for this lesson, Joshua 3-4, represents a major turning point in Israel's history. As we read, we will see a number of parallels and applications between this portion of Joshua and our own present-day journey with Jesus. Together, we will unpack both the literal and the figurative pictures of deliverance in these chapters.

To begin, read through Joshua 3 and 4 to get an overview of what's happening and then answer the following questions.

Snapshot
of Joshua 3

What river stands between Israel and the Promised Land?

Who and what does Joshua instruct the people to follow across this river?

Circle every occurrence of the word "ark" in Joshua 3-4.

Who is to gather the stones after they cross?

What seems to be the purpose of these stones?

Now, let's zoom in for a closer look. Joshua 3 is a treasure trove of symbolism!

Read Joshua 3:1-2.

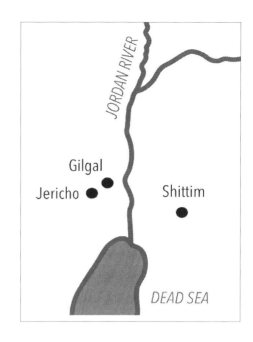

Upon hearing the report from the spies (Joshua 2:24), Joshua and the people of Israel set out for the Jordan River. In order to get our bearings, take a look at the map to see their journey.

1. Circle Shittim on the map and draw a dotted line across the Jordan River to Gilgal.

Imagine for a moment the emotions the Israelites must have experienced during this journey. Shittim is about seven miles east of the Jordan River. So, with all of their belongings and all of the memories of the past 40 years, they begin their walk toward the Promised Land. It probably takes Israel about a day to make the journey from Shittim to the Jordan River. [2]

2. What emotions do you think the Israelites experience as they approach the Jordan River?

We'll dig into this more in the coming days, but we learn later in Joshua 3 that the Jordan River is at flood stage at this time. During most of the year, the Jordan River is shallow enough to walk across, but in the spring, the winter rains combined with the melting snow from the mountains have swollen it to overflowing.

Even though the one obstacle between Israel and the Promised Land is teeming with water, Israel knows that if God is going to fulfill His promise to them, it will begin here. In this generation, only Joshua and Caleb have experienced God's deliverance through the Red Sea. Due to the previous generation's lack of faith, the rest have all died in the wilderness. But this was a new day, a new people, and they are full of hope as they forge ahead.

As this multitude reaches the Jordan River, they likely begin questioning the route and how they are going to get across. I picture a knowing, maybe even mischievous, glance being exchanged between Joshua and Caleb.

Read Joshua 3:3-4.

After they arrive at the Jordan and rest, the officers give the people their orders on the third day. Similar to the way they had followed the pillar of fire and the cloud of smoke in the wilderness, Joshua's officers instruct the people not to move until they see the priests setting out with the ark of the covenant. We're not told that there will be any sort of grand countdown, or time of day when the crossing will happen.

When the priests set out, so will the people. Imagine the incredible amount of anticipation as all of Israel fixes their attention on the ark. As David Guzik points out, "Israel would accomplish this impossible task as they set their eyes upon God's presence and followed the representation of His presence." [3]

In Joshua 3:4, the Israelites are told to get no closer than 2,000 cubits to the ark.

Did you know? A cubit was approximately 18 inches long and was measured from the elbow to the tip of the middle finger. [4] Based upon modern-day measurements, Joshua instructed the people to stay a 1,000 yards, or around a half mile, away from the ark.

We may initially think, based on other passages of Scripture, that the reason they should not come near the ark was to keep them from touching it. (Do you remember Uzzah's untimely death when he touched the ark to keep it from falling? (2 Samuel 6:3-8 and 1 Chronicles 13:7-11.) And certainly, that's a possible reason. Only the priests who were set apart to carry the ark could do so, and only if they strictly followed all the regulations (Numbers 4:15; 7:6-9, Exodus 25:14-15). But scholars also believe there was another reason. Practically, the distance would allow everyone to see the ark as they journeyed. At the time the ark reaches the edge of the water, the people will just be getting to the top of the gorge. They will be well positioned to see how God is going to move on their behalf.

3. Why is it crucial that they set their eyes on the ark? (Joshua 3:4)

The words "for you have not passed this way before" are words with which we can easily identify. Globally, over the past five years, the words, "unprecedented times," have become a household phrase. Worldwide pandemics, toilet paper shortages (help us, Lord), supply-chain problems, hurricanes, and wars have been experienced on a global scale.

But, what about your own "unprecedented times"?

Perhaps you have recently faced (or are currently facing) a path you've never been down before. It could be a challenge or heartache you're facing. Or, like the Israelites, it could be a new opportunity. A new day. Or it may just be the same old mundane day ahead of you. But make no mistake: **No matter what is before you (and none of us knows exactly what's before us), you must keep your eyes steadied on God's presence.**

4. In what area of your life is God calling you to fix your eyes on Him today?

Read Joshua 3:5-6.

5. From the text at the beginning of the lesson, fill in the blanks for verse 5:

The Joshua said to the people, "_____ yourselves, for tomorrow the Lord will

_____ among you."

God had called them to this same practice of consecration at Mount Sinai in Exodus 19. "Consecrate" is the translation of the Hebrew word, *qadas,* which means to dedicate, sanctify, set apart, to be holy. Richard Hess explains this consecration involved "washing their clothes and abstaining from sexual relations (Exodus 19:10-15)." [5] The people need to be cleansed so they can see and experience the wonder of what God is about to do.

Not even Joshua knows what is ahead. But he has seen God do wonders before. And he wants the people to be ready.

For those of us who are in Christ, we are already clean because of the Word He has spoken to us (John 15:3). And when we stand on the banks of our "Jordan," our eyes fixed on God's presence ahead of us, there is no limit to what the Father will do to show His power to deliver. Let's move forward.

Therefore, prepare your minds for action, keep sober in spirit, fix your hope completely
on the grace to be brought to you at the revelation of Jesus Christ.
1 Peter 1:13

DAY TWO
Joshua 3:7-13

Now, the Israelites are poised at the edge of the Jordan River, ready to cross over and take the land God has promised them. But first, something important has to take place.

Read Joshua 3:7.

Here, God speaks to Joshua for the first time since the instructions He gave in Joshua 1:1-9.

1. What promise does God make to Joshua before they move into the land? (v. 7)

To "exalt" means "to raise in rank, power, or character, to elevate by praise or in estimation." [6] As God speaks, He is affirming Joshua's rank as the commander of Israel and telling him the miracle about to be performed will confirm his leadership.

Up to this point, Moses is the leader the people of Israel have known. He is the one who led their ancestors across the Red Sea with the Egyptians in pursuit. Warren Wiersbe explains:

> This miracle magnified Moses before the people, and they recognized that he was indeed the servant of the Lord (Exodus 14:31). God would do the same thing for Joshua at the Jordan, and in so doing, He would remind the people that He was with Joshua just as He had been with Moses (Joshua 4:14; see 1:5, 9). Both Moses and Joshua had received their authority from the Lord before these miracles occurred, but the miracles gave them stature before the people. It takes both authority and stature to exercise effective leadership. [7]

At this critical moment when Israel needs a leader, God assures Joshua, "...just as I have been with Moses, I will be with you" (v. 7).

2. Why do you think it is important that the people recognize Joshua as a leader appointed by God?

Moving into the Promised Land is only the beginning. As we will see in chapters to come, this era of Scripture is known as the Conquest. Taking the land will not be easy, but God will continue to lead them. This miraculous crossing of the Jordan may have been just as much for Joshua's sake as it was for the entire people group.

Read Joshua 3:8-10.

God then gives Joshua instructions for the priests. Although all of Israel will participate in the miraculous crossing, the priests will initiate it as they step into the waters of the Jordan with the ark.

3. As they carry the ark, where are the priests to "stand still"? (v. 8)

In verse nine, Joshua addresses the people and essentially tells them, "Okay guys, here's how this is gonna go!" With the Jordan River swiftly flowing in the background, they hear what Joshua tells them in verse 10.

4. Fill in the blanks.

"By this you shall know that the _____ _____ __ _____ you...." (v. 10)

Note that Joshua does not emphasize his own leadership. Instead, he magnifies the Lord. As he speaks, Joshua is not delivering some type of pre-game pep talk, he is directing the focus of the Israelites to the Lord.

5. Read Zechariah 4:6. What was word of the Lord to Zerubbabel?

When we read a book titled "Joshua," we tend to think that the main character is, in fact, Joshua. And he's certainly a major contributor to what will take place. We even just read that God intends to exalt him before the people. **But the main character of this story, and every story in the Bible, is the Living God.** It is by His Spirit that the miraculous takes place.

The promise of verse 10 extends beyond just crossing the Jordan. It will be years before the Israelites conquer the Canaanites, Hittites, Hivites, Perizzites, Girgashites, Amorites, and Jebusites. But, before they ever even face those battles, God assures them that He will go before them and they will have the victory. The wonder that is about to take place will assure the Israelites that God will do what He has promised.

Did you know? The ark of the covenant represented the presence of God with His people. Robert Smith describes it this way: "The ark was a box made of acacia wood that was overlaid with gold; in fact, gold lined the inside of the box as well as its lid. There were carved angelic beings known as cherubim that faced each other and lifted up their wings toward Heaven in a posture of giving glory to God." [8] Inside the ark was "a golden jar holding the manna, and Aaron's rod which budded, and the tables of the covenant" (Hebrews 9:4). You can read Exodus 25:10-22 for more information about the ark of the covenant.

6. What evidence of God's power have you seen in your life recently? How does this give you hope for the future battles you may face?

Read Joshua 3:11-13.

7. What name does Joshua ascribe to God in verse 11?

The phrase "all the land" appears in the message the king of Jericho sends to Rahab in Joshua 2:3. There, the reference is to the land of Canaan. It may also be the understanding of the name Joshua uses for God in verse 11. Hess expounds on the meaning of "Lord of all the earth":

> God is Lord in the sense of "master" or "ruler." The term describes His sovereignty over the land of Canaan. Although its inhabitants do not yet acknowledge it, they will do so as the symbol which represents God's presence and power enters their land. Israel will witness a demonstration of this power at the miraculous crossing of the Jordan. [9]

8. What instruction does Joshua give the people regarding their tribes? (v. 12)

Hold on to that piece of info. We'll come back to it in a couple of days.

Joshua, speaking to a wide-eyed multitude, reveals to them in verse 13 exactly what will happen when the priests carry the ark into the water. It is something he had experienced himself at the Red Sea. Something the disciples would later experience on the Sea of Galilee. They would all see that God is indeed "the Lord of all the earth" (Joshua 3:13) and that "the earth is the Lord's, and everything in it" (Psalm 24:1, NLT). The swollen Jordan River is no match for the power of God.

What kind of a man is this, that even the winds and the sea obey Him?
Matthew 8:27

DAY THREE
Joshua 3:14-17

This may well be the most important day of this week's homework. It's certainly my favorite because of the richness we'll see from our creative, omniscient God. I can hardly wait to show you, but first, let's go back to the edge of the Jordan River.

Read Joshua 3:14-15.

As we saw yesterday, the first domino that has to fall as the Israelites begin their journey across the river rests solely with the priests. Until they move forward, the people will stay in their tents. But it is a specific group of priests, with a specific role, who will lead out in this endeavor.

1. What role do the priests have who initiate the crossing?

Three times in these two verses and ten times in this brief chapter, the ark of the covenant is mentioned. As Smith says, "This chapter is replete with the mentioning of the significance of the ark of the covenant. Everything begins and ends, it seems, with the ark of the covenant." [10]

To us, this emphasis on a box covered in gold can feel strange or even wrong. Is this idolatry? Did they carry the ark as some sort of lucky charm, or worse, as having some sort of power in and of itself to save them? The answer is a resounding no! As we saw yesterday, the ark was the *symbol* of God's presence among the people. It was the shadow of the reality.

2. In the following passages, what served as God's instrument or symbol of His presence among the Israelites?

Scriptures	God's Instrument or Symbol
Exodus 3:1-3	
Exodus 4:1-5, 17	
Exodus 13:21-22	
Exodus 25:8-9	

When I read about signs and wonders in the Old Testament, I think, "Wow! I wish I could've seen that!" But what Moses, Joshua, the Israelites, and the prophets longed for throughout history was to experience the Spirit of God. On this side of the cross, it's important to pause and try to realize the magnitude of what it means that Jesus, God in flesh, not only came and "dwelt among us" (John 1:14), but that His Spirit "dwells *within* us" (1 Corinthians 3:16).

Now, back to Joshua 3. Picture the scene in your mind as the priests hoist the ark of the covenant up by its poles and head down the steep riverbank toward the flooding waters of the Jordan River.

3. What action do the priests carrying the ark need to take? Circle the answer below:

     a. Jump into the river with abandon

     b. Swim across the river

     c. Dip their feet in the edge

     d. Caulk their wagons and float across

4. While there are many similarities between the moment at the Red Sea and this event at the Jordan, there is a difference. Read Exodus 14:21 and note the difference in God's instructions.

Did you know? If you've never seen the Jordan River in person, it is not as impressive as we might expect. At this portion across from Jericho, it's ordinarily about 50-60 yards wide. There are even areas and seasons where the Jordan is no more than three feet deep. But these weren't ordinary times. This was harvest time, meaning the river was at flood stage, when it would've been "twice as broad, and in ancient times, when the hills on the right and left were much more drenched with rain and snow than since the forests have disappeared." [11] God could've brought them to the crossing at any time. But in His sovereignty, He chooses the season when His power could be shown to a people who would desperately need to see it.

When the Israelites miraculously crossed the Red Sea 40 years earlier, their trust in the Lord should have been set in concrete. But then, that generation's faith faltered, and they spent decades wandering in the desert, learning about God's provision the hard way. Now, God is giving them a second chance to cross into the Promised Land. This time, standing at the banks of the Jordan, a step of faith will be required from them. *But only a step.*

5. Think about a time when God asked you to "dip your feet into the edge of the river." What did you learn about His character and power through that experience?

Read Joshua 3:16-17. Don't rush this. Read these two verses slowly.

In the ancient world, it was common for pagan armies to carry statues or standards representing their deities when they were headed into war. For the Israelites, it is the ark, Jehovah's standard representing His presence, that leads the Israelites across the Jordan into Canaan.

I love the way Ian Thomas describes this moment:

> They were out [of the Jordan] and they were in [to the Promised Land]!...How did they get through the Jordan? They put their feet in the waters of the Jordan and stood still. Why? God told them to! What happened? God divided the waters and they went through on dry land. Why? God said they would! [12]

At the edge of a flooded river, we do not and cannot see our way through. But the Lord does. The Lord can.

As we close today, we cannot rush past the not-so-hidden nugget someone once shared with me from these final verses. The answers to the following questions are simple and straight from the text – but ponder each one as you go:

6. The water stands in a heap a great distance away at what city? (v. 16)

7. The water is cut off that flows down toward which sea? (v. 16)

8. What is another common name for the Salt Sea? (A web search may help.)

9. What do the people do as God stops the waters? (vv. 16-17)

Here is the nugget: The curse of Genesis 3, when Adam's sin led to death for all mankind, was reversed at the cross of Jesus. **Because of Jesus, we have been given a path to cross from our wilderness *into the promise.***

> *He will swallow up death for all time, And the Lord God will wipe tears away from*
> *all faces, And He will remove the disgrace of His people from all the earth;*
> *For the Lord has spoken.*
> Isaiah 25:8, AMP

DAY FOUR
Joshua 4:1-18

Though today's reading carries us well into Joshua 4, there are a couple things we need to reach back and grab from Joshua 3. These two chapters make up one cohesive event for Israel. As Smith says, "Chapters 3 and 4 of Joshua share an inextricable relationship – they cannot be divided. They are not independent of each other; rather, they are interdependently related to each other." [13]

Read Joshua 4:1.

1. Now, look back at Joshua 3:17. What word is used to describe Israel in 4:1 and 3:17?

Lest we miss it, this alone is a promise that has been fulfilled.

2. Read Genesis 12:1-2 and Exodus 19:6. What promise from these verses has been fulfilled in Joshua 3 and 4?

Israel is no longer simply a multitude of people. They're no longer just freed slaves on the run. As promised, they are now a great nation, dwelling in a great land. The *ESV Study Bible* explains, "Israel is not called a 'nation' until now. In Egypt and in the wilderness, Israel was a 'people', now, with their having entered the Promised Land, the term 'nation' begins to apply." [14] Israel is one nation under one God.

Read Joshua 4:2-5.

Get this picture. The entire nation has crossed from the wilderness into the Promised Land, but the priests remain standing in the middle of the Jordan, still on dry ground. Why? Because God has not yet instructed Joshua to move them. Why? Because something else needs to take place.

We now discover the purpose for the 12 men God told Joshua to select in Joshua 3:12.

3. What are the 12 men to do? (Joshua 4:2-5)

Imagine what must have gone through the minds of these 12 men, "Go back into the middle of the Jordan?" It has likely taken a full day for the two million plus people to complete crossing the river. Yes, the waters are still piled high, and the ground is still dry, but how long will it stay that way?

Regardless of their concerns, the men obey. By faith, once again, they enter the riverbed.

4. Where are the men to carry the stones? (v. 3)

It's interesting to me that these men are instructed to carry stones from the middle of the Jordan. Why not just find some shiny, cool-looking rocks from the river's edge? Maybe even some rocks from the ground just inside the Promised Land, as a reminder of a promise fulfilled? But no. God's instructions are clear: Go to the middle of the Jordan, where the priests are still standing with the ark of the covenant, and pick up 12 stones.

5. Why do you think it was important to gather the stones from the middle of the Jordan rather than someplace else?

Read Joshua 4:6-7.

6. What will the stones be used for? (vv. 6-7)

7. Joshua 4:6 is where we find the title of this week's lesson. Write the title below:

We'll get to the broader answer to that question in our final lesson tomorrow. But there is an interesting qualifier in this question.

8. Fill in these blanks from verse 6: "What do these stones mean ____ _____?"

Let's come back to that in a moment.

Read Joshua 4:8-18.

Verse 8 records the obedience of the 12 men to do exactly as God had commanded. Their task is complete. But Joshua is not finished.

9. What does Joshua do next? (v. 9)

10. Why do you think Joshua wanted to leave a memorial in the middle of the Jordan?

Francis Schaeffer shares an interesting, practical perspective: "Occasionally, the Jordan gets very low, and the Israelites were able from time to time to see these twelve stones and to recall the great things God had done for them." [16]

There is no record in Scripture that God has instructed Joshua to do this. It appears to simply be a spontaneous act of worship for what God has done for Israel. Verse 9 tells us that Joshua places the stones where the priests had stood, where the symbol of God's presence had been. Perhaps Joshua saw this place as holy ground. And for Joshua, these stones might have represented a personal fulfillment of God's specific promise to him.

11. In what ways is Israel's obedience to God emphasized in Joshua 4:10-13?

Now let's look back again at our sister chapter, Joshua 3.

12. Compare Joshua 3:7 and Joshua 4:14. How is God's promise to Joshua fulfilled?

Hess draws another comparison between Joshua 3 and 4 as he notes that Joshua 4:15-18 resemble Joshua 3:8, 13, 15-16:

> There, the Lord speaks to Joshua and promises his exaltation. He instructs him to command the priests who carry the ark to stand in the river and, when they do, the waters of the Jordan cease. In Joshua 4:15-18, the Lord speaks again to Joshua and instructs him to command the priests. This time, however, they are to bring the ark up from the Jordan on to the dry ground of Canaan. Again, Joshua instructs the priests in what the Lord has said. Again, they do exactly as instructed and move the ark. [17]

Today's passage closes with the waters of the Jordan returning to their place. In fact, as soon as the priests carrying the ark of the covenant step out of the dry riverbed and onto the soil of the plains of Jericho, the water lapped at their heels as it "went over all its banks as before" (Joshua 4:18).

As the nation of Israel looks on, jaws on the ground, with a pile of stones nearby – I have to wonder how these individuals would answer the question, **"What do these stones mean to you?"**

13. As you look back on the obstacles God has helped you overcome – your Jordan, your Jericho, your wilderness – what do the reminders of God's faithfulness mean *to you*?

Consider gathering some rocks to serve as a literal memorial of God's faithfulness. Mark them with some sort of reminder of how you've seen God move on your behalf. Place them somewhere prominent in your house and be prepared to share of God's faithfulness anytime a friend or family member asks, "What do these stones mean to you?"

DAY FIVE
Joshua 3-4 | What do these stones mean?

Up to this point, the Israelites' entire history has been filled with ever-increasing anticipation. From the day the promise was given to Abraham, it has all come down to this moment. The wilderness is behind them and the land of milk and honey is before them. There is only one problem: The Promised Land is occupied. In fact, it could be said that the easy part is over. All the more reason why these stones of remembrance will serve a far greater purpose than simply a fond memory.

Read Joshua 4:19-24.

This week's warfare principle is:

> **Remembering what God has done builds a foundation of trust for what He will do.**

We've talked a lot about the similarities between the miracles at the Red Sea and the Jordan River. God parted the Red Sea so the Israelites could escape from Pharaoh. He did it again at the Jordan River so they could cross over into the Promised Land. But there is one major difference: At the Red Sea, their enemy had been behind them, chasing after them. At the Jordan, their enemies are ahead of them, along with battles they have not yet faced.

I don't have to tell you – you are going to face battles. You've faced them before, and you'll face them again. But it's our Red Sea moments that prepare us for our Jordan River moments. And it's our Jordan River moments that strengthen us to stand firm against the enemy that awaits us. Robert Morgan makes the connection, "The Lord then sends a trial into our lives to give us an opportunity to put His teachings into practice. As we trust Him and pass the test, we're strengthened for the future." [18]

Did you know? Gilgal, where Joshua set up the 12 stones of remembrance, is a place of great significance in the Old Testament, especially in the book of Joshua. According to Smith, "The word 'Gilgal' means 'roll.' Gilgal reminded the Israelites that the reproach, the embarrassment, and the shame of their 400 year servitude in Egypt had been rolled away." [19] Gilgal will serve as Joshua's military base throughout the conquest of Canaan and be a significant place in the history of Israel throughout Scripture.

1. On what date does the nation of Israel cross the Jordan River? (v. 19)

This is the same date that appears in Exodus 12:2-3, where the preparations for the Passover (which occurs on the fourteenth day of the month) are introduced. David Jackman observes that this is indicative of God's sovereignty, "Clearly the timing underlies the connection of the entry of the land with the exodus from Egypt some forty years earlier. The resting place chosen for their first night in the land is Gilgal (Joshua 4:19), where the memorial stones are set up (v. 20)." [20]

The memorials at Gilgal and in the Jordan are made of uncarved stone. In the days of Joshua, it was the custom of pagans to carve stone into images of people, animals, or symbols of nature to represent gods. God has already been clear in Exodus 20:4: No image formed by human hands is to represent Him.

The 12 stones that Joshua sets up at Gilgal have a very important purpose and a very specific audience.

2. How will these stones be used in the future? (Joshua 4:21-22)

Yesterday, we discussed the importance of personal testimony of God's goodness. We reflected on the question, "What do these stones mean to you?" Here, there is a broader focus on testifying to what God was willing to do for His people – a people that would face battle after battle in the coming years.

3. This is not the first time God has commanded His people to remember His character and power. Record what God commanded them to remember and why they should remember.

Passage	Remember	Why
Exodus 13:3		
Exodus 20:8		
Deuteronomy 5:15		
Deuteronomy 8:18		

This is merely a sampling of the times God tells the Israelites to remember what He has done for them: How He has brought them out of bondage, provided for them, and shown His might on their behalf. But this emphasis on "children" in Joshua 4 is noteworthy.

4. Read Psalm 78:1-8. Briefly summarize this passage.

In his book *Raising Spiritual Champions*, George Barna pulls no punches on the importance of raising children to be disciples of Jesus:

> Nationally, the body of Christ rejects the scriptural idea that children are born as spiritual beings and need to be prepared for spiritual battle at an early age. If you do not want to accept the cultural evidence of the significance of children, the Bible is very clear in that regard. We may not take the spiritual life and development of children seriously, but it is not because God has failed to exhort us to do so. [21]

Barna goes on to give examples in Scripture of God directing his people to share His faithfulness with the next generation – and we see it plainly in Joshua 4.

5. What two answers are the Israelites to give when their children ask about the stones? (v. 24)

-

-

One of the most beautiful things about children is their innocence – which is why it ignites so much pain and anger in us when it's stolen from them. Barring early tragedy, children are mostly spared from seeing the evil around us. But we are sorely mistaken if we pretend they won't. **And when the generation experiences the trials of this world, they must be able to look back and see our heap of stones.** It's up to us. We must tell them about the Lord's faithfulness, of His wonders and deliverance: How He parts the waters, calms the seas, slays the giants, walks with us through the fire, heals the hurting, died for us, forgives us, loves us, prays for us, and lives in us!

Just as Joshua commissioned the priests to lead the way into the Promised Land, God sent Jesus to be our Way into His promise of redemption. He "is the new and better ark of the covenant, God in flesh who dwelt among us. In knowing Christ, we hear God's proclamation and experience God's provision and power." [22]

Like the Israelites, we win the spiritual battle when we remember what God has done and we sing the song of Psalm 114:3, 5, "The sea looked and fled; the Jordan turned back...What ails you, O sea, that you flee? O Jordan, that you turn back?"

> *"Who is the King of glory? The Lord of Heaven's Armies – He is the King of glory."*
> Psalm 24:10, NLT

LESSON FOUR
Shout! For the Lord...

Israel Is Circumcised

[1] Now it came about when all the kings of the Amorites who were beyond the Jordan to the west, and all the kings of the Canaanites who were by the sea, heard how the Lord had dried up the waters of the Jordan before the sons of Israel until they had crossed, that their hearts melted, and there was no spirit in them any longer because of the sons of Israel.

[2] At that time the Lord said to Joshua, "Make for yourself flint knives and circumcise again the sons of Israel the second time." [3] So Joshua made himself flint knives and circumcised the sons of Israel at Gibeath-haaraloth. [4] This is the reason why Joshua circumcised them: all the people who came out of Egypt who were males, all the men of war, died in the wilderness along the way after they came out of Egypt. [5] For all the people who came out were circumcised, but all the people who were born in the wilderness along the way as they came out of Egypt had not been circumcised. [6] For the sons of Israel walked forty years in the wilderness, until all the nation, that is, the men of war who came out of Egypt, perished because they did not listen to the voice of the Lord, to whom the Lord had sworn that He would not let them see the land which the Lord had sworn to their fathers to give us, a land flowing with milk and honey. [7] Their children whom He raised up in their place, Joshua circumcised; for they were uncircumcised, because they had not circumcised them along the way.

[8] Now when they had finished circumcising all the nation, they remained in their places in the camp until they were healed. [9] Then the Lord said to Joshua, "Today I have rolled away the reproach of Egypt from you." So the name of that place is called Gilgal to this day.

[10] While the sons of Israel camped at Gilgal they observed the Passover on the evening of the fourteenth day of the month on the desert plains of Jericho. [11] On the day after the Passover, on that very day, they ate some of the produce of the land, unleavened cakes and parched grain. [12] The manna ceased on the day after they had eaten some of the produce of the land, so that the sons of Israel no longer had manna, but they ate some of the yield of the land of Canaan during that year.

[13] Now it came about when Joshua was by Jericho, that he lifted up his eyes and looked, and behold, a man was standing opposite him with his sword drawn in his hand, and Joshua went to him and said to him, "Are you for us or for our

adversaries?" ¹⁴ He said, "No; rather I indeed come now as captain of the host of the Lord." And Joshua fell on his face to the earth, and bowed down, and said to him, "What has my lord to say to his servant?" ¹⁵ The captain of the Lord's host said to Joshua, "Remove your sandals from your feet, for the place where you are standing is holy." And Joshua did so.

JOSHUA 6

The Conquest of Jericho

¹ Now Jericho was tightly shut because of the sons of Israel; no one went out and no one came in. ² The Lord said to Joshua, "See, I have given Jericho into your hand, with its king and the valiant warriors. ³ You shall march around the city, all the men of war circling the city once. You shall do so for six days. ⁴ Also seven priests shall carry seven trumpets of rams' horns before the ark; then on the seventh day you shall march around the city seven times, and the priests shall blow the trumpets. ⁵ It shall be that when they make a long blast with the ram's horn, and when you hear the sound of the trumpet, all the people shall shout with a great shout; and the wall of the city will fall down flat, and the people will go up every man straight ahead."

⁶ So Joshua the son of Nun called the priests and said to them, "Take up the ark of the covenant, and let seven priests carry seven trumpets of rams' horns before the ark of the Lord." ⁷ Then he said to the people, "Go forward, and march around the city, and let the armed men go on before the ark of the Lord." ⁸ And it was so, that when Joshua had spoken to the people, the seven priests carrying the seven trumpets of rams' horns before the Lord went forward and blew the trumpets; and the ark of the covenant of the Lord followed them. ⁹ The armed men went before the priests who blew the trumpets, and the rear guard came after the ark, while they continued to blow the trumpets. ¹⁰ But Joshua commanded the people, saying, "You shall not shout nor let your voice be heard nor let a word proceed out of your mouth, until the day I tell you, 'Shout!' Then you shall shout!" ¹¹ So he had the ark of the Lord taken around the city, circling it once; then they came into the camp and spent the night in the camp.

¹² Now Joshua rose early in the morning, and the priests took up the ark of the Lord. ¹³ The seven priests carrying the seven trumpets of rams' horns before the ark of the Lord went on continually, and blew the trumpets; and the armed men went before them and the rear guard came after the ark of the Lord, while they continued

to blow the trumpets. ¹⁴ Thus the second day they marched around the city once and returned to the camp; they did so for six days.

¹⁵ Then on the seventh day they rose early at the dawning of the day and marched around the city in the same manner seven times; only on that day they marched around the city seven times. ¹⁶ At the seventh time, when the priests blew the trumpets, Joshua said to the people, "**Shout! For the Lord** has given you the city. ¹⁷ The city shall be under the ban, it and all that is in it belongs to the Lord; only Rahab the harlot and all who are with her in the house shall live, because she hid the messengers whom we sent. ¹⁸ But as for you, only keep yourselves from the things under the ban, so that you do not covet them and take some of the things under the ban, and make the camp of Israel accursed and bring trouble on it. ¹⁹ But all the silver and gold and articles of bronze and iron are holy to the Lord; they shall go into the treasury of the Lord."

²⁰ So the people shouted, and priests blew the trumpets; and when the people heard the sound of the trumpet, the people shouted with a great shout and the wall fell down flat, so that the people went up into the city, every man straight ahead, and they took the city. ²¹ They utterly destroyed everything in the city, both man and woman, young and old, and ox and sheep and donkey, with the edge of the sword.

²² Joshua said to the two men who had spied out the land, "Go into the harlot's house and bring the woman and all she has out of there, as you have sworn to her." ²³ So the young men who were spies went in and brought out Rahab and her father and her mother and her brothers and all she had; they also brought out all her relatives and placed them outside the camp of Israel. ²⁴ They burned the city with fire, and all that was in it. Only the silver and gold, and articles of bronze and iron, they put into the treasury of the Lord. ²⁵ However, Rahab the harlot and her father's household and all she had, Joshua spared; and she has lived in the midst of Israel to this day, for she hid the messengers whom Joshua sent to spy out Jericho.

²⁶ Then Joshua made them take an oath at that time, saying, "Cursed before the Lord is the man who rises up and builds this city Jericho; with the loss of his firstborn he shall lay its foundation, and with the loss of his youngest son he shall set up its gates." ²⁷ So the Lord was with Joshua, and his fame was in all the land.

Shout! For the Lord...

*Enemy-occupied territory – that is what this world is. Christianity is the story of
how the rightful King has landed, you might say landed in disguise,
and is calling us to take part in His great campaign of sabotage.* [1]

~ C.S. Lewis

I remember the day like it was yesterday. My phone rang, I answered, and heard my husband say, "Honey, how would you feel about going on a mission trip to teach Pioneer Evangelism in Nigeria?" I was stunned. I wasn't sure how to respond. My mind spun off in a million directions. Only once before had I traveled outside the United States. I was pretty sure I was a most unlikely candidate for international missions. And then, there was the fact I thought Nigeria was in Central America, so we had to get that issue settled (Geography is not my strong suit!). We decided to attend an informational meeting about the trip, and there I caught the vision of what could be done to equip pastors to help their people evangelize, disciple, and plant churches. During the meeting, I sensed God's confirmation, and from that day on, I was all in!

To be honest, this was a pretty big endeavor for the two unseasoned travelers we were at the time. And we had never taught Pioneer Evangelism before, so the entire venture was going to be new to us. But, we were both strong on enthusiasm, and decided that had to count for something!

As the day drew near for our departure, we spent some time with our sons and their families. We talked excitedly about our grand adventure and they were genuinely excited, and even a bit proud of us. As we hugged them tightly, both sons whispered, "Please be careful." Aware of all the things that could go sideways – especially considering my track record of "crazy" – we reassured them we would be careful, and ended our visit with, "The only safe place is in the middle of God's will, and we believe this is God's will."

When we arrived in Nigeria, we quickly fell in love with the people, and were amazed at their profound faith in our Lord in the midst of difficult, and often dangerous, circumstances. While we were there, we had little access to internet, so we did not have much communication with our boys. However, on one occasion, when we did have access, we received this email from Dawson:

Dear Mom and Dad,

We are anxious to hear all about your trip. I know you are doing what God has called you to do. And I know that you are not afraid to trust the Lord, and we are not afraid for you. But this morning in my quiet time, I read 2 Kings 6:17, "Then Elisha prayed and said, 'O Lord, I pray, open his eyes that he may see,' and the Lord opened the servant's eyes and he saw; and behold, the mountain was full of horses and chariots of fire all around Elisha." I pray that God will open your eyes to see the Lord's army surrounding you.

Love, Dawson

As I began studying for this lesson, I was reminded of that email. As Joshua 5 opens, the Israelites are about to have their first encounter with their Canaanite enemy at Jericho, the city at the threshold of the Promised Land. It will be this new generation's first military engagement. Like Elisha, Joshua is going to need assurance of God's presence as they begin to claim Canaan. Fresh off the Jordan River crossing, they are riding high, bolstered by the experience. The entire nation is ready to step *into the promise*. But now, it is about to get real.

DAY ONE
Joshua 5:1

As we move into this portion of Scripture, Joshua is preparing for the first major battle in the Promised Land. Read through Joshua 5-6 to get the flow of the text we will be unpacking this week. Be mindful of the theme of these two chapters and look for repetitive words.

Let's create a snapshot of these two chapters to give us an overview before we take a deeper dive in.

Snapshot
of Joshua 5-6

What event prompts the Israelites to camp at Gilgal?

What is the condition of Jericho at the beginning of Joshua 6, and how does God instruct Joshua to approach it?

As you read Joshua 5-6, what theme did you sense developing in this passage? (Gathering the general idea of a passage is helpful as God writes His story in the book of Joshua.)

What recurring words or phrases did you notice in Joshua 5-6? (Repetition communicates the author's primary emphasis as the Spirit of God reveals the story through the pen of His chosen instrument.)

Ready to see some walls knocked down? Let's go!

Read Joshua 5:1.

The story of God's miraculous deliverance of His people from Egypt, and His parting of the Red Sea, has reached to the farthest recesses of the land. The reputation of the God of Israel produces terror in the hearts of His enemies.

Let's take a brief trip down memory lane to recall how the Israelites have gotten to this point in their history.

1. Read Deuteronomy 1:2. How long should the trip to the Promised Land have taken?

Kadesh-barnea was on the border of the Promised Land, and the spot intended to be the entry point for Israelites to take the land. Rebellion against the Lord (Numbers 14:10) caused Him to refuse to allow them to enter the Promised Land, relegating them to 40 years of wandering until those who rebelled died in the wilderness (Numbers 14:26-38). Only those who were 20 or younger would be able to claim Canaan, with the exception of Joshua and Caleb.

2. At some point in our lives, I'm pretty sure we have all gone through a season of rebellion against God's command. Think about a time in your walk with the Lord that you refused to obey Him. What were some of the consequences of such behavior?

When the trek of the Israelites stalled, we can assume it caused confusion for God's enemies and brought disgrace on the testimony of the Lord. For four decades, the Canaanites watched as the Israelites walked in circles without making any forward progress. But now, God's people are on the move. When the next generation of mostly young adults begin to march toward Canaan, the enemies of God take notice.

The inhabitants of Jericho are Amorites. The Amorites are descendants from one of the sons of Canaan (Genesis 10:15-16), and are one of the seven people groups spread throughout Canaan. God has promised to dispossess them before Israel (Joshua 3:10). The term "Canaanite" is often used as a general term for all of the inhabitants of Canaan. Richard Hess explains, "'Amorites' and 'Canaanites' are terms used to describe the same peoples. Their locations refer to peoples living between the Jordan and the Mediterranean." [2]

It is likely the king of Jericho and his fighting men know Israel is camped on the opposite of the Jordan. It would be hard to miss two and a half million people (more or less) setting up camp. It is likely the king of

Jericho thinks the Israelites will wait to cross the Jordan River until after the spring floods, when water levels would return to normal, and cause them to let down their guard.

I can only imagine the sight when the Israelites, unexpectedly, begin to line up in formation as they make preparations to cross over the raging Jordan. I wonder how long it took for Israel to cross? Some research on Mr. Google gave me this bit of information:

> The Bible does not really answer this question...But we can do some calculations to determine how long it would have taken. The Bible says that there were 600,000 fighting men. Scholars calculate that this would mean at least 2.5 million Israelites, including women, children, priests, and the elderly. The Bible also says that the Israelites had cattle, which would also have been driven across. Traveling several persons abreast, we could start by assuming that on average one person crossed every second, day and night for twenty-four hours a day. Two and a half million people would take up to 29 days to cross." [3]

Whether this calculation is accurate or not, we cannot be sure. God may have miraculously caused the Israelites to get across in record time, but I think God allowed this to play out in real time. I believe **He wanted His people to soak up this miracle and imprint it on their hearts.** God wants them to recount this event to the next generation with great accuracy and reverential enthusiasm. David Guzik explains how God was also sending a message to the inhabitants of Jericho, "The miraculous passage through the Jordan was not only a testimony to Israel, but also to the Canaanites. It was an additional warning to them that God's judgment was on the way, coming through the armies of Israel." [4]

Did you know? God had prophesied to Abram that when the iniquity of the Amorites reached its full measure (see Genesis 15:16), Israel would be God's instrument of judgment. God delayed His judgement for over 400 years out of mercy, giving them time and space to repent. The Amorites and other Canaanites were exceedingly wicked, worshipping idols and committing horrific sins. When the Amorites were entirely reprobate (beyond repentance), God brought Joshua and the children of Israel against them.

How kind of the Lord to allow this next generation of those who have come out of Egypt to experience a similar "Red Sea" miracle! Don't overlook the fact that the Lord not only parts the Jordan, but He also dries up the riverbed so that "all Israel crossed on dry ground" (Joshua 3:17), just as He had done at the Red Sea (Exodus 14:29). Have you ever waded across a stream or gone swimming in a creek? When you stand up, mud and silt squeeze up between your toes. This creates a suction that holds you fast as it threatens to drag you down into the water. Here, the Lord dries the muddy riverbed, allowing them to arrive on the other side with clean feet. I know all the mommas were glad.

3. I love to hear about God-stories in the lives of others. Hearing a testimony of His faithfulness always solidifies my confidence in His ability to move on my behalf. Will you share of a time when God stood strong for your benefit?

The nation of Israel arrives safely on the other side of the Jordan. God's miraculous deliverance totally demoralizes the Canaanites, who are at a loss to compete on any level with Israel's God.

4. In the text at the beginning of the lesson, underline the reaction of the Canaanites to the approaching Israelites. (Joshua 5:1b)

The stage is set for Israel to move into the land and possess it. The people of Jericho are growing increasingly unsettled as word of Israel's approach is noised about, sending shock waves through the city, from the king down to the lowest levels of servitude.

Although scholars agree that Jericho was fortified well enough to survive a siege for a year or more, the unknown element is Israel's God. Should He fight for the Israelites, no one would be able to withstand Him.

This dreadful realization of the likely annihilation of the city of Jericho led Rahab to salvation, which resulted in her deliverance as well as her family's – both physically and spiritually. The kings of the Amorites and Canaanites have heard of the exploits of Israel's God, but instead of fleeing to Him in faith as Rahab had done, their rebellious hearts sink in fear and immobilize them. Oh, that the enemies of God had responded with faith in Israel's God rather than fear!

The Israelites are now in the land, but they are not yet ready to confront the enemy. Their exposure to faith-walking is skewed at best, having lived among a people with a lackluster relationship with God, known for murmuring and complaining, and given to fear and rebellion. Besides overcoming the impact of their dysfunctional family life, they still have some spiritual lessons to learn before they can walk *Into the Promise*. Don't we all?

Dear Heavenly Father, Your mighty works in the Old Testament testify of Your power and presence in the parting of the Red Sea, and a similar miracle at the Jordan River. Your greatest work, the one that split the spectrum of time, was the cross of Jesus Christ. Christ died for our sins according to the Scriptures, was buried, was raised on the third day, and is now seated at Your right hand. Because of Him, I am now Your ambassador for Christ. May I be a testimony of Your power to redeem and Your indwelling presence of the Holy Spirit.

Amen and Amen.

DAY TWO
Joshua 5:2-9

Joshua's leadership has been established and Israel has crossed the Jordan. The miraculous nature of this venture fuels the people with exhilaration and anticipation. Now, positioned on the west side of the river, the excitement throughout the camp is palpable. If God is on their side, who can prevail against them?

Read Joshua 5:2-9.

God's people are encamped between the Jordan River and the city of Jericho. The nation of Israel is comprised of individuals 40 years and younger (Numbers 14:29). They are amped up, ready to claim their piece of real estate and set a move-in date. The women are beginning to dream about settling down in a permanent residence after years of a nomadic lifestyle. The children are sick of eating manna and have become tired and whiny. The livestock, which have been driven through the desert, are showing signs of wear. They are ready for a more sedentary life in a place where food is plentiful, and the shifting sand of the desert no longer blows and blinds their eyes. Standing at the threshold of a whole new way of living, God's people are eagerly awaiting what happens next.

The battle of Jericho is imminent. To a military strategist, it would seem Israel should seize this moment and move quickly to attack, while the people are still enthusiastic and motivated and while the citizens of Jericho are panic-stricken. From a human viewpoint, this is the perfect time to marshal the troops and thrash their opponents. But just like that, God hits the pause button.

We live in a fast-paced world that is burdened with F.O.M.O. (fear of missing out). We want immediate gratification. Waiting is a concept we intentionally resist. And being asked to wait patiently is out of the question. Patience is a quality most of us struggle to evoke or maintain.

Here are some interesting statistics that prove the point:

- 96 percent of Americans will knowingly consume extremely hot food or drink that burns their mouth; and 63 percent do so frequently.
- More than half hang up the phone after being on hold for one minute or less.
- 71 percent frequently exceed the speed limit to get to their destination faster.
- Americans will binge-watch an average of seven TV episodes in a single sitting.
- Nearly a third of respondents aged 18-24 admit to waiting less than one second before bypassing someone walking slower in front of them.
- Generation Y-ers check their phones an average of eight times when waiting to hear back from someone they've dated.
- When waiting for a table at a restaurant, nearly a quarter of respondents ages 18-24 wait less than one minute before approaching the host again after the wait period has passed. [5]

Were it not for God working the fruit of the Spirit within us, we would never know the joy of operating in this virtue (Galatians 5:22-23). In the process of spiritual growth, we often find ourselves being sent to what I call God's waiting room. And we don't like it, because we don't like to wait. **But God knows that delayed gratification is useful in our character development, making us more like Christ and less like a spoiled child that demands her way.**

1. Can you think of a time when God caused you to wait for an answer to prayer? Write down the circumstances and the lesson you learned in the process.

When my husband and I first married, we bought a tiny cabin on a lake in Eads, Tennessee. It was the perfect size for the two of us, and for several years we lived happily in our tiny home. But then, we started our family. With the addition of two little boys in two years, our tiny space seemed to shrink overnight. As we sought the Lord, we sensed He was giving us permission to relocate.

Trying to check out real estate with two little people in tow proved to be more challenging than expected. And trying to find a home that was reasonably priced and would meet our needs for years to come only added to the difficulty. Weeks rolled into months as we waited on the Lord. Several homes seemed to meet our specifications, but after putting in multiple competitive offers, offer after offer was declined. Understand that with each house, I had mentally redecorated – ripping up carpet, moving walls, adding a garage, and redoing the landscaping. I became emotionally attached to every home we considered, so each loss felt like the death of a vision.

In addition, trying to keep our little cabin showcase ready with two toddlers was proving to be more than I could reasonably do. Every time our real estate agent called to show our home, our oldest would holler out, "Momma, get the vacuum!" Moving was quickly rising to the top of the list of things I never wanted to do again! And frankly, I was growing weary of sitting in God's waiting room, where time seems to stand still and emotions escalate easily. During that time, a dear older saint shared this verse with me and it was God's word for us, "Therefore will the Lord wait, that He may be gracious unto you" (Isaiah 30:18, KJV).

After months of waiting and a few tears (and by a few, I mean buckets), God moved on our behalf. A sweet couple wanted to move to the country, and our cabin was just what they wanted. And then, suddenly, we found the perfect house for our family. **When God makes us wait on His perfect will, He is at work behind the scenes on our behalf for the best possible solution.** And when He acts, it may appear to be a sudden resolution, but in reality it is the culmination of preparation, obedience, and anticipation. Beloved, only God could have orchestrated the circumstances and the resolution. Indeed, God was (and continues to be) gracious to us.

One of the life lessons learned in God's waiting room is that He is not concerned with time; He is all about the timing. Joshua and the children of Israel are about to learn this lesson.

2. In a move that seems counterintuitive, what does God tell Joshua to do? (v. 2)

Circumcision is an outward physical sign of the eternal covenant between God and the Jewish people. Biblical scholars Kenneth Gangel and Max Anders help us understand this Old Testament sacred ritual:

> Circumcision, the physical sign of the Abrahamic covenant, goes back to Genesis 17 where God said to Abraham, "You are to undergo circumcision, and it will be a sign of the covenant between me and you. For the generations to come every male among you who is eight days old must be circumcised" (Genesis 17:12). This was a visible sign of commitment to God. It proclaimed a national distinctive: "We are different and we belong to you." It also reminded the nation of God's promise to Abraham to make them a great people and give them the land. How important then to have the sign in place when preparing to enter this promised land. [6]

Camped in the shadows of the enemy walls, God asks Joshua to do the unthinkable and incapacitate his entire army. For Joshua, it will take great faith to submit to God's command, which is contrary to wise military strategy.

Joshua acts with immediate obedience (Joshua 5:3), as do all the sons of Israel, who have submitted themselves to God's command through Joshua (v. 8). This act of obedience is essential if the people of Israel are to know God's presence and serve God's purposes.

3. Why is it necessary to circumcise all the men who had been born in the wilderness? (Joshua 5:4-7)

This command was apparently ignored in the wilderness by an entire generation. In Joshua 5:2, God repeats the command of this covenant mark "the second time." Having arrived in the Promised Land, it is vital that they renew their covenant relationship with the Lord.

This physical mark in the flesh is meant to symbolize a spiritual operation on the heart. Deuteronomy 10:16 says, "So circumcise your heart, and stiffen your neck no longer." Warren Wiersbe debunks the notion that the ritual of circumcision counts towards salvation, "But over the years, the Jews came to trust in the external mark of the covenant and not in the God of the covenant who wanted to make them a holy people. They thought that as long as they were God's covenant people, they could live just as they pleased!" [7]

4. What is the meaning behind the name Gilgal? (v. 9)

You will remember from our last lesson that the reproach refers to the ridicule of their enemies when Israel failed to trust God at Kadesh-barnea and were denied the right to enter the Promised Land. Their rebellion resulted in a forty-year death march through the wilderness. At times, God grew so weary of His rebellious people that He considered exterminating them and beginning again.

5. Look up the following passages, examples of times when the Lord lost patience with His petulant people. In both instances, Moses pleads with the Lord to stay His hand of judgment against them. Jot down your insights.

Scripture	Israel's Sin	The Reproach of the Egyptians
Exodus 32:1-14		
Numbers 14:11-19		

Why did Moses plea with the Lord to spare the Israelites? Because he did not want the Egyptians to spread the word that Israel's God was not able to finish what He had started, or even worse, that He had abandoned His chosen people.

Now, standing inside the borders of the Promised Land, Israel has been careful to obey God, and reenact the sacred ritual of circumcision. Warren Wiersbe explains the significance of the place called Gilgal:

> No matter what the Egyptians and the other nations had said about Israel because of their sin at Kadesh-barnea, that reproach was now completely gone. Each man bore on his body the mark that reminded him that he belonged to God, he was a son of the covenant, and the land was his to conquer and possess. [8]

What a hallelujah day for God's people!

In Colossians 2:11-12, Paul writes, "In Him you were also circumcised with a circumcision made without hands, in the removal of the body of the flesh by the circumcision of Christ; having been buried with Him in baptism, in which you were also raised up with Him through faith in the working of God, who raised Him from the dead." David Jackman helps us shift our understanding of the covenant sign of believers from the Old Testament to the New Testament:

> The covenant sign moves from circumcision to baptism in the new order, whereby the outward and visible sign speaks of an inward and spiritual grace. That grace means "putting off...the flesh," the old sinful, self-centered way of life. This is the spiritual reality of regeneration, accomplished in us by and through the saving work of Christ. [9]

In the familiar words of John 3:16, "For God so loved the world, that He gave His only begotten Son, that whoever believes in Him shall not perish, but have eternal life." God's invitation to come to Jesus to be saved is inclusive, but the way to salvation is very specific. Salvation is through Jesus Christ alone. In John 14:6, "Jesus said to him, I am the way, and the truth, and the life; no one comes to the Father but through Me." He is the only way to be reconciled to God. In Romans 1:16, Paul writes, "For I am not ashamed of the gospel, for it is the power of God for salvation to everyone who believes, to the Jew first and also to the Greek." The body of Christ is made "from every tribe and tongue and people and nation" (Revelation 5:9), of all who has repented of their sin, believed on the Lord Jesus, and received Him by faith. "For whosoever shall call upon the name of the Lord shall be saved" (Romans 10:13, KJV). God's grace is truly amazing! So step *Into the Promise* of eternal life with Christ!

Amazing grace! how sweet the sound,
That saved a wretch; like me!
I once was lost, but now am found,
Was blind, but now I see. [10]

DAY THREE
Joshua 5:10-15

In yesterday's lesson, we saw how the Israelites reinstated the ritual of circumcision as they were preparing to take the Promised Land. Today, we will examine a second act of obedience that needs to take place prior to the conquest.

Read Joshua 5:10.

1. Now look back at Joshua 4:19. How long have the Israelites been encamped at Gilgal? (5:10)

2. What holiday do the Israelites celebrate on the fourteenth day? (v. 10)

The observance of Passover had first been instituted the night before the Israelites' exodus from Egypt (Exodus 12-13). The second time was "in the wilderness of Sinai, in the first month of the second year after they had come out of the land of Egypt" (Numbers 9:1). There is no account of the Israelites celebrating it again in the years of the wilderness wandering. Exodus 12:48 (NKJV) states, "No uncircumcised person may eat of [the passover meal]." The fact that the new generation were not circumcised in the wilderness would have prevented them from participating in this holy celebration. Now, having stepped into the Promised Land and completed the ritual of circumcision, the nation stands ready to celebrate the Passover.

Read the story of the first Passover in Exodus 12:1-13. Remember the death of the firstborn was the tenth and final plague. This is on the heels of nine plagues which have created chaos in Egypt. Pharaoh had every reason to believe Israel's God would deliver on His promise.

3. What instructions were given concerning the Passover lamb (or goat)? (Exodus 12:5-10)

4. The Passover meal was to be eaten in a particular fashion. What was that? (v. 11)

5. What was the judgment God declared He would bring down throughout the land of Egypt? (v. 12)

6. What would stay God's hand of judgment? (v. 13)

7. Reread Exodus 12:1-13. What imagery of the Lord Jesus do you see in the Passover?

With the exception of Joshua and Caleb, none of the Israelites have ever celebrated Passover. However, they most certainly would have heard stories about it, since oral history was the means used to pass information from one generation to another.

Try to imagine the great joy that accompanies the reinstatement of this celebration in the Promised Land. In addition, there is a very significant event tucked into this passage.

Read Joshua 5:11-12.

8. What becomes the new source of food for the Israelites? (v. 11)

9. When does the food the Israelites are eating change? (v. 11)

10. What do the Israelites quit receiving on the same day? (v. 12)

After 40 years of eating the same thing, day in and day out, what a blessed relief that must have been!

To enrich our study and enhance our understanding of some of the hidden meaning of manna, Harry Ironside shares this:

> Morning by morning it came from Heaven to earth. It was not upon the high trees or on the mountains where the people would have to climb to obtain it; nor was it down in the deep ravines where they would have to descend and search for it. It lay all about them upon the ground, on the dew, which is a type of the Holy Spirit. The manna occupied so low a place that every Israelite, when he stepped out of his tent door in the morning, had to do one of two things: he either had to gather it or trample on it. And this is exactly the place which our Lord Jesus has taken in His infinite love and grace. We may well pause and ask ourselves the question: Are we trampling on His loving-kindness or have we received Him as our blessed, adorable Savior? [11]

Read Joshua 5:13-15.

We can assume that shortly after the Passover, Joshua begins to work on preparations for the conquest of Canaan. All that is lacking is a battle plan and the go-order from God.

11. Where does this next scene take place? (v. 13)

At sunset, Joshua is walking near Jericho, probably on a secret reconnaissance mission to see for himself the enemy's walled city and plan his strategy for attack. Phillip Keller uses poetic language to give us a mental image of what Joshua sees: "Across the low plain, a short distance from Gilgal, stood Jericho. Its perimeter of rough brown walls, pierced by huge gateways, now barred and bolted, looked impregnable. Like a tawny, maned lion, crouched upon the hot valley floor, it was a formidable fortress." [12]

As Joshua scouts out Jericho, his senses are on high alert lest an enemy solider get the drop on him. Suddenly, he sees the shadowy figure of "a man was standing opposite him with his sword drawn in his hand" (Joshua 5:13).

Did you know? Manna "was the food God gave the Israelites in the wilderness. It was white, small, round, and flaky, similar to coriander seeds. It tasted like wafers made from honey or fresh oil. It fell from the sky with the dew every morning, except on the Sabbath. The Israelites ground, beat, baked, and boiled manna. The Israelites named manna 'man,' which comes from the Hebrew word for 'what' or 'what is it.'" [13]

12. Joshua questions the soldier as to whether he is an enemy or an ally. What is his response? (v. 14)

This visitation is considered by many Bible scholars to be the preincarnate Son of God, which in theological terms is called a Christophany. A Christophany is the visible manifestation of Jesus Christ to humans before His birth in Bethlehem.

13. What does Joshua do? (v. 14)

The Captain of the host of the Lord has come, not to take sides, but to take charge. He tells Joshua to remove his sandals because he is standing on holy ground. This is Joshua's burning bush experience, similar to the one Moses experienced in Exodus 3:5.

Having submitted to the rite of circumcision and celebrated the Passover, Israel is ready as a nation to move against the enemy. Robert Smith shows us how this preparation pictures Christ and he ties these Old Testament events together for New Testament believers:

> Circumcision represents when Jesus was cut off from the Father at Calvary because He was the sin bearer. There he was abandoned and cried out, "My God, my God, why have you abandoned me?" (Mark 15:34, NLT). In the Passover, Jesus is our Passover Lamb. John the Baptist declared, "Look, the Lamb of God, who takes away the sin of the world!" (John 1:29). He does not come to bring an offering; He is the offering. Finally, the divine presence of Christ as the captain of the Lord's heavenly armies means Christ has come to be King of Kings and Lord of Lords. [14]

This chapter closes with Joshua on his face before the Lord. Joshua had gone out to survey his problem and found himself face-to-face with the Lord! He is the One who will dictate the battle strategy. He is the One who will deliver Jericho into His people's hands. He is the One who will take His people *into the promise.*

Beloved, just as Joshua is completely surrendered to the Lord, may we learn to humbly submit to His authority. He is the One who will deliver us from our spiritual enemies and lead us *Into the Promise* of His eternal life.

The free gift of God is eternal life in Christ Jesus our Lord.
Romans 6:23

DAY FOUR
Joshua 6:1-27

The Israelite army is now ready to fight its first battle in Canaan, and Joshua is ready to lead them.

Read Joshua 6:1-5.

1. What defensive precautions has the city of Jericho taken? (v. 1)

In verses 2-5, the Lord gives Joshua the battle plan to take the heavily fortified city of Jericho. Wiersbe notes, "It's possible that the Lord spoke these words to Joshua when He confronted him at Jericho (5:13-15)." [15]

The strategy Joshua is given is unusual to say the least. The Israelite militia are poorly equipped and are an inexperienced body of fighting men. On a human level, it seems unlikely that this rather rag-tag band of fighters can win against the foreboding citadel called Jericho. But God.

Did you know? In the Bible, numbers are significant. "Biblical numerology is the study of numbers in the Bible... The number 7 signifies completion or perfection." [17]

God takes delight in operating in seemingly impossible situations and doing what only He can do. When the angel spoke to Mary concerning the birth of Jesus, he said, "For nothing will be impossible with God" (Luke 1:37). And Jericho is, humanly speaking, an impossible situation. Robert Smith gives us a description of the city, "Jericho was major city in Canaan. It was surrounded by an outer wall forty feet high and an inner wall twenty feet high, each one being about six feet thick." [16]

2. Underline the words of the Lord, "See, I have given Jericho into your hand" in Joshua 6:2. What is the significance of the verb tense God uses?

God's statement in the future perfect tense to Joshua indicates there is not a shred of doubt concerning the outcome. Jackman adds this, giving us insight into the source of Israel's confidence:

> There is not a shred of doubt about the outcome. It is an echo of the promise back in 1:3, which came with the command to go over the Jordan: "Every place that the sole of your foot will tread upon I have given to you." It is not yet yours in experience, but the fact that it will be is so certain, in the providence of your sovereign, all-powerful God, that the future can be expressed by a tense of completed action ("I have given..."). [18]

On that basis, the Lord gives Joshua the battle plan.

Read Joshua 6:3-17.

3. Summarize God's plan to conquer Jericho (vv. 3-5).

For six days (vv. 3-4a)	On the seventh day (vv. 4b-5)

4. Look at the text of Joshua 6 in your workbook. Circle every time the number seven (or a form of it) is mentioned in Joshua 6:4-16. How many did you count?

Seven priests, seven trumpets, seven days of marching, and seven marches around Jericho on the seventh day. Wiersbe notes that God's use of the number seven is noteworthy:

> The Hebrew word translated "seven" (shevah) comes from a root that means "to be full, to be satisfied." When God finished His work of creation, He rested on the seventh day and sanctified it (Genesis 2:3), and this helped give the number seven its sacred significance. The Jews noted that there were seven promises in God's covenant with Abraham (12:1-3) and seven branches on the candlestick in the tabernacle (Exodus 37:17-24). Anything involving the number seven was especially sacred to them. It spoke of God's ability to finish whatever He started. [19]

5. What specific instructions does Joshua give to the priests? (Joshua 6:6)

6. What is the order in which the people are to march around Jericho? (vv. 6-9)

7. What is the only sound that is to be heard during the first six days? (vv. 7-10)

Wiersbe observes, "If the week's schedule was a test of their patience, the divine command of silence was a test of their self control." [20] Considering the relatively young age of the fighting men and their lack of experience in battle, we would expect some push back when Joshua explains the plan. But these men are fresh off the experience of crossing the Jordan on dry land. Therefore, the battle plan, which humanly speaking appears on the surface to be a suicide mission, is met with obedience.

Every time our faith is challenged by difficult circumstances, and we run to Jesus "so that we may receive mercy and find grace to help in time of need" (Hebrews 4:16), our faith is built up and bolstered. As God continues to write our story, we begin to see a pattern of God's faithfulness in our lives. He is the Way Maker, the Miracle Worker, and the Promise Keeper! Then, in every subsequent season of suffering, we find the ability to more fully trust in the sovereignty of God, believing He is at work for our good and His glory. I do not intend to minimize anyone's pain or dismiss the hard places we are often faced with, but I can personally testify to the great value of the historical record of God's ways in my life.

8. Write about a time when God proved Himself faithful in a difficult season in your life. Then spend a few minutes in prayer, thanking and praising Him for His goodness.

For six days, the Israelites follow the Lord's command (Joshua 6:11-14). For six days, the residents of Jericho wonder what the God of Israel is going to do to Jericho.

9. What happens on the seventh day? (vv. 15-16)

Read Joshua 6:17-27.

All of Jericho falls under God's judgment, with one exception.

10. Who does God allow to live? (v. 17)

God saves Rahab and her family because of their faith in Him. Verses 22-25 gives the details of her rescue. Wiersbe explains the reason Rahab and her family were initially put "outside the camp":

> Rahab and her relatives were put "outside the camp" initially because they were unclean Gentiles, and "outside the camp" was the place designated for the unclean (Numbers 5:1-4;

12:14; Deuteronomy 23:9-14). The men in the family would have to be circumcised in order to become "sons of the covenant," and all of the family would have to submit to the law of Moses. What grace that God spared Rahab and her loved ones, and what abundant grace that He chose her, an outcast Gentile, to be an ancestress of the Savior! [21]

11. What happens to the city? (v. 24)

12. What happens to all the precious metals found in Jericho? (v. 24)

The articles of silver, gold, bronze, and iron are to go into the treasury of the Lord, but the people and the livestock are to be put to death. Divine justice of the Canaanite conquest is a strong theme in the Old Testament, and one that is challenging to understand. Judgment is always God's final resort, and in this case, it comes after generations of provocation. Jackman helps us with this dilemma as we try to reconcile God's grace with His judgment: "All that has been discovered about Canaanite paganism only serves to confirm the gross and barbaric manifestations of evil that were endemic in their idolatrous culture. So there can be no accusations of injustice against the Creator God of perfect righteousness and justice." [22] Incest and sexual perversions of every kind, along with child sacrifice, mark out the inhabitants of Canaan for God's judgment (Leviticus 18).

After burning the city with fire, Joshua makes an oath, "Cursed before the Lord is the man who rises up and builds this city Jericho; with the loss of his firstborn he shall lay its foundation, and with the loss of his youngest son he shall set up its gates" (Joshua 6:26). This prophecy would be fulfilled in the days of the ungodly King Ahab (1 Kings 16:34). May we remember that what God has cursed is to be avoided at all costs.

"So the Lord was with Joshua, and his fame was in all the land" (Joshua 6:27). God fulfills His promise to Joshua, "Just as I have been with Moses, I will be with you; I will not fail you or forsake you" (Joshua 1:5). Beloved, just as God led Joshua and the Israelites *Into the Promise*, He can be trusted to fulfill His promises to us as well!

> *Jesus, may we fix our eyes on You, the Author and Finisher of our faith (Hebrews 12:2).*
> *When faced with the enemy, my prayer is that we will be strong in the Lord and in the*
> *strength of His might, in order to stand firm against his schemes (Ephesians 6:10-11).*
> *Our confidence rests in You, O Lord. You give us hinds' feet for high places (Habakkuk 3:19, KJV).*
> *You train our hands for battle. Our hope is in You.*
> *Amen and Amen.*

DAY FIVE
Joshua 5-6 | Shout! For the Lord...

One of the greatest spiritual warfare weapons we have in our arsenal is praise. When we praise the Lord, we take our focus off ourselves and put it back on God. In our selfie-focused world, we need to be reminded that life is not all about us. It is all about Jesus! We all have a natural bent towards selfishness, but when we engage in praise from a pure heart, everything shifts dramatically towards the Lord. Psalm 34:1 says, "I will bless the Lord at all times; His praise shall continually be in my mouth."

As we are continuing to work our way through Joshua, the warfare principle for this lesson is:

> **Praise declares the sovereignty of God and defeats the scheme of the enemy.**

Think about the walking tour the Israelites take around of Jericho for those seven days. The city is heavily fortified and built to evoke fear in its enemies' hearts, giving pause to any who might attempt to breach it. The city walls are so wide that chariots ride on the top of them, and they are considered a military impossibility to penetrate or scale. The walls, "at least 13 feet (4 metres) in height and backed by a watchtower or redoubt some 28 feet tall, were intended to protect the settlement and its water supply from human intruders." [23] The men of war are well-trained and battle ready, thoroughly equipped with weapons designed for mass destruction. The warriors of Jericho are known to be fearsome and bloodthirsty. Most likely, as the Israelites parade past, these warriors are standing in battle dress on top of the wall, looking down on them, while hurling vile threats and heckling the people.

1. Revisit Joshua 6:10. What does Joshua command the people to do?

The silence magnifies the taunts of the Jericho inhabitants and prevents any retorts from the rank and file of the Israelites. Yet, after each trek around Jericho, the Israelites simply "[return] to the camp" (Joshua 6:14). It is noteworthy that the Scripture does not record any murmuring or make mention of fear among the Israelites. Remember that the parents of this generation were well-known for that kind of behavior. God's people have broken the strongholds of their parents, having seen the terrible end of such behavior. This generation of Israelites have made a conscious decision to put their faith in God and trust Him. On the seventh day on the seventh trip around the city, they give a shout of praise and the walls collapse.

God's instructions do not line up with any military strategy. But by faith, the Israelites shout to the Lord, trusting His sovereign plan. Just as God's people used praise as a weapon against Jericho, we can use praise to defeat our spiritual enemy, the devil. This includes praise uttered in prayer, lifted in a song or hymn, or spoken aloud to the Lord. Praise has the ability to attract the manifest presence of God, and thwart the devices of the enemy.

2. Look up Psalm 22:3-5. According to this passage, what are the advantages of praising the Lord?

Praising the Lord invites His presence and shifts our focus to Him. And it disturbs and hinders the enemy. He is forced to flee as his plan of destruction implodes in shambles. James writes, "Resist the devil, and he will flee from you" (James 4:7). The best way to resist the enemy is to praise the Lord with all of your heart.

3. Read Psalm 150 and if you mark in your Bible, make note of each time the word praise is used. Thirteen times in six verses the psalmist tells us to praise God. How and where should we praise the Lord?

Praise helps us to focus on God and recognize our deep need for His presence. During a particularly difficult time in my life as caregiver for my aging parent, I knew I needed to begin to come to grips with the imminent loss. I was meditating on Psalm 23. The familiarity of this psalm was like a soothing salve to my troubled soul, but something caught my attention that I had never noticed before. Psalm 23:5 says, "You prepare a table before me *in the presence of my enemies*." (emphasis mine) Beloved, when we are surrounded by the enemy, but we stand firm, undaunted and unflustered by his attacks, the Lord sets a banqueting table for us and invites us to dine. As we choose to commune with our King, even in difficult circumstances, He forces our enemies to watch. I believe they must hate that!

4. Read 1 Samuel 16:21-23. King Saul was being terrorized by an evil spirit. His servants suggested finding a skillful musician to play for him. David was brought to him. What did David do and what effect did it have on King Saul?

From this text we are reminded that praise causes the enemy to flee. **Praise pushes back the darkness and gives entrance to the Light of the world.**

5. Think of a time when the enemy was coming after you and you began to praise the Lord, causing the devil to flee. Share your experience. Recounting your God-story will fortify your faith and bless your heart.

Beloved, praise is one of the languages of faith. It opens the gates of Heaven and doors of blessing. Praise dissolves worry and fear. Praise ushers us into the presence of the King. "Enter His gates with thanksgiving and His courts with praise" (Psalm 100:4). And the joy that is generated during a praise-fest strengthens our faith while it amplifies our courage.

Praise destroys walls: walls of frustration, failure, shame, loss, and sadness. And these are just a few of the walls that fall when we praise the Lord. Praise tears down negative thoughts and builds courage. It turns our heart towards the Lord so that we can receive a fresh filling of His love and blessing. Praise lifts our earth-bound heart to Heaven and gives us a fresh vision and insight. If you are looking for the keys to a heavenly view, just keep praising Jesus and He will bring you *Into the Promise* of His everlasting joy!

Dear Lord, We praise You today for Your goodness to us and for Your faithfulness.
Even when we are faithless, You remain faithful. We praise You for Your might and power.
And we praise You for Your unconditional love. We praise You that You will never leave nor
forsake us. We thank You for Your abundant grace upon grace and Your mercies that are new
every morning. We are so grateful for so great a salvation! We ask You to draw us near and work
Your purposes in and through us. Our eyes are fixed on You, the author and Finisher of our faith.
In the precious name of Jesus Christ,
Amen and Amen.

LESSON FIVE
Do not fear

JOSHUA 7

Israel Is Defeated at Ai

[1] But the sons of Israel acted unfaithfully in regard to the things under the ban, for Achan, the son of Carmi, the son of Zabdi, the son of Zerah, from the tribe of Judah, took some of the things under the ban, therefore the anger of the Lord burned against the sons of Israel.

[2] Now Joshua sent men from Jericho to Ai, which is near Beth-aven, east of Bethel, and said to them, "Go up and spy out the land." So the men went up and spied out Ai. [3] They returned to Joshua and said to him, "Do not let all the people go up; only about two or three thousand men need go up to Ai; do not make all the people toil up there, for they are few."

[4] So about three thousand men from the people went up there, but they fled from the men of Ai. [5] The men of Ai struck down about thirty-six of their men, and pursued them from the gate as far as Shebarim and struck them down on the descent, so the hearts of the people melted and became as water.

[6] Then Joshua tore his clothes and fell to the earth on his face before the ark of the Lord until the evening, both he and the elders of Israel; and they put dust on their heads.

[7] Joshua said, "Alas, O Lord God, why did You ever bring this people over the Jordan, only to deliver us into the hand of the Amorites, to destroy us? If only we had been willing to dwell beyond the Jordan! [8] O Lord, what can I say since Israel has turned their back before their enemies? [9] For the Canaanites and all the inhabitants of the land will hear of it, and they will surround us and cut off our name from the earth. And what will You do for Your great name?"

[10] So the Lord said to Joshua, "Rise up! Why is it that you have fallen on your face? [11] Israel has sinned, and they have also transgressed My covenant which I commanded them. And they have even taken some of the things under the ban and have both stolen and deceived. Moreover, they have also put them among their own things. [12] Therefore the sons of Israel cannot stand before their enemies; they turn their backs before their enemies, for they have become accursed. I will not be with you anymore unless you destroy the things under the ban from your midst. [13] Rise up! Consecrate the people and say, 'Consecrate yourselves for tomorrow, for thus the Lord, the God

of Israel, has said, "There are things under the ban in your midst, O Israel. You cannot stand before your enemies until you have removed the things under the ban from your midst." [14] In the morning then you shall come near by your tribes. And it shall be that the tribe which the Lord takes by lot shall come near by families, and the family which the Lord takes shall come near by households, and the household which the Lord takes shall come near man by man. [15] It shall be that the one who is taken with the things under the ban shall be burned with fire, he and all that belongs to him, because he has transgressed the covenant of the Lord, and because he has committed a disgraceful thing in Israel.'"

The Sin of Achan

[16] So Joshua arose early in the morning and brought Israel near by tribes, and the tribe of Judah was taken. [17] He brought the family of Judah near, and he took the family of the Zerahites; and he brought the family of the Zerahites near man by man, and Zabdi was taken. [18] He brought his household near man by man; and Achan, son of Carmi, son of Zabdi, son of Zerah, from the tribe of Judah, was taken. [19] Then Joshua said to Achan, "My son, I implore you, give glory to the Lord, the God of Israel, and give praise to Him; and tell me now what you have done. Do not hide it from me." [20] So Achan answered Joshua and said, "Truly, I have sinned against the Lord, the God of Israel, and this is what I did: [21] when I saw among the spoil a beautiful mantle from Shinar and two hundred shekels of silver and a bar of gold fifty shekels in weight, then I coveted them and took them; and behold, they are concealed in the earth inside my tent with the silver underneath it."

[22] So Joshua sent messengers, and they ran to the tent; and behold, it was concealed in his tent with the silver underneath it. [23] They took them from inside the tent and brought them to Joshua and to all the sons of Israel, and they poured them out before the Lord. [24] Then Joshua and all Israel with him, took Achan the son of Zerah, the silver, the mantle, the bar of gold, his sons, his daughters, his oxen, his donkeys, his sheep, his tent and all that belonged to him; and they brought them up to the valley of Achor. [25] Joshua said, "Why have you troubled us? The Lord will trouble you this day." And all Israel stoned them with stones; and they burned them with fire after they had stoned them with stones. [26] They raised over him a great heap of stones that stands to this day, and the Lord turned from the fierceness of His anger. Therefore the name of that place has been called the valley of Achor to this day.

JOSHUA 8

The Conquest of Ai

[1] Now the Lord said to Joshua, "**Do not fear** or be dismayed. Take all the people of war with you and arise, go up to Ai; see, I have given into your hand the king of Ai, his people, his city, and his land. [2] You shall do to Ai and its king just as you did to Jericho and its king; you shall take only its spoil and its cattle as plunder for yourselves. Set an ambush for the city behind it."

[3] So Joshua rose with all the people of war to go up to Ai; and Joshua chose 30,000 men, valiant warriors, and sent them out at night. [4] He commanded them, saying, "See, you are going to ambush the city from behind it. Do not go very far from the city, but all of you be ready. [5] Then I and all the people who are with me will approach the city. And when they come out to meet us as at the first, we will flee before them. [6] They will come out after us until we have drawn them away from the city, for they will say, 'They are fleeing before us as at the first.' So we will flee before them. [7] And you shall rise from your ambush and take possession of the city, for the Lord your God will deliver it into your hand. [8] Then it will be when you have seized the city, that you shall set the city on fire. You shall do it according to the word of the Lord. See, I have commanded you." [9] So Joshua sent them away, and they went to the place of ambush and remained between Bethel and Ai, on the west side of Ai; but Joshua spent that night among the people.

[10] Now Joshua rose early in the morning and mustered the people, and he went up with the elders of Israel before the people to Ai. [11] Then all the people of war who were with him went up and drew near and arrived in front of the city, and camped on the north side of Ai. Now there was a valley between him and Ai. [12] And he took about 5,000 men and set them in ambush between Bethel and Ai, on the west side of the city. [13] So they stationed the people, all the army that was on the north side of the city, and its rear guard on the west side of the city, and Joshua spent that night in the midst of the valley. [14] It came about when the king of Ai saw it, that the men of the city hurried and rose up early and went out to meet Israel in battle, he and all his people at the appointed place before the desert plain. But he did not know that there was an ambush against him behind the city. [15] Joshua and all Israel pretended to be beaten before them, and fled by the way of the wilderness. [16] And all the people who were in the city were called together to pursue them, and

they pursued Joshua and were drawn away from the city. ¹⁷ So not a man was left in Ai or Bethel who had not gone out after Israel, and they left the city unguarded and pursued Israel.

¹⁸ Then the Lord said to Joshua, "Stretch out the javelin that is in your hand toward Ai, for I will give it into your hand." So Joshua stretched out the javelin that was in his hand toward the city. ¹⁹ The men in ambush rose quickly from their place, and when he had stretched out his hand, they ran and entered the city and captured it, and they quickly set the city on fire. ²⁰ When the men of Ai turned back and looked, behold, the smoke of the city ascended to the sky, and they had no place to flee this way or that, for the people who had been fleeing to the wilderness turned against the pursuers. ²¹ When Joshua and all Israel saw that the men in ambush had captured the city and that the smoke of the city ascended, they turned back and slew the men of Ai. ²² The others came out from the city to encounter them, so that they were trapped in the midst of Israel, some on this side and some on that side; and they slew them until no one was left of those who survived or escaped. ²³ But they took alive the king of Ai and brought him to Joshua.

²⁴ Now when Israel had finished killing all the inhabitants of Ai in the field in the wilderness where they pursued them, and all of them were fallen by the edge of the sword until they were destroyed, then all Israel returned to Ai and struck it with the edge of the sword. ²⁵ All who fell that day, both men and women, were 12,000—all the people of Ai. ²⁶ For Joshua did not withdraw his hand with which he stretched out the javelin until he had utterly destroyed all the inhabitants of Ai. ²⁷ Israel took only the cattle and the spoil of that city as plunder for themselves, according to the word of the Lord which He had commanded Joshua. ²⁸ So Joshua burned Ai and made it a heap forever, a desolation until this day. ²⁹ He hanged the king of Ai on a tree until evening; and at sunset Joshua gave command and they took his body down from the tree and threw it at the entrance of the city gate, and raised over it a great heap of stones that stands to this day.

³⁰ Then Joshua built an altar to the Lord, the God of Israel, in Mount Ebal, ³¹ just as Moses the servant of the Lord had commanded the sons of Israel, as it is written in the book of the law of Moses, an altar of uncut stones on which no man had wielded an iron tool; and they offered burnt offerings on it to the Lord, and sacrificed peace offerings. ³² He wrote there on the stones a copy of the law of Moses, which he had written, in the presence of the sons of Israel. ³³ All Israel with their elders and

officers and their judges were standing on both sides of the ark before the Levitical priests who carried the ark of the covenant of the Lord, the stranger as well as the native. Half of them stood in front of Mount Gerizim and half of them in front of Mount Ebal, just as Moses the servant of the Lord had given command at first to bless the people of Israel. [34] Then afterward he read all the words of the law, the blessing and the curse, according to all that is written in the book of the law. [35] There was not a word of all that Moses had commanded which Joshua did not read before all the assembly of Israel with the women and the little ones and the strangers who were living among them.

Do not fear

O man, made in the image of God,
O man, who is not merely determined by chemistry, society, or psychology,
O man, who is a man – you have a choice. Choose! [1]
~ Francis Schaeffer

The walls of Jericho have fallen. Sin has been judged, and God's promises have been fulfilled. The Lord is with Joshua, and his reputation has spread throughout the land (Joshua 6:27).

For Israel, Jericho was an undisputable victory, a "mountaintop" experience. It would have been a great ending to an action-packed suspense movie. And it was, indeed, a magnificent triumph for Joshua and the people of God.

But as Warren Wiersbe poignantly observes about the Christian life, "We can't have mountains without valleys." [2]

As we march forward in the book of Joshua, the Israelites will go through a "valley" following this mountaintop victory orchestrated and provided by the sovereign, mighty hand of God. Joshua and all of Israel will have choices to make: Fear or faith. Life or death.

We, too, face the same choices. God, in His infinite power, could certainly make the choice for us. But He does not. From the beginning, He has given humanity the freedom to choose. And still today, in His perfect love, He gives us a choice. His heart's desire *then* was to usher His children into the Promised Land, a land of abundance. He desires the same for you *now*...to usher you into the Promised Life.

What will you choose today?

DAY ONE
Joshua 7:1-15

But. This one little three-letter word strikes an ominous shift in the narrative. As we turn the page to Joshua 7, it captures our attention and sets the stage for a contrast to what has just happened in Jericho. Francis Schaeffer says this word "stands in antithesis to chapter 6, for it tells a tale of defeat." [3]

Before you begin reading today, take a moment to prepare your heart by reading Romans 5:18-21 and 1 John 1:6-9. Prayerfully consider any unconfessed sin in your life. If the Holy Spirit reveals any sin to you, confess it immediately and receive the forgiveness He has promised you through His Son, Jesus Christ.

As we begin this week's lesson, read Joshua 7-8 in its entirety and then create a brief snapshot of these two chapters using the following questions:

Snapshot
of Joshua 7-8

What key events occur in Joshua 7-8?

Who are the main characters in these two chapters?

Using the scripture at the beginning of your lesson, mark when God is directly speaking.

In what ways does Ai represent our flesh?

Now, let's dive into our passage today.

Read Joshua 7:1.

Right out of the gate, verse 1 sets up the situation which the rest of chapter will expose. We are told what has happened before we read the account so that we will have a spiritual understanding of what follows. However, Joshua and the rest of Israel will not know about it until about halfway through the story. They are totally unaware that they are about to experience a sudden reversal, as they are snatched from the jaws of victory and land on the plane of defeat.

1. What event leads to the upcoming defeat of the Israelites? (v. 1)

"Things under the ban" in Joshua 7:1 is the Hebrew word, *herem*, and is translated "the devoted things" in the NIV and ESV.

2. Review Joshua 6:17-19. What things are to be "designated" (set apart) for the Lord?

3. Read Deuteronomy 20:16-18. Why is what has happened such a serious offense?

4. Who is the culprit in the story? (Joshua 7:1)

Before we move ahead, it will help us to understand something about the culture of the Old Testament. Israel (and the entire ancient Near East) was a collectivist culture. This kind of culture stands in stark contrast to the individualistic culture of our western mindset. In ancient Israel, a person's identity was linked directly to their people group, and the people as a whole were viewed as one unit. Morality was a community concern: When one person sinned, the group shared the responsibility.

Did you know? *Achan*, or *Achar*, means "trouble." Achan is known in Bible history as the man who troubled Israel (Joshua 7:25). Because of his disobedience, Israel is defeated at Ai. Israel's first and only military defeat in Canaan is forever associated with Achan's name. [4] (We will take a more in-depth look at Achan's sin on Day 2.)

Read Joshua 7:2-5.

In preparation for their next attack, and as was his custom, Joshua sends some of his men to spy out the town of Ai. Ai is located in the hill country, about 1,700 feet above sea level. Some 15 miles from Jericho, Joshua may have chosen Ai because the city would provide a secure position that could not be reached by Egyptian and Canaanite chariots. [5]

5. What do Joshua's men come back and report to him? (vv. 2-3)

A hasty decision is made. Perhaps Joshua is overly confident and becomes prideful. Or, maybe he is just zealous following the victory at Jericho and wants to maintain the momentum. Whatever the case may be, he does not go before the Lord and seek Him for guidance and direction. Wiersbe observes,

> No doubt the impressive victory at Jericho had given Joshua and his army a great deal of self-confidence, and self-confidence can lead to presumption. Since Ai was a smaller city than Jericho, victory seemed inevitable from the human point of view. But instead of seeking the mind of the Lord, Joshua accepted the counsel of his spies. [6]

6. Can you reflect on a time when you responded or made a decision without first taking it before the Lord? What did you learn in that experience?

Unfortunately, I can quickly recount instances in my own life where I knew (or thought I knew) what I needed to do. Surely God would be okay with my response. It made perfect sense to me!

Our own reasoning most often leads to disaster and disappointment. We think we know best. We mistakenly compare our circumstances to that of another person or previous experience. We allow the enemy to infiltrate our thoughts and push us to a rash and hasty decision, usually plagued by pride.

7. What is the result of Joshua's rash decision? (v. 5)

Death is the consequence for going ahead of an omniscient God. Phillip Keller sheds light on this overwhelming defeat: "In a matter of hours his fighting forces had turned from being triumphant victors to craven cowards." [7] We also see in verse five that "the Israelites were paralyzed with fear...and their courage melted away" (NLT). What a tragedy! Because Joshua chose to lean into his understanding, the Israelites have plummeted into discouragement and fear.

Child of God, look up. **When decisions need to be made, when a response is warranted, and when you find yourself at a crossroads, look to your Heavenly Father.** The One who knows all, sees all, and controls all. The One Who loves you more than anyone. The One who holds your plans for the future, plans to prosper you and not to harm you. The One Who will reward your obedience with blessing and revelation. Do not substitute God's perfect plan with your prideful presumption. As Keller points out, "It is incumbent upon us as God's children to walk humbly with Christ. We need always to seek the direction of His Spirit in our decisions. Always we must keep our Father's perspective and view of life." [8]

Read Joshua 7:6-9.

Following this horrific defeat and loss of life, Joshua and the leaders find themselves totally undone.

8. How do Joshua and the elders respond to their humiliating defeat? (vv. 6-9)

The ark of the covenant appears for the first time in this chapter in verse 6. Richard Hess makes an insightful comment, "As a symbol of God's presence and of Israel's past victories, its absence in the first five verses demonstrated the lack of divine support and suggested the ensuing disaster." [9]

In dismay, Joshua goes before the Lord with the age-old question, "Why, Lord?" Robert Smith notes that Joshua's questions to God do not stem from disrespect, but from dejection and disappointment, and then gives this helpful insight:

> God is not fragile; He is omniscient. We must be aware that God knows what we will think before we think it. He is strong enough to handle our honest questions and deepest pain. He is not temperamental. He knows the end before the beginning begins. Joshua could ask God what was on his heart. His honesty demonstrates his trust in the Master. [10]

In verses 8-9, it becomes clear to Joshua that Israel's defeat has robbed God of His glory. And for this, Israel must repent. Wiersbe helps us understand the necessity of this repentance: "The important thing was...the glory of the God of Israel. Joshua's concern was not for his own reputation but for the 'great Name' of Jehovah. Joshua had learned this lesson from Moses (Exodus 32:11-13; Numbers 14:13-16), and it's a lesson the church needs to learn today." [11]

In humility and repentance, Joshua and the elders stay before the ark until evening. Then the Lord speaks to Joshua.

Read Joshua 7:10-15.

9. What does the Lord tell Joshua to do first? (v. 10)

10. What is the true reason for Israel's defeat at Ai? (vv. 11-12)

11. What will be the remedy for this sin? (vv. 13-15)

We see God being very direct, maybe even a little brusque in His response. And if we are honest, we prefer a more gentle, feel-good type of answer. However, God's abrupt and straightforward response not only charges Joshua to get up and get moving, but He also begins to unfold the details of Achan's sin and what needs to be done to purge the camp.

Here, God reveals His heart to redeem and restore. This is Who He is. The very nature of our God is on display! He is walking Joshua and the Israelites *Into the Promise*, and He will stop at nothing to do the same for you and me!

The Lord also will be a stronghold for the oppressed,
a stronghold in times of trouble;
And those who know Your name will put their trust in You,
For You, O Lord, have not forsaken those who seek You.
Psalm 9:9-10

DAY TWO
Joshua 7:16-26

God is holy! And because He is holy, we will only experience victory when we have a cleansed heart.

Let's do a quick review of where we left off yesterday. Reread Joshua 7:13-15. The *Life Application Study Bible* notes, "The Israelites had to undergo purification rites like those mentioned in [Joshua] 3:5 when they were preparing to cross the Jordan River. Such rites prepared the people to approach God and constantly reminded them of their sinfulness and His holiness." [12]

Pause for just a moment and let the goodness of God soak in right here. God is holy, and we are sinful. Facing consequences for our sin is unavoidable. But, in His goodness, faithfulness, and graciousness, He longs to clean us up and restore us to a right relationship with Himself. This is the work of the cross! When Adam and Eve sinned in the Garden, God immediately made a way for redemption (eternal life). When you and I sin, He makes a way for redemption and restoration (abundant life). We must only go to Him and confess our sins, and He is "faithful and just to forgive us our sins and to cleanse us from all unrighteousness" (1 John 1:9, ESV).

Here, we see God doing the same for Joshua and the camp. Sin has been committed and God is laying out a specific plan to identify it and purge it, so that they can once again experience victory. (Spoiler alert, that is coming in chapter 8!) **Redemption and restoration are at the center of God's heart.**

At the close of yesterday's lesson, we saw that God had a plan for exposing the sin in the camp. We are about to see that plan unfold.

Read Joshua 7:16-21.

1. In the text at the beginning of the lesson, underline the names of those "taken" from the tribe of Judah when Joshua "arose early" the next morning (vv. 16-18).

2. What instruction does Joshua give to Achan and how does he respond? (vv. 19-20)

Joshua tells Achan that he can give glory to the Lord by telling the truth, by confessing what he has done. Nothing we do is hidden from God (Hebrews 4:13). Schaeffer says, "While it is wonderful to have an infinite God, this means we must take His omniscience into account in our daily lives." [13] Think about the choices you made just yesterday. Did you walk, talk, behave, and even think in a way that shows reverence and acknowledgment of God's omniscience? Yes, I know...this can be a painful consideration. I feel it too. But what a powerful truth to consider as we strive to live out a Spirit-filled life. We cannot be full of the Spirit and produce good fruit if we are living in a way that denies His omniscience.

3. What has Achan specifically taken from the plunder and what has he done with it? (v. 21)

Let's pause here and take notice of Achan's words as he gives the details of what he has stolen and hidden. Here, we see a common thread in sin, especially involving material possessions, affluence, and prestige.

4. What reason does Achan give for taking the robe, silver, and gold? (v. 21b)

Did you know? The metals taken from the Canaanite cities have been assigned to the sanctuary, meaning what Achan has taken actually belongs to the Lord. And this is no small heist! "There are about five or six pounds of silver and about a pound and a half ingot of gold in Achan's treasure trove. That represents what it would take the average worker a lifetime to earn." [14]

"I wanted them so much" (NLT). Achan's sin is a result of coveting, setting his eyes on something that does not belong to him and then wanting it for himself. His sin began with a thought. Our mind is the battleground. The sin is not seeing it. The sin is not acknowledging its appeal or beauty. The sin is *wanting* it. The last of the Ten Commandments is, "You must not covet" with specific examples of things not to covet. This final commandment sums up the list of commandments given by God to His people. It serves as a bookend to them all, a wrapping up of sorts for how to live a life pleasing to God.

5. Compare Joshua 7:21 with Genesis 3:6. What similarities do you see?

Just like Eve, covetousness is Achan's downfall. J. Vernon McGee says of Achan, "He saw, he coveted, he took. These are the steps of the sin of the flesh." [15] A dangerous progression both he and Eve share. Achan's unwillingness to refuse the thought led to his choice, his destruction, and the demise of his entire family. What a weighty and consequential choice!

6. What does the Bible teach us about our thoughts in 2 Corinthians 10:5?

I love John Piper's insight into this verse. He says, "We submit everything we think – all our ideas, all our worldview, all our viewpoints – to God, and we say, 'Let Your Word dismantle me if necessary.'" He goes on to say, "If anything is out of sync with the Bible's teaching, we should let it be destroyed." [16]

7. Practically speaking, what are some ways you can take your thoughts captive every day? (Sharing this with your small group can help equip others.)

While Achan does not repent until his sin is exposed, he does, nevertheless, confess. And he does so specifically. Achan does not just give a blanket statement like, "I'm sorry, God. Forgive me of all my sins." As he confesses his sin in front of the entire congregation, he specifically names his sin (coveting) and then lists each item he has taken and what he has done with them. Achan includes all the details. This is important as we confess our sin as well. McGee notes, "True confession does not deal in generalities. There can be no joy in your life; there can be no power in your life; there can be no victory in your life until there is confession of sin." [17]

This proves to be true in this account from Joshua. Only after Achan's confession of sin (and purging of the camp of sin) do the Israelites experience joy, power, and victory.

Read Joshua 7:22-26.

Joshua sends his men in to conduct a search of Achan's tent. Everything is just as Achan has said. They bring all the items and lay them before the Lord. The Valley of Achor ("Trouble Valley") is a remorseful pun on Achan's name.

8. What happens to Achan, his family, and his possessions in the Valley of Achor? (vv. 24-25)

It's painful to read the cost of Achan's sin, isn't it? The depth of it. The reach of it. The horrific consequences of it. The effects of his sin are not only felt by the nation, but also by his own family. The *Life Application Study Bible* helps us understand the far-reaching consequences of his sin:

> Why did Achan's entire family pay for his sin? The biblical record does not tell us if they were accomplices to his crime, but in the ancient world, the family was treated as a whole. Achan, as the head of his family, was like a tribal chief. If he prospered, the family prospered with him. If he suffered, so did they. Achan's entire family was to be stoned along with him so that no trace of the sin would remain in Israel. In our permissive and individualistic culture we have a hard time understanding such a decree, but in ancient cultures this punishment was common. The punishment fit the crime: Achan had disobeyed God's command to destroy everything in Jericho; thus, everything that belonged to Achan had to be destroyed. Sin has drastic consequences, so we should take drastic measures to avoid it. [18]

In our modern society, we do not experience consequences in this same manner, but the principle is the same. Your sin does not only affect you. Your sin affects your family, your friends, your church, your community, and your nation. **You fall prey to the enemy of your soul when you erroneously believe your sin will not do any harm beyond your own life.**

9. What takes place in verse 26?

It's hard to ignore the connection between this pile of stones and the earlier sets of memorial stones that were erected at the Jordan River. The reason for each pile is different, but both remained in their place "until this day" (4:9; 7:26). While the first pile was a reminder of God's presence, the second pile served as a reminder of the consequences of sin.

Chapter 7 closes with a dramatic warning for each of us: God is holy and just and will not overlook or tolerate sin in our lives. He will deal with us, and our "camp" will suffer as a result. There is no getting around it.

We would be remiss (foolish really) to study such a powerful passage of Scripture and not allow the Lord to shine His Holy Spirit spotlight into the corners of our hearts. We all sin and fall short of God's glory (Romans 3:23). Maybe you are not guilty of stealing or taking things that do not belong to you. But what about gossip, covetousness, discontentment, lust, an ungrateful heart, unforgiveness, bitterness, addiction, anger, laziness, cursing, pride, neglecting church, a critical spirit, arrogance, complaining, greed, jealousy, impure thoughts, lying, and unbelief? If we lay our hearts bare before the Lord, we can all raise our hand to at least one of these as a point of struggle or weakness. And we must call it what it is: sin.

Left unchecked, buried, and hidden, we invite destruction and disaster into our lives, and into our "camp."

Take the next few moments and spend time before the Lord in a quiet place. Allow Him to speak to you about any sin, whether it is quickly recognized or deeply buried. He longs to purge your life of anything that hinders your fellowship with Him. Just as sin's consequences are far reaching, even more so are the blessings of God.

Know therefore that the Lord your God is God, the faithful God
Who keeps covenant and steadfast love with those who love Him
and keep His commandments, to a thousand generations...
Deuteronomy 7:9, ESV

DAY THREE
Joshua 8:1-29

When you surrender to the Lord, no defeat is permanent
and no mistake is beyond remedy. [19]
~ Warren Wiersbe

If you are like me, you often find yourself thinking, "I sure wish I could hear God's voice like those in the Old Testament!" We think it would make it easier to know the will of God and walk in obedience if we could. I admit that I have entertained these thoughts myself. And yes, it would be incredible to hear His voice audibly. What a day that will be when we stand before Him, face-to-face, and hear His voice.

But, before you go thinking they had it better back then, consider this: We have the complete Word of God at our fingertips, in many languages and dozens of translations. And we have the Spirit of God living in us. *In* us! We sometimes lose sight of this truth and the power of it.

As you begin today's study, prepare your heart to receive a word from the Living God by the power of the Holy Spirit. We have seen the despair of defeat, the sorrow of sin, and the consequences of a covetous heart. Now, we are moving into a new beginning. Even after grievous mistakes have been made, God cleanses His people, and is now "free to speak to them in mercy and direct them in their conquest of the land." [20] He is "eager to give us cleansing, forgiveness, and strength." [21]

Chapter 8 opens with a mighty command from the Lord, words that will ensure an Israelite victory over Ai.

Read Joshua 8:1-2.

1. What does the Lord say to Joshua right away? (v. 1a)

Keep in mind the disastrous loss – militarily, physically, and spiritually – that Israel has just experienced. Ponder the goodness of God in this generous encouragement. These same words will empower us and guarantee the same victory over our flesh.

2. What assurances does God give as it relates to Ai, it's king, town, and land? (v. 1b)

Wiersbe says, "The answer to our discouragement and fear is in hearing and believing God's Word." [22] If we are discouraged by or fearful of what is to come because of past failures, the antidote is to hear God's Word and believe it. To battle fear and discouragement (two of the devil's favorite tactics), you must immerse yourself in the Word of God. And then you must take it a step further. Believe it! What good is reading God's Word if we do not believe what it says?

God has clearly commanded that Joshua not be afraid or give in to discouragement, and He lays out His provision and promise to him. Joshua hears it, believes it, and acts accordingly.

3. What is God's strategy for battle? (v. 2)

In a nutshell, the strategy is to take Ai by ambush, leaving the city unprotected and vulnerable to attack. Keller points out, "None of these tactics were the sort normally employed by forces with enormous military superiority. They were, instead, the cunning and craftiness used when a force was heavily outnumbered." [23] And Joshua knows this. It is a sign of his "genuine humility before God that he [does] not hesitate to comply promptly with such subversive strategy." [24] Joshua is determined to conduct this mission according to God's plan, no questions asked. He has learned his lesson of doing things his own way.

This time, unlike the battle at Jericho, God gives His people the right to claim the spoils. Keller explains, "Where Israel had been strictly forbidden to loot or pillage Jericho, here that edict was removed and the invaders would be given a free hand to plunder the captured city and claim their prize of battle." [25]

If only Achan had waited.

Take a moment to consider the heart of your Father. Read slowly this insight from Keller as it relates to pressing on following consequences, correction, and cleansing: "He takes no delight in our disasters. He finds no pleasure in our distress. He longs only to pick us up and set us on our way again in joyous company with Himself." [26]

4. How does this quote impact you?

Read Joshua 8:3-13.

5. How many warriors does Joshua select? (v. 3)

6. Summarize the battle instructions Joshua gives to these men (vv. 4-8).

Wiersbe notes, "The strategy for Ai was based on Israel's previous defeat, for God was organizing victory out of Joshua's mistakes. The people of Ai were overconfident because they had defeated Israel at the first attack, and this overconfidence would be their undoing." [27]

7. Who is leading Israel's army? (v. 8)

At night, Joshua and his army make the fifteen-mile trek from Gilgal to Ai. Joshua then sets up the plan for the ambush (vv. 9-13).

Read Joshua 8:14-17.

The stage is set for Joshua to be victorious.

8. What does the king of Ai see and do? (v. 14)

9. What does the king of Ai not know? (v. 14)

10. How does Joshua's plan work? (vv. 15-17)

Read Joshua 8:18-29.

Aware that this battle belongs to the Lord, Joshua waits upon Him for further instructions.

11. What does God tell Joshua to do? (v. 18)

This is the signal for the army to move into the city and burn it. Wiersbe observes that Joshua holds "up his spear until the victory [is] won, an action that reminds us of the battle Joshua fought against Amalek when Moses held up his hands to the Lord (Exodus 17:8-16)." [28]

In verses 19-29, we see that the plan is a success. All of Ai's soldiers are killed, the army of Israel is able to enter the city unhindered, and the entire population is wiped out. All that is left is the plunder for which God has given permission to take for their own.

12. What does Joshua do following the destruction of Ai? (vv. 28-29)

Israel is restored and experiences the joy of victory, even after knowing the heavy weight of loss and defeat. We, too, can walk in the power of the Holy Spirit and have victory, even on the heels of defeat. Let's examine how Ai represents our flesh and what we must do to defeat it.

First, we must admit that "self" is often our greatest enemy. Just as the Lord laid out a specific plan for the defeat of Ai, we too must have a plan in place to have victory over our flesh.

13. What does Luke 9:23 tell us we must do to follow Christ and walk in spiritual victory?

Second, we cannot fight in our own strength and expect to win. Joshua and his spies foolishly underestimated the enemy in Chapter 7, but following the cleansing of sin, their eyes were opened to their need for God's plan, not their own. Joshua clung to the promises of God and fought *His* way. The same goes for us. **We cannot control our flesh in our own strength (nor do we have to).**

14. What does Galatians 2:20 tell us about the power of the Spirit (Christ in me)?

Billy Graham reminds us, "Only in the power of the Spirit can we live a life that glorifies God. We cannot glorify God in the energy of the flesh." [29]

Imagine the sight of the hanging corpse of the king of Ai that is later buried under a pile of stones. Both the city and the king are reduced to a heap of stones. This has to strengthen the faith of the Israelites. It is important to keep in mind the annihilation of the people of Ai is "not the 'slaughter of innocent people' but the judgement of God on an evil society that had long resisted His grace and truth." [30] As gruesome as these details are, we must remember the seriousness of sin and the high cost that comes with refusing to turn from it.

The people of Israel are able to clearly distinguish what happens when they do things their own way versus following the ways of the Lord. His Word and His promises do not fail. Wiersbe makes this powerful observation about the grace of God, "The disgrace and defeat caused by Achan had now been erased, and Israel was well on her way to conquering the Promised Land." [31]

As you experience the victory that comes from choosing to walk in the power of the Spirit rather than the power of the flesh, you can make a similar statement about your own life: "The disgrace and defeat caused by my sin and failure has been erased. I am well on my way *Into the Promise*."

> *I can have real spiritual power to the extent that I look to the finished work of Christ*
> *and allow Him to produce His fruit through me into the external world.* [32]
> ~ Francis Schaeffer

DAY FOUR
Joshua 8:30-35

God's people may try all sorts of other tactics,
but only compliance with His commands assures us of conquest. [33]

~ Phillip Keller

The first round at Ai proved to be a painful lesson for Joshua and his people, leading to a great defeat. However, the second time around, Joshua carefully listened to the instructions from the Lord and did exactly as He commanded, leading to a great victory. Praise the Lord for second chances!

As we open today's text, we immediately see a heart characterized by humility and gratefulness. Following the victory at Ai, Joshua and his army do not move quickly to settle in the land before them. Rather, Joshua leads the Israelite nation to come before God with thanksgiving.

Read Joshua 8:30-35.

1. Following the king of Ai's burial under a heap of stones, what does Joshua do? (v. 30)

2. Where and why does Joshua build an altar? (v. 30)

Commenting on Deuteronomy 27:4-7, Schaeffer gives us helpful context, "Moses, before he died, gave an express command that after the Israelites were in the land, they were to go to Ebal and Gerizim. At this place were to occur certain events that would remind them of their relationship to God." [34] Joshua does not delay in his obedience. Hampton Keathley offers insight regarding this moment, "This illustrates the principle of first priorities. Many Christians continually face defeat in their walk because they fail to take time to get alone with the Lord and reflect on Him and put on their spiritual armor." [35]

Are you facing defeat? Fear, doubt, or discouragement? Are you faithfully spending time with the Lord – seeking His face, obeying Him, thanking Him, and putting on your spiritual armor?

3. Are there changes you need to make as you consider the questions above?

4. What specific instruction is given about the stones for the altar and why? (v. 31, Exodus 20:25)

The altar is not to have any manmade work, no shaping or chiseling with a tool, just simply made of earth and stones. Schaeffer shares that in this, "We are reminded in both Exodus and Joshua that the approach to God must always be through sacrifice and not through the keeping of the law or any other work people may do themselves." [36]

5. How does Paul reiterate this truth in Ephesians 2:8-9?

Did you know? The burnt offering is an "act of worship to express devotion or commitment to God. It was also used as an atonement for unintentional sin. The peace offering was a sacrifice of thanksgiving and fellowship followed by a shared meal." [37]

The Israelites in the Old Testament needed to understand that it was not their doing that made them righteous before God, but only by way of sacrifice. And we, as New Testament believers on this side of the cross, must know and believe the same. We can do no work for our souls to be eternally saved. It is not of ourselves, but only because of the free gift from God in His Son, Jesus Christ. May we follow Paul's lead in declaring, "May I never boast except in the cross of our Lord Jesus Christ" (Galatians 6:14, NIV).

6. Back to Joshua 8, what type of offerings are made at the altar? (v. 31)

About these two offerings, Wiersbe writes, "By these sacrifices, the nation of Israel is assuring God of their commitment to Him and their fellowship with Him." [38] They had reason to celebrate, and Joshua's heart is resolved to lead his people just as Moses had commanded him.

Following this time of thanksgiving and worship, Joshua copies the instructions given by Moses onto the altar stones, and then the people are divided into two groups.

7. Make a list of the people who are "standing on both sides of the ark before the Levitical priests" (v. 33).

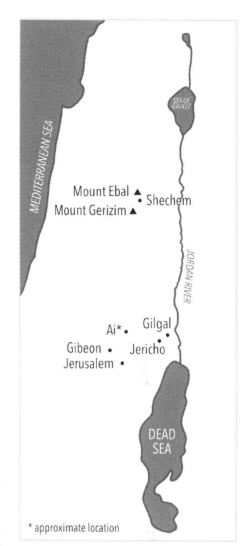

Schaeffer offers noteworthy details about these two mountains between which God's people would stand to hear His Word proclaimed:

> Ebal and Gerizim are about a mile and a half apart at the top but only about 500 yards apart at the bottom. Gerizim reaches to approximately 2,895 feet above sea level, Ebal to 3,077 feet. This means that Gerizim stands about 800 feet above the valley and Ebal about 1,000 feet.
>
> From the top of Ebal or Gerizim we can see a great deal of the Promised Land. At one place a natural amphitheater exists, and as we stand on the top or on the sides of these mountains, we can see and hear everything occurring on both of the mountains and in the valley below. This is God's own amphitheater. [39]

8. Why is this reading of the commandments taking place at Mount Ebal and Mount Gerizim? (Deuteronomy 11:26-32)

Joshua is following Moses' instructions in reading the blessings and curses as the people stand between these two mountains.

9. What does Joshua 8:34-35 tell us about Joshua's reading of the book of the Law?

Joshua reads every word of the Law in its entirety. The people (citizens and foreigners alike) stand and listen to the whole law as it rings out loud and clear in this natural amphitheater perfectly fashioned by Creator God.

It is as though their physical placement (on one side or the other) is a representation of a decision to be made. In Deuteronomy, Moses pled for the people to hear the Word of God and choose obedience, thus choosing blessing. In Joshua 8, we see Joshua doing the same as he reads these familiar words once again, beckoning the people to obey and live under the blessing of God.

The same is true for us. Almighty God, by the power of the Holy Spirit, gives an earnest plea throughout the pages of Scripture. The Bible tells us that Jesus is the way, the truth, and the life, and there is no other way to the Father (John 14:6). The Bible also tells us that Jesus is the only Source of abundant life on this earth (John 10:10). Will you choose Jesus or allow the world to fill you? As a child of God, are you choosing to be crucified with Christ (Galatians 5:24), and no longer gratifying your fleshly desires, or are you allowing those sinful desires to rule? Do you love the Lord with all your heart, soul, mind, and strength (Mark 12:30), or are your affections set on the things of the world?

The choice laid out for the Israelites — first by Moses, and later by Joshua — is the same for us today. Blessing or curse. Life or death. Thy will or my will. Jesus or self.

Choose Jesus. Choose life and blessing.

In Christ believers are blessed with "every spiritual blessing" (Ephesians 1:3)
because of the grace of God. For them life means the blessings of Gerizim
and not the curses of Ebal. Let's give thanks that Jesus bore the curse
of the law for us on the cross and that He bestows all the blessings
of the heavenlies on us through the Spirit. [40]
~ Warren Wiersbe

DAY FIVE
Joshua 7-8 | Do not fear

A walk of spiritual victory is not a matter of one step at a time,
but rather one choice at a time. [41]

~ Jim Logan

As I ponder this week's study, my heart is stirred with a fresh urgency to do battle according to the ways of the Lord, and to encourage you to do the same. As I went through discipleship many years ago, this was an area of my spiritual life that was non-existent, not due to unbelief or unwillingness, but from a lack of knowledge and understanding. Regarding spiritual warfare, Chip Ingram aptly states, "We cannot afford to be indifferent. In this case, ignorance is not bliss; it is devastating." [42]

The spiritual warfare principle for this lesson is:

> ### Sin exposes you to attacks from the enemy.

We saw this play out disastrously in the life of Achan and his family. Not only does our sin expose us to Satan's attacks, but when we sin, we invite him in to attack those we love the most.

Learning to pray (primarily using Scripture) over my own life and the lives of my family have been the most powerful, life-transforming spiritual disciplines I have ever learned. Through discipleship, and through the teaching of my pastor and his wife, my eyes were opened to this incredible truth. And it has changed my life.

Many Christians shy away from the topic of spiritual warfare out of fear. But, if you are a child of God, His Spirit lives in you, and "greater is He who is in you than he who is in the world" (1 John 4:4). We have nothing to fear! The same power that raised Jesus Christ from the dead (and defeated the devil) lives in you! The devil has no power over you except that which you give him.

In his book, *Reclaiming Surrendered Ground*, Jim Logan opens with these words, "The first recorded attack of Satan was upon the family." [43]

And he surely has not backed off from his original scheme. He will stop at nothing in taking down your family. He is no respecter of persons or age. We must be prepared to do battle in prayer on behalf of our families. This applies to every Christ follower, regardless of your age or stage of life.

First things first. Before we kneel in prayer to lift our loved ones before the throne, we must allow the Lord to cleanse us from our own sin. Jack Taylor reminds us, "We cannot engage in anything that would give the devil breathing space. [We] must have no weak places where the devil could walk in. If there is a weak place in the character, he will eventually find it." [44]

Begin by using this prayer from Sylvia Gunter's *For the Family*:

> Father, in Jesus' name, show me areas where I need to take back ground that I have conceded to Satan. Identify for me my key issues. I submit to You, resist the devil, and he must flee. By Your Spirit, I covenant to keep a clean slate with You every day. [45]

1. Write Psalm 139:23-24 in the space below and pray it as you write each word.

2. Are there specific areas that come to mind as you pray and listen to the Holy Spirit?

Once you have allowed the Lord to inspect and cleanse your heart, you are ready to approach the throne of grace with boldness and confidence (Hebrews 4:16).

Our focus this week is "do not fear." **The devil is a liar and wants you to live in fear. God is truth and calls you to live by faith.** As you battle in prayer for you and your family, you can do it by faith because you are doing it from a place of victory! You do not have to be perfect to bow in prayer for your family. However, refusing to acknowledge and turn away from sin hinders your prayers and opens the door to the enemy. Just as Achan's choice to steal the goods for which he coveted brought great disaster upon his family, so do our sinful choices. It's as though we swing the door wide open and invite the devil in to have his way in our lives, our homes, and our families.

The following is a list of some of the things I have learned over the years and practice daily. Remember, the devil knows the Word of God and he knows the power of prayer. He will do everything in his power to keep you distracted, discouraged, disheartened, and doubtful. He wants to keep you from saturating your mind in the truth of God's Word, and from covering yourself and your family in the power of prayer. He will stop at nothing to keep you from it.

- Spend time in God's Word each day. Do not allow this time to be compromised. You must saturate your mind daily in the truths of God's Word to victoriously combat the lies of the enemy and this world.

- Thank the Lord for who He is. Name attributes and characteristics that you have witnessed in recent days. Praise Him! God inhabits the praises of His people, and the devil must flee!

- Walk through the halls of your home in the early morning hours, praying the fruit of the Spirit over your home and your family. Touch bedroom doors, walk into empty bathrooms, extend your hands as a welcome invitation to the Holy Spirit to fill every corner before the day begins.

- As you fold laundry, pray over the bodies that will fill those clothes: head, arms, hands, feet, heart. Ask the Lord to cover your family head to toe, both physically and spiritually.

- Enter the rooms of those who live in your home, touching beds where they will lie down and ask the Spirit of the Lord to be over them, to speak and make Himself known.

- Pray daily. Set aside time each morning to pray in the secret place, just you and God.

- Pray continually. Be sensitive to the Spirit as you go about your day. Make an effort to have quiet moments. Turn off the tv and music, put the phone down. As He brings things to mind about your family (strengths, weaknesses, strongholds, and struggles), present them to the Lord. You can go about the business of your day and pray as you go.

- Pray Scripture. As you do, you are praying the will of God.

3. Do any of these areas need attention in your life? If so, which one(s)?

4. What are some other ways you do battle in the spiritual realm?

Precious sister, for many years of my life, I lived the Christian life apart from victory, without freedom. I plead with you to choose today: faith over fear, life over death, freedom over bondage, victory over defeat. Jesus Christ, the Son of God, left the glory of Heaven and stepped into this world of sin and rejection to die on a cross for you and me.

The devil is a defeated foe. God is the Victor. And we have the victory! I echo the words of Taylor, "Retreat not; yours is the victory!" [46]

Repent and turn away from sin. Choose the Spirit-filled life. Allow the Lord to satisfy your soul. Remind the devil of his future as you pray from a place of victory and power. Live the promised life Jesus died to give you.

As you prepare for battle each day by reading and praying the Word of God, hear the Word of the Lord, "Do not be afraid; do not be discouraged" (Joshua 8:1, NIV).

Here and now, I draw a boundary
Against every weapon that's formed
The thief and his plans will pass over
When he sees the red on the door
I plead the blood

The enemy can't take my family
'Cause this home belongs to the Lord
So, I'm not afraid to remind him
That he has no claim in this war

I plead the blood
I plead the blood of Jesus
I plead the blood
I plead the blood of Jesus

'Cause my future is glory to glory
And my freedom's been purchased in full
For all of the weight of His suffering
The Lamb will receive His reward

I plead the blood
I plead the blood of Jesus
It's more than enough
I plead the blood of Jesus

My shield and my shelter
It's my defense
I claim it over and over again
I plead the blood
I plead the blood of Jesus

Plead the blood, plead the blood
Oh, thank You for the blood
Thank You for the blood! [47]

LESSON SIX
The Lord fought

JOSHUA 9

Guile of the Gibeonites

¹ Now it came about when all the kings who were beyond the Jordan, in the hill country and in the lowland and on all the coast of the Great Sea toward Lebanon, the Hittite and the Amorite, the Canaanite, the Perizzite, the Hivite and the Jebusite, heard of it, ² that they gathered themselves together with one accord to fight with Joshua and with Israel.

³ When the inhabitants of Gibeon heard what Joshua had done to Jericho and to Ai, ⁴ they also acted craftily and set out as envoys, and took worn-out sacks on their donkeys, and wineskins worn-out and torn and mended, ⁵ and worn-out and patched sandals on their feet, and worn-out clothes on themselves; and all the bread of their provision was dry and had become crumbled. ⁶ They went to Joshua to the camp at Gilgal and said to him and to the men of Israel, "We have come from a far country; now therefore, make a covenant with us." ⁷ The men of Israel said to the Hivites, "Perhaps you are living within our land; how then shall we make a covenant with you?" ⁸ But they said to Joshua, "We are your servants." Then Joshua said to them, "Who are you and where do you come from?" ⁹ They said to him, "Your servants have come from a very far country because of the fame of the Lord your God; for we have heard the report of Him and all that He did in Egypt, ¹⁰ and all that He did to the two kings of the Amorites who were beyond the Jordan, to Sihon king of Heshbon and to Og king of Bashan who was at Ashtaroth. ¹¹ So our elders and all the inhabitants of our country spoke to us, saying, 'Take provisions in your hand for the journey, and go to meet them and say to them, "We are your servants; now then, make a covenant with us."'

¹² This our bread was warm when we took it for our provisions out of our houses on the day that we left to come to you; but now behold, it is dry and has become crumbled. ¹³ These wineskins which we filled were new, and behold, they are torn; and these our clothes and our sandals are worn out because of the very long journey." ¹⁴ So the men of Israel took some of their provisions, and did not ask for the counsel of the Lord.

¹⁵ Joshua made peace with them and made a covenant with them, to let them live; and the leaders of the congregation swore an oath to them.

[16] It came about at the end of three days after they had made a covenant with them, that they heard that they were neighbors and that they were living within their land. [17] Then the sons of Israel set out and came to their cities on the third day. Now their cities were Gibeon and Chephirah and Beeroth and Kiriath-jearim. [18] The sons of Israel did not strike them because the leaders of the congregation had sworn to them by the Lord the God of Israel. And the whole congregation grumbled against the leaders. [19] But all the leaders said to the whole congregation, "We have sworn to them by the Lord, the God of Israel, and now we cannot touch them. [20] This we will do to them, even let them live, so that wrath will not be upon us for the oath which we swore to them." [21] The leaders said to them, "Let them live." So they became hewers of wood and drawers of water for the whole congregation, just as the leaders had spoken to them.

[22] Then Joshua called for them and spoke to them, saying, "Why have you deceived us, saying, 'We are very far from you,' when you are living within our land? [23] Now therefore, you are cursed, and you shall never cease being slaves, both hewers of wood and drawers of water for the house of my God." [24] So they answered Joshua and said, "Because it was certainly told your servants that the Lord your God had commanded His servant Moses to give you all the land, and to destroy all the inhabitants of the land before you; therefore we feared greatly for our lives because of you, and have done this thing. [25] Now behold, we are in your hands; do as it seems good and right in your sight to do to us." [26] Thus he did to them, and delivered them from the hands of the sons of Israel, and they did not kill them.

[27] But Joshua made them that day hewers of wood and drawers of water for the congregation and for the altar of the Lord, to this day, in the place which He would choose.

JOSHUA 10

Five Kings Attack Gibeon

[1] Now it came about when Adoni-zedek king of Jerusalem heard that Joshua had captured Ai, and had utterly destroyed it (just as he had done to Jericho and its king, so he had done to Ai and its king), and that the inhabitants of Gibeon had made peace with Israel and were within their land, [2] that he feared greatly, because Gibeon was a great city, like one of the royal cities, and because it was greater than Ai, and all its men were mighty. [3] Therefore Adoni-

zedek king of Jerusalem sent word to Hoham king of Hebron and to Piram king of Jarmuth and to Japhia king of Lachish and to Debir king of Eglon, saying, ⁴ "Come up to me and help me, and let us attack Gibeon, for it has made peace with Joshua and with the sons of Israel." ⁵ So the five kings of the Amorites, the king of Jerusalem, the king of Hebron, the king of Jarmuth, the king of Lachish, and the king of Eglon, gathered together and went up, they with all their armies, and camped by Gibeon and fought against it.

⁶ Then the men of Gibeon sent word to Joshua to the camp at Gilgal, saying, "Do not abandon your servants; come up to us quickly and save us and help us, for all the kings of the Amorites that live in the hill country have assembled against us." ⁷ So Joshua went up from Gilgal, he and all the people of war with him and all the valiant warriors. ⁸ The Lord said to Joshua, "Do not fear them, for I have given them into your hands; not one of them shall stand before you." ⁹ So Joshua came upon them suddenly by marching all night from Gilgal. ¹⁰ And the Lord confounded them before Israel, and He slew them with a great slaughter at Gibeon, and pursued them by the way of the ascent of Beth-horon and struck them as far as Azekah and Makkedah. ¹¹ As they fled from before Israel, while they were at the descent of Beth-horon, the Lord threw large stones from heaven on them as far as Azekah, and they died; there were more who died from the hailstones than those whom the sons of Israel killed with the sword.

¹² Then Joshua spoke to the Lord in the day when the Lord delivered up the Amorites before the sons of Israel, and he said in the sight of Israel,

"O sun, stand still at Gibeon,
And O moon in the valley of Aijalon."
¹³ So the sun stood still, and the moon stopped,
Until the nation avenged themselves of their enemies.

Is it not written in the book of Jashar? And the sun stopped in the middle of the sky and did not hasten to go down for about a whole day. ¹⁴ There was no day like that before it or after it, when the Lord listened to the voice of a man; for **the Lord fought** for Israel.

¹⁵ Then Joshua and all Israel with him returned to the camp to Gilgal.

Victory at Makkedah

¹⁶ Now these five kings had fled and hidden themselves in the cave at Makkedah. ¹⁷ It was told Joshua, saying, "The five kings have been found hidden in the cave at Makkedah."

[18] Joshua said, "Roll large stones against the mouth of the cave, and assign men by it to guard them, [19] but do not stay there yourselves; pursue your enemies and attack them in the rear. Do not allow them to enter their cities, for the Lord your God has delivered them into your hand." [20] It came about when Joshua and the sons of Israel had finished slaying them with a very great slaughter, until they were destroyed, and the survivors who remained of them had entered the fortified cities, [21] that all the people returned to the camp to Joshua at Makkedah in peace. No one uttered a word against any of the sons of Israel.

[22] Then Joshua said, "Open the mouth of the cave and bring these five kings out to me from the cave." [23] They did so, and brought these five kings out to him from the cave: the king of Jerusalem, the king of Hebron, the king of Jarmuth, the king of Lachish, and the king of Eglon. [24] When they brought these kings out to Joshua, Joshua called for all the men of Israel, and said to the chiefs of the men of war who had gone with him, "Come near, put your feet on the necks of these kings." So they came near and put their feet on their necks. [25] Joshua then said to them, "Do not fear or be dismayed! Be strong and courageous, for thus the Lord will do to all your enemies with whom you fight." [26] So afterward Joshua struck them and put them to death, and he hanged them on five trees; and they hung on the trees until evening. [27] It came about at sunset that Joshua gave a command, and they took them down from the trees and threw them into the cave where they had hidden themselves, and put large stones over the mouth of the cave, to this very day.

[28] Now Joshua captured Makkedah on that day, and struck it and its king with the edge of the sword; he utterly destroyed it and every person who was in it. He left no survivor. Thus he did to the king of Makkedah just as he had done to the king of Jericho.

Joshua's Conquest of Southern Palestine

[29] Then Joshua and all Israel with him passed on from Makkedah to Libnah, and fought against Libnah. [30] The Lord gave it also with its king into the hands of Israel, and he struck it and every person who was in it with the edge of the sword. He left no survivor in it. Thus he did to its king just as he had done to the king of Jericho.

[31] And Joshua and all Israel with him passed on from Libnah to Lachish, and they camped by it and fought against it. [32] The Lord gave Lachish into the hands of Israel;

and he captured it on the second day, and struck it and every person who was in it with the edge of the sword, according to all that he had done to Libnah.

33 Then Horam king of Gezer came up to help Lachish, and Joshua defeated him and his people until he had left him no survivor.

34 And Joshua and all Israel with him passed on from Lachish to Eglon, and they camped by it and fought against it. 35 They captured it on that day and struck it with the edge of the sword; and he utterly destroyed that day every person who was in it, according to all that he had done to Lachish.

36 Then Joshua and all Israel with him went up from Eglon to Hebron, and they fought against it. 37 They captured it and struck it and its king and all its cities and all the persons who were in it with the edge of the sword. He left no survivor, according to all that he had done to Eglon. And he utterly destroyed it and every person who was in it.

38 Then Joshua and all Israel with him returned to Debir, and they fought against it. 39 He captured it and its king and all its cities, and they struck them with the edge of the sword, and utterly destroyed every person who was in it. He left no survivor. Just as he had done to Hebron, so he did to Debir and its king, as he had also done to Libnah and its king.

40 Thus Joshua struck all the land, the hill country and the Negev and the lowland and the slopes and all their kings. He left no survivor, but he utterly destroyed all who breathed, just as the Lord, the God of Israel, had commanded. 41 Joshua struck them from Kadesh-barnea even as far as Gaza, and all the country of Goshen even as far as Gibeon. 42 Joshua captured all these kings and their lands at one time, because the Lord, the God of Israel, fought for Israel. 43 So Joshua and all Israel with him returned to the camp at Gilgal.

JOSHUA 11

Northern Palestine Taken

1 Then it came about, when Jabin king of Hazor heard of it, that he sent to Jobab king of Madon and to the king of Shimron and to the king of Achshaph, 2 and to the kings who were of the north in the hill country, and in the Arabah—south of Chinneroth and in the lowland and on the heights of Dor on the west— 3 to the Canaanite on the east and on the west, and the Amorite and the Hittite and the

Perizzite and the Jebusite in the hill country, and the Hivite at the foot of Hermon in the land of Mizpeh. [4] They came out, they and all their armies with them, as many people as the sand that is on the seashore, with very many horses and chariots. [5] So all of these kings having agreed to meet, came and encamped together at the waters of Merom, to fight against Israel.

[6] Then the Lord said to Joshua, "Do not be afraid because of them, for tomorrow at this time I will deliver all of them slain before Israel; you shall hamstring their horses and burn their chariots with fire." [7] So Joshua and all the people of war with him came upon them suddenly by the waters of Merom, and attacked them. [8] The Lord delivered them into the hand of Israel, so that they defeated them, and pursued them as far as Great Sidon and Misrephoth-maim and the valley of Mizpeh to the east; and they struck them until no survivor was left to them. [9] Joshua did to them as the Lord had told him; he hamstrung their horses and burned their chariots with fire.

[10] Then Joshua turned back at that time, and captured Hazor and struck its king with the sword; for Hazor formerly was the head of all these kingdoms. [11] They struck every person who was in it with the edge of the sword, utterly destroying them; there was no one left who breathed. And he burned Hazor with fire. [12] Joshua captured all the cities of these kings, and all their kings, and he struck them with the edge of the sword, and utterly destroyed them; just as Moses the servant of the Lord had commanded. [13] However, Israel did not burn any cities that stood on their mounds, except Hazor alone, which Joshua burned. [14] All the spoil of these cities and the cattle, the sons of Israel took as their plunder; but they struck every man with the edge of the sword, until they had destroyed them. They left no one who breathed. [15] Just as the Lord had commanded Moses his servant, so Moses commanded Joshua, and so Joshua did; he left nothing undone of all that the Lord had commanded Moses.

[16] Thus Joshua took all that land: the hill country and all the Negev, all that land of Goshen, the lowland, the Arabah, the hill country of Israel and its lowland [17] from Mount Halak, that rises toward Seir, even as far as Baal-gad in the valley of Lebanon at the foot of Mount Hermon. And he captured all their kings and struck them down and put them to death.

[18] Joshua waged war a long time with all these kings. [19] There was not a city which made peace with the sons of Israel except the Hivites living in Gibeon; they took

them all in battle. [20] For it was of the Lord to harden their hearts, to meet Israel in battle in order that he might utterly destroy them, that they might receive no mercy, but that he might destroy them, just as the Lord had commanded Moses.

[21] Then Joshua came at that time and cut off the Anakim from the hill country, from Hebron, from Debir, from Anab and from all the hill country of Judah and from all the hill country of Israel. Joshua utterly destroyed them with their cities. [22] There were no Anakim left in the land of the sons of Israel; only in Gaza, in Gath, and in Ashdod some remained. [23] So Joshua took the whole land, according to all that the Lord had spoken to Moses, and Joshua gave it for an inheritance to Israel according to their divisions by their tribes. Thus the land had rest from war.

JOSHUA 12

Kings Defeated by Israel

[1] Now these are the kings of the land whom the sons of Israel defeated, and whose land they possessed beyond the Jordan toward the sunrise, from the valley of the Arnon as far as Mount Hermon, and all the Arabah to the east: [2] Sihon king of the Amorites, who lived in Heshbon, and ruled from Aroer, which is on the edge of the valley of the Arnon, both the middle of the valley and half of Gilead, even as far as the brook Jabbok, the border of the sons of Ammon; [3] and the Arabah as far as the Sea of Chinneroth toward the east, and as far as the sea of the Arabah, even the Salt Sea, eastward toward Beth-jeshimoth, and on the south, at the foot of the slopes of Pisgah; [4] and the territory of Og king of Bashan, one of the remnant of Rephaim, who lived at Ashtaroth and at Edrei, [5] and ruled over Mount Hermon and Salecah and all Bashan, as far as the border of the Geshurites and the Maacathites, and half of Gilead, as far as the border of Sihon king of Heshbon. [6] Moses the servant of the Lord and the sons of Israel defeated them; and Moses the servant of the Lord gave it to the Reubenites and the Gadites and the half-tribe of Manasseh as a possession.

[7] Now these are the kings of the land whom Joshua and the sons of Israel defeated beyond the Jordan toward the west, from Baal-gad in the valley of Lebanon even as far as Mount Halak, which rises toward Seir; and Joshua gave it to the tribes of Israel as a possession according to their divisions, [8] in the hill country, in the lowland, in the Arabah, on the slopes, and in the wilderness, and in the Negev; the Hittite, the Amorite and the Canaanite, the Perizzite, the Hivite and the Jebusite: [9] the king of Jericho, one; the king of Ai, which is beside Bethel, one; [10] the king of

Jerusalem, one; the king of Hebron, one; [11] the king of Jarmuth, one; the king of Lachish, one; [12] the king of Eglon, one; the king of Gezer, one; [13] the king of Debir, one; the king of Geder, one; [14] the king of Hormah, one; the king of Arad, one; [15] the king of Libnah, one; the king of Adullam, one; [16] the king of Makkedah, one; the king of Bethel, one; [17] the king of Tappuah, one; the king of Hepher, one; [18] the king of Aphek, one; the king of Lasharon, one; [19] the king of Madon, one; the king of Hazor, one; [20] the king of Shimron-meron, one; the king of Achshaph, one; [21] the king of Taanach, one; the king of Megiddo, one; [22] the king of Kedesh, one; the king of Jokneam in Carmel, one; [23] the king of Dor in the heights of Dor, one; the king of Goiim in Gilgal, one; [24] the king of Tirzah, one: in all, thirty-one kings.

The Lord fought

Théoden: I will not risk open war.
Aragon: Open war is upon you,
whether you would risk it or not. [1]
~ J.R.R. Tolkien

In early December 1944, the German army was making a desperate attempt to regain lost territory in France along the 88 mile front that was being defended by the Allied Forces. Heavy rain and thick fog was keeping Allied planes and forces on the ground, aiding the Axis powers in their attempts. On the morning of December 8, 1944, Father James Hugh O' Neill, Chief Chaplain of the Third Army, answered the phone and heard a familiar voice say, "This is General Patton; do you have a good prayer for weather? We must do something about those rains if we are to win the war." O'Neill could not find a prayer in his prayer books, so he typed up the following on an index card:

> *Almighty and most merciful Father, we humbly beseech Thee, of Thy great goodness, to restrain these immoderate rains with which we have had to contend. Grant us fair weather for battle. Graciously hearken to us as soldiers who call upon Thee that, armed with Thy power, we may advance from victory to victory, and crush the oppression and wickedness of our enemies and establish Thy justice among men and nations. Amen.*

The chaplain added a Christmas greeting and then took it to Patton for his approval. Patton signed the prayer, and directed that 250,000 copies be made and distributed to every man in the Third Army. Then Patton asked O'Neill, "Chaplain, how much praying is being done in the Third Army?" The chaplain replied, "Does the General mean by chaplains, or by the men?" "By everybody," he replied. To this O'Neill responded,

> I am afraid to admit it, but I do not believe that much praying is going on. When there is fighting, everyone prays, but now with this constant rain — when things are quiet, dangerously quiet, men just sit and wait for things to happen. Prayer out here is difficult. Both chaplains and men are removed from a special building with a steeple. Prayer to most of them is a

formal, ritualized affair, involving special posture and a liturgical setting. I do not believe that much praying is being done.

Patton then told O'Neill, "I am a strong believer in prayer," and instructed the chaplain to send out a training letter to all the army chaplains on prayer. He then said, "We've got to get not only the chaplains but also every man in the Third Army to pray. We must ask God to stop these rains...If we all pray...it will be like plugging in on a current whose source is in Heaven. I believe that prayer completes that circuit. It is power."

Between December 11 and 14, a quarter of a million prayer cards and 486 training letters were distributed to the soldiers and chaplains of the Third Army. From December 16 to 19, the rain continued as the Third Army fought bravely against an almost invisible enemy. Then, on the morning of December 20, although rain was still forecasted, the skies cleared and the rain ceased. For most of the next week, clear skies created perfect flying weather. The Allies were able to defeat the Germans and cut off any chance that they would receive reinforcements.

Several days later, Patton saw the chaplain and said, "Well, Padre, our prayers worked. I knew they would." [2] There was no doubt in Patton's mind: The Lord fought for them.

Throughout the Old Testament, Satan repeatedly resists the purposes of God in an attempt to prevent the coming of the One who will ultimately crush the serpent's head (Genesis 3:15). At this point in Joshua, as the promise of the land is being realized by Israel, it is not surprising that the opposition from the enemy increases. The events in Joshua 9-12 reveal the cosmic spiritual conflict between the forces of evil and God, as the conquest of the Promised Land continues. God is giving the Israelites the land, but He doesn't just hand it to them on a silver platter. As they continue in their conquest, their responsibility will often call for them to fight, and always require them to seek the Lord and be obedient to Him. As they fulfill their commission, He will fight for them.

Joshua believed God would fight for Israel against the Canaanites. Patton believed God would fight against the maniacal evil of Hitler. Do you honestly, genuinely believe God will fight for you?

DAY ONE
Joshua 9:1-2

Let's begin our study this week by reading the entire passage, Joshua 9-12. As you read, circle any key words you see. I know this will take a few minutes, but doing so will give us an overview of what is happening in these four chapters before we dive in for a deeper study. Before you begin, ask the Lord to open your heart to what He wants to say to you through His Word today.

Let's capture a brief snapshot of what takes place in these four chapters.

Snapshot of Joshua 9-12

Who are the main characters in Joshua 9?

What significant event takes place in Joshua 9?

In Joshua 10, how does God intervene in Israel's battle with the five kings?

In Joshua 11, what is the response of the coalition of northern kings to Israel's conquests?

How many kings do the Israelites defeat on the east side of the Jordan River? (Joshua 12)

What are some of the key words in Joshua 9-12?

Up to this point, Israel has chosen its military objectives and targets in the Promised Land. The Canaanite kings have been on the defensive as the Israelites have mounted their offensive strategy. But that is about to change.

Read Joshua 9:1-2.

1. List the six nations in verse 1.

-
-
-
-
-
-

2. Read Deuteronomy 20:16-18. These are the same six nations mentioned in Joshua 9:1. What did God tell Israel to do to them and why?

Did you know? The six nations mentioned in Joshua 9:1 were city-states, autonomous provinces consisting of a city and surrounding territory. On the international stage, Egypt exercised some control over Palestine, but did not officially rule over these city-states. However, there was some reciprocity between the city-states and Egypt, because it was the only overland trade route in and out of Egypt. Over 400 letters have been discovered between the kings of these city-states and Egyptian pharaohs during the first half of the fourteenth century B.C. These Armana letters (named for the location where they were found) document the threat the invading Israelites were to the kings of Canaan. In these letters, the kings appeal to Egypt to send troops to help them deal with the Habiru, a term used to describe nomadic invaders into the region, which included the Israelites. [3]

The geographical description given shows that the kings opposing Israel come from the main regions of Canaan:

- The "hill country" – The central highlands from above Shechem to below Hebron, considered to be the backbone of the country.

- The "lowland" – The western region of rocky hills between the central highland and the coastal plains, extending south from the Valley of Ayalon to Beersheba.

- "All of the coast of the Great Sea" – The entire coast of the Mediterranean Sea as far north as Lebanon.

The only area not mentioned is "the plain," which is already firmly in Israel's control.

At the end of Joshua 9:1, the word, "it," is a reference to the defeat of Jericho and Ai.

3. What do the kings of Canaan do in reaction to the news about Israel's victories at Jericho and Ai? (v. 2)

While Israel is worshiping the Lord and reviewing God's law at Mount Ebal and Mount Gerizim (Joshua 8:30-35), the kings of Canaan gather to form a coalition against God's people. Warren Wiersbe explains the reasoning of the kings:

> They had heard about the defeat of Jericho and Ai and were not about to give up without a fight. It was time for them to go on the offensive and attack these Jewish invaders. The city-states in Canaan were not always friendly with one another, but local rivals can often come together when they have a common enemy. [4]

4. Turn back and read Joshua 2:10-13. What did Rahab say happened to the people of Jericho when they "heard" what God had done for Israel at the Red Sea, and how they "utterly destroyed" the two Amorite kings, Sihon and Og?

5. Now, look back at Joshua 5:1. How did the Amorite kings react when they "heard" how God had dried up the Jordan River so that Israel could walk across?

In both cases, what they "heard" about God's power on Israel's behalf "melted" their hearts with fear. However, that is not the case with the kings from the cities south of Ai who are uniting to fight against Israel in Joshua 9.

So, what has changed? Why no fear now? The difference is the initial defeat Israel experienced at Ai. That is what gives the kings a glimmer of hope. The possibility now exists that Israel can lose in battle. Of course, they are not aware (as we are) that Israel was routed due to the debilitating effect of sin in their midst. Achan's sin has not only caused a delay in Israel's possession of the land, but has also infused courage, instead of fear, into the coalition of their opponents. This is exactly what Joshua had predicted would happen in Joshua 7:9, "'For the Canaanites and all the inhabitants of the land will hear of it, and they will surround us and cut off our name from the earth.'"

If Achan had not sinned, perhaps the events in Joshua 9 would not have happened. It is even possible that all of Israel's enemies might have surrendered, as Rahab had done earlier, and the battle at Ai could have been Israel's last. But, as it was with Adam and Eve in the Garden, so it is with Israel in the Promised Land – one sin has long-term consequences. [5] Sin takes you further than you want to go, keeps you longer than you want to stay, and costs you more than you want to pay. Always.

What is happening in Joshua 9:1-2 is a typical strategy of Satan. Let's remember that the Israelites have just returned from a mountain-top spiritual experience at Mount Ebal and Mount Gerizim. It had been a time of spiritual victory. Now, powerful alliances are being formed to come against Israel. In the place of tribal warfare that has existed for years, former enemies are uniting to wage war against God's people. The list of nations in verse 1 underscores the vast number of people and size of the armies who are gathering to fight Israel.

Righteous activity attracts unrighteous activity.

What these kings do not understand is that in resisting Israel, they are resisting God. Their rebellion against Him gives evidence that the sins of the Canaanites and Amorites "warrant their destruction" (Genesis 15:16, NLT). These pagan races know about the judgment of God upon Egypt but are not moved to seek God. Instead, they worship false gods and participate in evil and perversion of the worst kind. Phillip Keller writes, "The cup of their iniquity had overflowed. So now in response the cup of divine judgment was to be poured out upon them. God's direct instructions to Joshua were simply to liquidate the offenders." [6] And the Israelites will not be fighting in their own strength; God will fight for them:

> The Lord your God who goes before you will Himself fight on your behalf, just as He did for you in Egypt before your eyes...No one will be able to stand against you as long as you live. For I will be with you as I was with Moses. I will not fail you or abandon you (Deuteronomy 1:30, Joshua 1:5, NLT).

Like the Israelites, we are engaged in a war on this battlefield called earth. Nothing on this planet is more powerful than a born again, Spirit-filled, disciple of Jesus. And nothing is more humanly devastating to the domain of darkness than a believer who chooses to stand in faith and believe God's Word. Remember His promises to fight for you and stand victorious in the battle by the promises of God.

> *Do not fear them, for the Lord your God is the one fighting for you* (Deuteronomy 3:22).

> *For by their own sword they did not possess the land, and their own arm did not save them, but Your right hand and Your arm and the light of Your presence, for You favored them* (Psalm 44:3).

> *You will not have to fight this battle. Take up your positions; stand firm and see the deliverance the Lord will give you* (2 Chronicles 20:17, NIV).

DAY TWO
Joshua 9:3-27

We are most vulnerable to making an error in judgment when we least expect it. When things are going well in our lives, when we are experiencing the blessing of God, we tend to let our guard down. When that happens, Satan is sure to find the crack in our armor. And that is what is about to happen to Joshua.

Let's backtrack a little and recall what has been going on in Joshua's life. He faced the initial defeat at Ai courageously. Difficult as it was, Joshua dealt with Achan's sin. Then, he built an altar and "offered burnt offerings" and "peace offerings" to the Lord at Mount Ebal and Mount Gerizim. There, all of Israel assembled and worshipped God. To reaffirm Israel's commitment to God's commands, Joshua wrote a copy of the law God had given to Moses on stones and read it to the people. Everything appeared to be in order for Israel to move forward victoriously in their continued conquest of the land.

But then, Joshua is caught off guard, and he falls for a scheme of the enemy. Gene Getz expounds:

> Make no mistake about it! Satan is a subtle enemy. If he cannot reach his insidious goals by causing us flagrantly to disobey the Word of God, on occasions he will appear as an "angel of light" and actually use God's Truth to trip us. He did this to Joshua, and, unfortunately, this Old Testament leader made a decision that was irreversible. [7]

Read Joshua 9:3-13.

Among those represented at the summit meeting of the kings are leaders from Gibeon.

The city of Gibeon is about seven miles southwest of Ai and only twenty-five miles from Gilgal, where the Israelites are camped. [8] Gibeon is one of the larger cities in Canaan. Joshua 10:2 describes Gibeon as "a great city, like one of the royal cities...it was greater than Ai, and all its men were mighty." Since there is no mention of a king in Gibeon, it is believed that the city's political structure was a republic governed by a body of elders who represented the people.

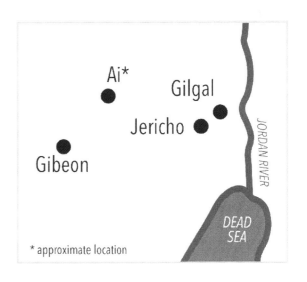

Like the rest of Canaan, the Gibeonites have heard what "Joshua had done to Jericho and to Ai." But unlike those who have formed a coalition to fight against Israel, the Gibeonites devise another course of action. Although they are pagans, the Gibeonites know enough to understand that behind Joshua, stands the God of the universe. To their credit, they realize that they don't stand a chance against Israel and their God. So, instead of waiting for Israel to show up on their doorstep, the leaders of Gibeon send a delegation to meet with Joshua.

1. Who do the Gibeonite envoys pretend to be? (vv. 4-6)

Robert Smith describes the Gibeonites' appearance when they arrive at Gilgal:

> The Gibeonites, who were Hivites, pulled off an Oscar-worthy performance in their theatrical debut. They took old sacks and loaded them on their donkeys. They carried tattered and torn wineskins, wore old and patched sandals, and dressed in old garments. To make the Gibeonite ambassadors more convincing to Joshua and the Israelite elders, they brought dry and moldy bread, contending it was hot and fresh the day they left their homes in a far and distant land. [9]

2. What request do the men from Gibeon make? (v. 6)

The word "covenant" in verse 6 is the Hebrew word, *berit*, the same word used in 7:11 and 24:25. [10] Just as Israel had a covenant with the Lord, Gibeon wants a treaty with Israel by which Gibeon will become subjects to Israel. From a human point of view, this is an ingenious strategy and reveals that the leaders of Gibeon have knowledge of the instructions God had given to the Israelites:

> "I will fix your boundary from the Red Sea to the sea of the Philistines, and from the wilderness to the River Euphrates; for I will deliver the inhabitants of the land into your hand, and you will drive them out before you. You shall make no covenant with them or with their gods. They shall not live in your land, because they will make you sin against Me; for if you serve their gods, it will surely be a snare to you" (Exodus 23:31-33).

The Gibeonites know that no city in Canaan is to be spared. But, they are also aware that God has made provision for cities outside of Canaan to be saved. Moses had made this clear:

> "When you approach a city to fight against it, you shall offer it terms of peace. If it agrees to make peace with you and opens to you, then all the people who are found in it shall become your forced labor and shall serve you. However, if it does not make peace with you, but makes war against you, then you shall besiege it" (Deuteronomy 20:10-12).

This is the strategy behind the Gibeonites ruse. They must appear to come from a country outside of Canaan for their plan to make peace to succeed.

3. What lies do the Gibeonites tell Joshua when he questions them? (vv. 7-13)

The Gibeonites have done their research. They avoid any mention of Jericho and Ai or reference to any other Canaanite city to give the impression that they know nothing about the land. Their disguise is brilliant and well-executed. And what is most impressive (and deceptive), they acknowledge "the fame" (v. 9) of the God of Israel.

Read Joshua 9:14-15.

4. What is the mistake Joshua and the men of Israel make that leads them to agree to a covenant? (vv. 14-15)

The men of Israel examine the bread and agree that it is old and moldy. Once again, they rely on their senses instead of seeking "the counsel of the Lord" (v. 14). This is a repeat of the mistake they made the first time at Ai when they trusted their senses and thought a smaller army would be able to defeat the city. Smith notes, "They lost that battle because they relied on what they could see and did not inquire of the Lord whom they could not see." [11] As one philosopher has said, "Those who cannot remember the past are condemned to repeat it." [12] Because Joshua and the leaders rely on their own understanding instead of asking God what they should do, they make a bad decision that, unfortunately, cannot be reversed.

Read Joshua 9:16-20.

5. How long does it take for Israel to discover the truth? (v. 16)

Ultimately, deception always comes out. No one can lie indefinitely and not be caught.
6. How do the Israelites discover that they have been tricked? (vv. 16-17)

To their credit, Joshua and the leaders of Israel are men of their word, and do not attack Gibeon when they arrive.

7. How do the Israelites respond to their leaders' mistake? (v. 18)

Wiersbe expounds on the cause of the grumbling:

> This covenant with Gibeon would cost the soldiers dearly in plunder they would never get from the protected cities. Furthermore, the Gibeonites and their neighbors might influence the Jews with their pagan practices and lead them away from the Lord. Moses had given Israel stern warnings against compromising with the people of the land (Deuteronomy 7), and now they had foolishly made a covenant with the enemy. [13]

Wiersbe then ponders, "However, we wonder what decisions the common people would have made had they been in the place of the leaders. It's easy to criticize after the fact!" [14]

8. If Israel had broken an oath sworn in the name of the Lord, what would have happened? (vv. 19-20)

Read Joshua 9:21-27.

Just because the Gibeonites broker a peace treaty with Israel does not mean that there will be no consequences for their deception.

9. What decision do the leaders of Israel make regarding the Gibeonites? (vv. 21-23)

10. What reason do the Gibeonites give for their deception? (vv. 24-25)

In an act of unconditional surrender, the Gibeonites basically throw themselves at the mercy of Israel. Although they are consigned to a role of servitude, their lives are spared.

11. How does Joshua live up to the meaning of his name, "Salvation," in the way he deals with the Gibeonites? (vv. 26-27)

Joshua puts them to work hauling water and wood for the Tabernacle, where both are used in abundance. Although the Gibeonites deserve to die, they receive undeserved mercy and grace. Not only are their lives spared, but they participate in the sacrificial service of God by serving at His altar.

As we reflect on all that happens in Joshua 9, rather than point our finger at Joshua and the leaders of Israel for being caught off guard in this whole Gibeonite blunder, let's ask ourselves: How often do we do the same thing? How often do we just plunge ahead with a course of action based upon our own judgment or lack of judgment?

When we act without seeking the Lord, we are easily deceived. Deception is a scheme of Satan who "disguises himself as an angel of light" and has "his servants also disguise themselves as servants of righteousness" (2 Corinthians 11:14-15). As Wiersbe points out, "It's much easier for us to identify the lion when he's roaring than to detect the serpent when he's slithering into our lives." [17] Joshua 9 serves to reinforce the truth of Proverbs 3:5-6: "Trust in the Lord with all your heart and do not lean on your own understanding. In all your ways acknowledge Him, and He will make your paths straight."

But, an even greater truth that emerges from this story is the sovereignty of God. This incident is a cunning attempt by Satan to destroy Israel from within by infiltrating the Israelites with Canaanite idolatry and immorality through the Gibeonites. So, what does God do? He turns the tables and makes the Gibeonites servants in the temple, assisting the Israelites in their worship of Him. And then, in His amazing grace, He allows the lives of the Gibeonites to be spared and incorporates them into the community of Israel. David Jackman gives us this beautiful summary:

Did you know? Years later, the Gibeonites were part of the Nethinim, servants who were assigned to the Levites in service to the temple. The city of Gibeon was assigned to the priestly family of Aaron and became a seminary of sorts, a training ground in God's Word and worship. Wiersbe notes, "It's likely that their service in the tabernacle, and later in the temple, influenced them to abandon their idols and worship the God of Israel." [15] The Nethinim are mentioned in 1 Chronicles 9:2; Ezra 2:43, 58; and Nehemiah 3:26 in relation to the Israelites' return from exile, and were given the same protection from taxes as the Levites. After the Jews returned from exile in Babylon, the Gibeonites were included in the list of those who could prove Jewish heritage (Nehemiah 7:25). Most scholars believe that the Nethinim were absorbed into the general population of Israel or assimilated into the Levites. [16]

> This is the glory of Yahweh. He cannot be outmaneuvered by human cunning or hindered by human fallibility. That glory is shown in the grace that can turn a curse into a blessing, that can use our mistakes and foolishness to bind us more closely than ever to Him, that can reveal where we went wrong and make it become the means by which we can begin to go right...Neither the Gibeonites or the Israelites came out of the story untainted, but the grace of God superabounds over all human sin and failure. He is the hero of the story. [18]

And it is that same grace that is lavished on us because of Christ's death at Calvary and reminds us that:

> The free gift is not like the transgression. For if by the transgression of the one the many died, much more did the grace of God and the gift by the grace of the one Man, Jesus Christ, abound to the many...so that, as sin reigned in death, even so grace would reign through righteousness to eternal life through Jesus Christ our Lord (Romans 5:15, 21).

Hallelujah and Amen!

DAY THREE
Joshua 10

After the collapse of Jericho, the victory at Ai, and the treaty with Gibeon, a considerable portion of the southern part of Canaan is now in the possession of Israel.

Read Joshua 10:1-5.

When the king of Jerusalem hears about Gibeon, he decides that these traitors must be punished. Wiersbe explains the reason for Adoni-zedek's alarm: "If a great city like Gibeon capitulated to the Jews, then one more barrier was removed against the advancement of Israel in the land. It was important for the Canaanites to recover that key city, even if they had to take it by force." [19]

1. What does Adoni-zedek do? (vv. 3-4)

2. Draw lines to match the four kings Adoni-zedek sends a message to with their city (v. 3).

Debir	Hebron
Piram	Eglon
Hoham	Lachish
Japhia	Jarmuth

3. How do the four kings respond to Adoni-zedek's request? (v. 5)

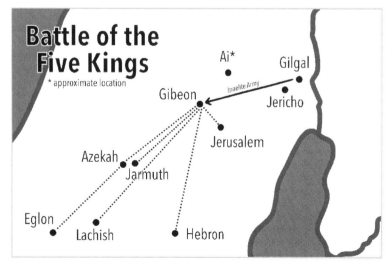

The four kings are strategically chosen by Adoni-zedek because of their location: Jarmuth will serve as a line of defense for Jerusalem from the west. Lachish, Eglon, and Hebron will form a line across the southern Shephelah and hill country. All of these cities benefit from trade with Jerusalem and its access to routes in the north. [20] The four kings know that if they cannot stop Israel at Jerusalem, it will not be long until their own cities face destruction.

Read Joshua 10:6-15.

After the five kings join forces, they sweep down from the hills and encamp around Gibeon, taking the Gibeonites by surprise. Their once friends are now their foes. And to make it worse, Gibeon is outnumbered five to one.

Jackman gives us insight into the two-prong significance of the attack on Gibeon:

> First, it is an act of revenge against Gibeon for their betrayal of the Canaanite cause and subsequent provision of a potential base for the Israelites within their own area. But secondly, it will test the quality of the Israelites' alliance with Gibeon and either draw them both into the conflict, so the alliance can kill the two birds with one stone or demonstrate that the Israelites' promises are worthless. [21]

4. What appeal do the Gibeonites make to Joshua? (v. 6)

5. How does Joshua respond? (v. 7)

Joshua does not hesitate. He is quick to move his army from Gilgal to Gibeon to fulfill the commitment he has made to the Gibeonites.

6. What promise does God make to Joshua about the impending battle? (v. 8)

God's promise to Joshua recalls His previous words in Joshua 1:5, 9. Granted, Joshua may feel like the battle they are about to fight is the result of the mistake he made when he was deceived by the Gibeonites. But in a Romans 8:28 moment, God is going to turn the defense of Gibeon into the defeat of five enemy cities, all in the space of one day.

The urgency of the situation at Gibeon prompts Joshua to lead his army on a night-long march of about 20 miles involving a climb to higher terrain. The text in Joshua 9:17 says that it took Joshua three days to reach Gibeon the first time. To make the trip in an eight to ten hour span highlights the remarkable feat of Joshua and his army. Joshua's strategy pays off and causes confusion among the Amorite armies as they see Israel approaching in the early morning.

7. What is the outcome of the battle at Beth-horon? (v. 10)

Richard Hess explains that the Israelite victory is summarized in verses 7-10 and then gives us a helpful outline for the remainder of the chapter:

> The Israelite victory is...developed in three "panels": God's assistance (vv. 11-15), Joshua and Israel's defeat of the enemy (vv. 16-27), and the systematic destruction of southern towns (vv. 28-39). A summary of the activities of the campaign concludes the account as Israel returns to where it began, at the worship centre of Gilgal (vv. 40-43). [22]

8. How does God kill more of the enemy than the sons of Israel do? (v. 11)

God not only supernaturally assists the travel-weary Israelites by sending a hailstorm, but in an even more miraculous act, God's aim is so precise that the hail stones only hit the Amorite soldiers. And then, something even more miraculous happens.

9. What request does Joshua make of God during the battle? (v. 12)

From where Joshua is standing as he prays, the sun is over Gibeon, to the southeast, and the moon is over the valley of Aijalon, to the southwest. [23]

10. How does God answer Joshua's prayer? (v. 13)

Did you know? Scholars believe the Book of Jasher was a collection of Hebrew songs and poems written in praise of the heroes of Israel and their accomplishments in battle. The book itself is lost and is not part of Scripture. However, it is referenced in Joshua 10:12-13 as well as 2 Samuel 1:18-27, the funeral lament David writes after the deaths of Saul and Jonathan. [24]

God suspends the laws of nature because Joshua's prayer aligns with His will. While many attempts have been made to reconcile what happened that day with a scientific explanation, they all fall short. The only explanation is that God performed a miracle that day as He "fought for Israel" (v. 14).

Meanwhile, the five kings have fled and are in hiding.

Read Joshua 10:16-27.

11. Where are the Amorite kings hiding? (vv. 16-17)

12. To ensure that they don't escape, what instruction does Joshua give? (v. 18)

13. Then, what command does Joshua give to his army? (v. 19)

With the five kings trapped in the cave, Joshua leads his army to chase down any of the remaining enemy, "slaying them with a very great slaughter" (v. 20). Although a few fugitives escape to fortified cities, they have no chance of survival because those cities will eventually be destroyed.

When Joshua returns to camp the next day, he orders the five kings to be brought out of the cave and put face down in the dirt. Wierbse explains, "This humiliating posture announced that Joshua had won a total victory and their end had come." [25]

Wiersbe then goes on give the details of what happens next:

> But there was more. He called for his officers to put their feet on the necks of the kings, symbolic not only of the past victory but also of the victories the Lord would give His people in the days ahead. The kings were slain and the five corpses hung on five trees until sundown. Then their bodies were put into the cave, with a pile of stones closing up the entrance. This pile of stones was another monument in the land speaking of the power and victory of the Lord. [26]

It was an ancient custom for victorious kings to place their feet on the necks of those they conquered. The foot was considered the lowest part of the body in status, and the head, the most exalted. This degrading act implied that the foe's most honored parts were lower than the victor's least ones. For the believer, this is also a picture of Satan's ultimate defeat (1 Corinthians 15:24-28). Because of Christ's death and resurrection, we fight the enemy from a position of victory. As Paul writes in Romans 16:20, "The God of peace will soon crush Satan under your feet."

In Joshua 10:27, we see another stone memorial. Jackman explains:

> Just as the stones from the Jordan were an eloquent reminder of the powerful grace that rescues and preserves (4:21-24) and the stones that buried Achan and his family were a permanent memorial to God's righteous wrath (7:26), so the cave at Makkedah spells out what will happen to all who set themselves against God and His purposes. [27]

Read Joshua 10:28-43.

14. In the text at the front of the lesson, underline the cities Israel captures after the five kings are defeated and killed (vv. 28-39).

15. What is the final outcome of Israel's southern campaign? (vv. 40-43)

16. What happens to the inhabitants of all the cities? (v. 40)

City after city collapses under attack from Joshua's advancing army. Five times in verses 28-40, the writer notes that Joshua left "no survivor" in the town, demonstrating the obedience of Israel to God's instructions in Deuteronomy 20:10-18.

Keller summarizes God's faithfulness to Israel up to this point:

> God had brought Joshua and his people into Canaan. God had gone ahead by His Spirit to prepare the path for certain conquest. God had worked actively behind the scenes to demoralize the Amorites within their walled towns. Now God had granted Israel tremendous courage and energy to attack the enemy forces. God had performed miracles in the midst of combat. Now God had given glorious victories beyond their highest hopes. [28]

At the end of Joshua 10, Israel's sweep south is completed, with the dominant theme being, "The Lord fought for Israel" (v. 14). But wait, there's more.

DAY FOUR
Joshua 11-12

In the Kingdom of God, partial obedience is disobedience. God has commanded the Israelites to utterly destroy the Canaanite residents of the Promised Land because He knows they will threaten Israel's devotion to Him. In particular, they pose a risk to the preservation of the tribe of Judah, the tribe through which the Messiah will come.

In obedience to God, Israel's military campaign forges ahead in Joshua 11 as they shift their campaign to the north.

Read Joshua 11:1-15.

Joshua 9, 10, and 11 begin the same way. The enemies of Israel hear what God is doing on their behalf and determine to resist their further advance.

1. Who solicits help from other kings in the northern part of Canaan? (v. 1)

Hazor is a key city in northern Canaan, the largest and best protected city. Geographically, it covers about 200 acres, with an estimated population of about 30,000. [29]

2. In your text, underline the cities and people groups (the "ites") the enemy armies represent (vv. 1-3).

These forces will be daunting to overcome as they have "as many people as the sand that is on the seashore" (v. 4). Even more impressive is their military technology, including "very many horses and chariots." But God is at work on behalf of His people to give them the Promised Land, no matter the odds, the size of the army, or the might of their weapons.

3. Although there is no dramatic miracle this time, how does the writer make it clear that the battle is the Lord's? (vv. 6, 8)

Like Rahab and the Gibeonites, all of these Canaanites have had the opportunity to turn to God, but instead, they resist Him. They choose battle over belief and fighting over faith.

4. What is the outcome of the battle? (vv. 7-9)

5. What happens to the king, city, and people of Hazor? (vv. 10-11)

6. What happens to the rest of the cities and their inhabitants? (vv. 12-14)

Joshua's conquest is directly related to his obedience to God as he leaves nothing God had commanded to Moses "undone" (v. 15).

Read Joshua 11:16-23.

This section wraps up the conquest and highlights Joshua's accomplishments as Israel's leader. The territory conquered in verses 16-17 is a summary of the northern campaign. Note the area in the Promised Land that Israel now possesses.

7. How long has the conquest taken? (v. 18)

Wiersbe explains that the "long time" in verse 18 is around seven years:

> Israel's failure at Kadesh-barnea (Deuteronomy 2:14), at which time Caleb was forty years old (Joshua 14:7), to their crossing of the Jordan was thirty-eight years. He was eighty-five when the conquest was over (v. 10), which means that at least seven years had been devoted to the campaign. [30]

Did you know? Hazor has the distinction of joining Jericho and Ai as the only three cities burned by the Israelites. The other cities are left intact (although the inhabits are all killed), so that Israel will inherit "great and splendid cities which you did not build, and houses full of all good things which you did not fill, and hewn cisterns which you did not dig, vineyards and olive trees which you did not plant, and you eat and are satisfied" (Deuteronomy 6:10-11).

8. Why do none of the cities make peace with Israel (with the exception of the Gibeonites)? (vv. 19-20)

Similar to what God did to Pharaoh's heart the generation before, the stubborn hearts of the Canaanites are due to God's hardening process. Marten Woudstra comments, "God gives up to their own wickedness those who have shown that they prefer the lie to the truth." [31] In the end, the Canaanites bring about their own demise.

9. What people group does Joshua destroy in verses 21-22?

The Anakim, a race of giants, are the same people who terrified the ten unbelieving men who had spied out Canaan and returned with a bad report (Numbers 13:22, 28, 33). The two believing spies, Joshua and Caleb, did not fear them and returned with a good report. The rebellion at Kadesh-barnea and the subsequent 40 years wandering in the wilderness was due to these imposing giants. It seems fitting that the chronicle of Israel's conquests ends with victory over the inhabitants they had once feared.

10. After the land has been conquered, what is Joshua's next responsibility? (v. 23)

Wiersbe explains the apparent contradiction between Joshua 11:23 and what God says to Joshua in 13:1, "You are old and advanced in years, and very much of the land remains to be possessed":

> Joshua and his army did take control of the whole land by destroying the key cities with their kings and people. Israel didn't take every little city or slay every citizen or ruler, but they did enough to break the power of the enemy and establish control over the land. Once this was accomplished and there was rest in the land, Joshua was able to assign each tribe its inheritance, and within each inheritance, the tribes had to gain mastery over the remaining inhabitants who were still there. Even after the death of Joshua and his officers, there was additional land to be taken (Judges 1-3). [32]

Joshua 11 then concludes on a note of shalom: "Thus the land had rest from war."

Read Joshua 12.

This chapter is a compilation of the 33 kings God helped Moses and Joshua defeat. Sihon and Og were conquered under the leadership of Moses. Joshua 12:9-16 records the 16 kings defeated in Joshua's southern campaign and verses 17-24 list the 15 kings overcome in the northern campaign.

As you wrap up your time in God's Word today, take a few minutes and recall some of the things in your life that God has helped you conquer. Then, spend time in prayer thanking Him for the victory He has given to you.

In all these things we overwhelmingly conquer through Him who loved us.
Romans 8:37

DAY FIVE
Joshua 9-12 | The Lord fought

In Tolkien's *The Lord of the Rings,* Sauron the Dark Lord of Mordor, assembles massive armies to gain control over all of Middle-earth and spread his reign of evil. Peter Jackson does a masterful job portraying the enormous scope and scale of these armies in his movie depictions of the trilogy. Repeatedly, it appears as if the enemy will overpower Gandalf, Aragon, and the rest of the Fellowship. However, because of their resolute hope and steadfast courage, they consistently prevail in battle. [33]

I couldn't help but picture some of those scenes from *The Lord of the Rings* trilogy as Joshua and the Israelites were continually outnumbered in Joshua 9-12. The spiritual conflict in these chapters is intense. The enemy has been entrenched in this part of the world for centuries as the sins of the Amorites have multiplied. Jackman writes,

> The pot was overflowing with wickedness, all of which constituted an assault upon the righteous character of their Creator. The conquest is a divine initiative to cleanse the land of its iniquity. So it is not going to happen without diabolic resistance, which means conflict. [34]

But, over and over, God prevails, giving the Israelites victory in their quest.

Russian revolutionary Leon Trotsky wrote, "Whoever longs for a quiet life has been born in the wrong generation." [35] Truly, there has never been a generation that has not experienced conflict. And certainly, no believer is immune from spiritual conflict. So, we should not be surprised when we find ourselves in battle "against the rulers, against the powers, against the world forces of this darkness, against the spiritual forces of wickedness in the heavenly places" (Ephesians 6:12).

Since conflict with Satan and his evil forces is inevitable, being able to recognize "the devil's schemes" will keep us from getting sidelined or defeated in the daily battle. In Joshua 9-12, we see two specific ways Satan attacks: through deception and discouragement. Let's take a moment and examine the enemy's scheming ways:

Satan deceives. In the Joshua 9 narrative with the Gibeonites, Joshua and the leaders of Israel fall prey to Satanic deception based upon the way things appear. Satan is a master of deception.

1. Complete the following chart to see some of the ways he disguises himself.

Scripture	Satan's Disguise
Matthew 16:21-24	
2 Corinthians 11:14	
1 Peter 5:8	
Revelation 12:9	

2. What is a way that Satan has attempted to deceive you?

Satan discourages. The account of Beth-horon in Joshua 10, when the kings of the Canaanites band together and come roaring down against Joshua and the Israelites, is a picture of what happens when Satan tries to overwhelm us with discouragement. The devil is a roaring lion (1 Peter 5:8) who will resort to anything in an attempt to shatter our faith. But from Joshua's example, we learn what to do when the enemy is bringing all he has against us: Stand fast in faith. Joshua prayed, stood firm, and waited on God to work a miracle. Like Joshua, we must learn to stand firm against the enemy. As Paul tells us in Ephesians 6:13: "Therefore, take up the full armor of God, so that you will be able to resist in the evil day, and having done everything, to stand firm."

Unlike the miraculous victory God gives to Israel in Joshua 10, in Joshua 11, there is no visible divine intervention that precipitates their victory. As they face the northern kings, Israel will have to fight. But there is no doubt as to the Source of their triumph. Again, this battle is the Lord's, "The Lord delivered them into the hand of Israel, so that they defeated them, and pursued them as far as Great Sidon and Misrephoth-maim and the valley of Mizpeh to the east; and they struck them until no survivor was left to them" (Joshua 11:8).

After soundly defeating the enemy, Joshua obeys the Lord and destroys all of the weapons of the enemy. Without a doubt, Joshua could have used these Canaanite weapons in future battles. But, Joshua obeys God, and disabling the horses and burning all the chariots. Here, we see another principle in spiritual warfare:

You can't fight God's battles with the enemy's weapons.

Israel prevailed in battle for one reason and one reason only: God was with them. As David writes, "For by their own sword they did not possess the land, and their own arm did not save them, but Your right hand and Your arm and the light of Your presence, for You favored them" (Psalm 44:3).

Let's face it, friend. We are in a war. It often seems like right in the middle of a wonderful day, we find ourselves on the front lines standing against the enemy. But, we must be careful not to use the enemy's tools when we engage in battle. David Guzik makes an apt observation, "Many Christians do not hesitate to use the 'horses and chariots' of their spiritual enemy. Perhaps they should believe that God wants them to fight the battle on a different level – a level of complete trust in Him." [36] The tools of the enemy include any deeds of the flesh (Galatians 5:19-21). **When we pick up the worldly weapons of control, manipulation, anger, gossip, dissension, and strife, we are fueling chaos instead of peace.** Paul reminds us that we don't fight the way the world does: "The weapons we fight with are not the weapons of the world. On the contrary, they have divine power to demolish strongholds" (2 Corinthians 10:4, NIV).

So, how do we fight to win the battle we are facing today? Paul tells us in Ephesians 6:13, "Therefore, take up the full armor of God, so that you will be able to resist in the evil day, and having done everything, to stand firm." Chip Ingram explains that the way we resist the enemy is "by putting on the full armor of God, standing firm, taking the sword of the Spirit, and wielding that powerful weapon against all the deception." [37]

3. Read Ephesians 6:17. How does Paul define the Christian's sword?

The Greek word most often used in the New Testament for "word" is *logos*. However, that is not the case in Ephesians 6:17. Here, the Greek word is *rhema*, the specific spoken Word of God. W.E. Vines notes that this reference is not to the entire Bible, but rather "to the individual scripture which the Spirit brings to our remembrance for use in time of need, a prerequisite being the regular storing of the mind with Scripture." [38]

We learn best how to do this from Jesus' example. Matthew 4 relates how Jesus was tempted by Satan in the wilderness at the end of His forty-day fast.

4. Read Matthew 4:1-11. What trio of words does Jesus use three times in response to the attacks from Satan? (vv. 4, 6, 7)

All three times Jesus is assaulted by the enemy, He counters back with "It is written" and then quotes a specific scripture to Satan. Ingram writes that Jesus was "quoting the *logos* of God, but He was battling with the *rhema* of God – the *logos* applied to His specific situation." [39] The Word of God made flesh (John 1:14) quoted the written Word of God to defeat the enemy's attack. And when He did, Satan left

(Matthew 4:11). **When we come under attack from the enemy, "It is written" should be our response. God's Word is the weapon that will silence the lies from the enemy.**

Let's consider Paul's words in 2 Corinthians 10:4 once again. This time, let's read it in the ESV: "For the weapons of our warfare are not of the flesh but have divine power to destroy strongholds." Did you notice that the power in our weapons comes from beyond our own authority? While we are the ones who wield the sword of the Spirit, it is the powerful hand of God that enables it to send the enemy running.

5. Read the following verses from Psalm 119 and note the impact of the Word of God in our lives.

Scriptures	God's Word...
Psalm 119:9	
Psalm 119:11	
Psalm 119:105	

Over and over, we see the importance of the Word of God in our lives. In fact, Moses instructed the Israelites to take to heart every word he commanded them, "For it is not an idle word for you; indeed it is your life" (Dueteronomy 32:47). To effectively fight the enemy and his demonic forces, you must know the Word of God. Jesus took His weapons right out of Deuteronomy (8:3; 6:16; 6:13). How well are you using the Word of God to defeat the enemy's attacks in your life?

6. Make a list of Bible verses to use as weapons against Satan when he attacks. Choose one or two verses and memorize them. Write some of these verses on index cards and put them in strategic places as reminders.

Whatever battle you are in today, you are not in it alone. Remember, through Christ, the victory over sin and death has already been won. Satan knows his doom is sure. One day, Jesus will return, and evil will be no more. Until then, you have the armor of God to protect you, the ultimate weapon of the Word of God that will bring you victory, and the Lord of Hosts Who is fighting for you.

Father, in the name of Jesus, I take up the sword of the Spirit, the Word of God, and advance confidently into the battle. May the truth of Your Word be my guiding light today, exposing every lie of the enemy. Help me to use the sword of the Spirit to shatter every stronghold of deception and discouragement in my life. Give me the wisdom to bring Your Word against the enemy and empower me to live a life of victory. I pray this in the conquering name of Jesus,
Amen.

LESSON SEVEN

*Because you have
followed the Lord...fully*

JOSHUA 13

Canaan Divided among the Tribes

[1] Now Joshua was old and advanced in years when the Lord said to him, "You are old and advanced in years, and very much of the land remains to be possessed. [2] This is the land that remains: all the regions of the Philistines and all those of the Geshurites; [3] from the Shihor which is east of Egypt, even as far as the border of Ekron to the north (it is counted as Canaanite); the five lords of the Philistines: the Gazite, the Ashdodite, the Ashkelonite, the Gittite, the Ekronite; and the Avvite [4] to the south, all the land of the Canaanite, and Mearah that belongs to the Sidonians, as far as Aphek, to the border of the Amorite; [5] and the land of the Gebalite, and all of Lebanon, toward the east, from Baal-gad below Mount Hermon as far as Lebo-hamath. [6] All the inhabitants of the hill country from Lebanon as far as Misrephoth-maim, all the Sidonians, I will drive them out from before the sons of Israel; only allot it to Israel for an inheritance as I have commanded you. [7] Now therefore, apportion this land for an inheritance to the nine tribes and the half-tribe of Manasseh."

[8] With the other half-tribe, the Reubenites and the Gadites received their inheritance which Moses gave them beyond the Jordan to the east, just as Moses the servant of the Lord gave to them; [9] from Aroer, which is on the edge of the valley of the Arnon, with the city which is in the middle of the valley, and all the plain of Medeba, as far as Dibon; [10] and all the cities of Sihon king of the Amorites, who reigned in Heshbon, as far as the border of the sons of Ammon; [11] and Gilead, and the territory of the Geshurites and Maacathites, and all Mount Hermon, and all Bashan as far as Salecah; [12] all the kingdom of Og in Bashan, who reigned in Ashtaroth and in Edrei (he alone was left of the remnant of the Rephaim); for Moses struck them and dispossessed them. [13] But the sons of Israel did not dispossess the Geshurites or the Maacathites; for Geshur and Maacath live among Israel until this day.

[14] Only to the tribe of Levi he did not give an inheritance; the offerings by fire to the Lord, the God of Israel, are their inheritance, as He spoke to him.

[15] So Moses gave an inheritance to the tribe of the sons of Reuben according to their families. [16] Their territory was from Aroer, which is on the edge of the valley of the Arnon, with the city which is in the middle of the valley and all the plain by Medeba; [17] Heshbon, and all its cities which are on the plain: Dibon and Bamoth-baal and

Beth-baal-meon, [18] and Jahaz and Kedemoth and Mephaath, [19] and Kiriathaim and Sibmah and Zereth-shahar on the hill of the valley, [20] and Beth-peor and the slopes of Pisgah and Beth-jeshimoth,

[21] even all the cities of the plain and all the kingdom of Sihon king of the Amorites who reigned in Heshbon, whom Moses struck with the chiefs of Midian, Evi and Rekem and Zur and Hur and Reba, the princes of Sihon, who lived in the land. [22] The sons of Israel also killed Balaam the son of Beor, the diviner, with the sword among the rest of their slain.

[23] The border of the sons of Reuben was the Jordan. This was the inheritance of the sons of Reuben according to their families, the cities and their villages.

[24] Moses also gave an inheritance to the tribe of Gad, to the sons of Gad, according to their families. [25] Their territory was Jazer, and all the cities of Gilead, and half the land of the sons of Ammon, as far as Aroer which is before Rabbah; [26] and from Heshbon as far as Ramath-mizpeh and Betonim, and from Mahanaim as far as the border of Debir; [27] and in the valley, Beth-haram and Beth-nimrah and Succoth and Zaphon, the rest of the kingdom of Sihon king of Heshbon, with the Jordan as a border, as far as the lower end of the Sea of Chinnereth beyond the Jordan to the east. [28] This is the inheritance of the sons of Gad according to their families, the cities and their villages.

[29] Moses also gave an inheritance to the half-tribe of Manasseh; and it was for the half-tribe of the sons of Manasseh according to their families. [30] Their territory was from Mahanaim, all Bashan, all the kingdom of Og king of Bashan, and all the towns of Jair, which are in Bashan, sixty cities; [31] also half of Gilead, with Ashtaroth and Edrei, the cities of the kingdom of Og in Bashan, were for the sons of Machir the son of Manasseh, for half of the sons of Machir according to their families.

[32] These are the territories which Moses apportioned for an inheritance in the plains of Moab, beyond the Jordan at Jericho to the east. [33] But to the tribe of Levi, Moses did not give an inheritance; the Lord, the God of Israel, is their inheritance, as He had promised to them.

JOSHUA 14

Caleb's Request

¹ Now these are the territories which the sons of Israel inherited in the land of Canaan, which Eleazar the priest, and Joshua the son of Nun, and the heads of the households of the tribes of the sons of Israel apportioned to them for an inheritance, ² by the lot of their inheritance, as the Lord commanded through Moses, for the nine tribes and the half-tribe.

³ For Moses had given the inheritance of the two tribes and the half-tribe beyond the Jordan; but he did not give an inheritance to the Levites among them. ⁴ For the sons of Joseph were two tribes, Manasseh and Ephraim, and they did not give a portion to the Levites in the land, except cities to live in, with their pasture lands for their livestock and for their property. ⁵ Thus the sons of Israel did just as the Lord had commanded Moses, and they divided the land.

⁶ Then the sons of Judah drew near to Joshua in Gilgal, and Caleb the son of Jephunneh the Kenizzite said to him, "You know the word which the Lord spoke to Moses the man of God concerning you and me in Kadesh-barnea. ⁷ I was forty years old when Moses the servant of the Lord sent me from Kadesh-barnea to spy out the land, and I brought word back to him as it was in my heart. ⁸ Nevertheless my brethren who went up with me made the heart of the people melt with fear; but I followed the Lord my God fully. ⁹ So Moses swore on that day, saying, 'Surely the land on which your foot has trodden will be an inheritance to you and to your children forever, **because you have followed the Lord my God fully**.' ¹⁰ Now behold, the Lord has let me live, just as He spoke, these forty-five years, from the time that the Lord spoke this word to Moses, when Israel walked in the wilderness; and now behold, I am eighty-five years old today. ¹¹ I am still as strong today as I was in the day Moses sent me; as my strength was then, so my strength is now, for war and for going out and coming in. ¹² Now then, give me this hill country about which the Lord spoke on that day, for you heard on that day that Anakim were there, with great fortified cities; perhaps the Lord will be with me, and I will drive them out as the Lord has spoken."

¹³ So Joshua blessed him and gave Hebron to Caleb the son of Jephunneh for an inheritance. ¹⁴ Therefore, Hebron became the inheritance of Caleb the son of Jephunneh the Kenizzite until this day, because he followed the Lord God of Israel

fully. [15] Now the name of Hebron was formerly Kiriath-arba; for Arba was the greatest man among the Anakim. Then the land had rest from war.

JOSHUA 15

Territory of Judah

[1] Now the lot for the tribe of the sons of Judah according to their families reached the border of Edom, southward to the wilderness of Zin at the extreme south. [2] Their south border was from the lower end of the Salt Sea, from the bay that turns to the south. [3] Then it proceeded southward to the ascent of Akrabbim and continued to Zin, then went up by the south of Kadesh-barnea and continued to Hezron, and went up to Addar and turned about to Karka. [4] It continued to Azmon and proceeded to the brook of Egypt, and the border ended at the sea. This shall be your south border. [5] The east border was the Salt Sea, as far as the mouth of the Jordan. And the border of the north side was from the bay of the sea at the mouth of the Jordan. [6] Then the border went up to Beth-hoglah, and continued on the north of Beth-arabah, and the border went up to the stone of Bohan the son of Reuben.

[7] The border went up to Debir from the valley of Achor, and turned northward toward Gilgal which is opposite the ascent of Adummim, which is on the south of the valley; and the border continued to the waters of En-shemesh and it ended at En-rogel. [8] Then the border went up the valley of Ben-hinnom to the slope of the Jebusite on the south (that is, Jerusalem); and the border went up to the top of the mountain which is before the valley of Hinnom to the west, which is at the end of the valley of Rephaim toward the north. [9] From the top of the mountain the border curved to the spring of the waters of Nephtoah and proceeded to the cities of Mount Ephron, then the border curved to Baalah (that is, Kiriath-jearim). [10] The border turned about from Baalah westward to Mount Seir, and continued to the slope of Mount Jearim on the north (that is, Chesalon), and went down to Beth-shemesh and continued through Timnah. [11] The border proceeded to the side of Ekron northward. Then the border curved to Shikkeron and continued to Mount Baalah and proceeded to Jabneel, and the border ended at the sea. [12] The west border was at the Great Sea, even its coastline. This is the border around the sons of Judah according to their families.

¹³ Now he gave to Caleb the son of Jephunneh a portion among the sons of Judah, according to the command of the Lord to Joshua, namely, Kiriath-arba, Arba being the father of Anak (that is, Hebron). ¹⁴ Caleb drove out from there the three sons of Anak: Sheshai and Ahiman and Talmai, the children of Anak. ¹⁵ Then he went up from there against the inhabitants of Debir; now the name of Debir formerly was Kiriath-sepher.

¹⁶ And Caleb said, "The one who attacks Kiriath-sepher and captures it, I will give him Achsah my daughter as a wife." ¹⁷ Othniel the son of Kenaz, the brother of Caleb, captured it; so he gave him Achsah his daughter as a wife. ¹⁸ It came about that when she came to him, she persuaded him to ask her father for a field. So she alighted from the donkey, and Caleb said to her, "What do you want?" ¹⁹ Then she said, "Give me a blessing; since you have given me the land of the Negev, give me also springs of water." So he gave her the upper springs and the lower springs.

²⁰ This is the inheritance of the tribe of the sons of Judah according to their families.

²¹ Now the cities at the extremity of the tribe of the sons of Judah toward the border of Edom in the south were Kabzeel and Eder and Jagur, ²² and Kinah and Dimonah and Adadah,

²³ and Kadesh and Hazor and Ithnan, ²⁴ Ziph and Telem and Bealoth, ²⁵ and Hazor-hadattah and Kerioth-hezron (that is, Hazor), ²⁶ Amam and Shema and Moladah,

²⁷ and Hazar-gaddah and Heshmon and Beth-pelet, ²⁸ and Hazar-shual and Beersheba and Biziothiah, ²⁹ Baalah and Iim and Ezem, ³⁰ and Eltolad and Chesil and Hormah,

³¹ and Ziklag and Madmannah and Sansannah, ³² and Lebaoth and Shilhim and Ain and Rimmon; in all, twenty-nine cities with their villages.

³³ In the lowland: Eshtaol and Zorah and Ashnah, ³⁴ and Zanoah and En-gannim, Tappuah and Enam, ³⁵ Jarmuth and Adullam, Socoh and Azekah, ³⁶ and Shaaraim and Adithaim and Gederah and Gederothaim; fourteen cities with their villages.

³⁷ Zenan and Hadashah and Migdal-gad, ³⁸ and Dilean and Mizpeh and Joktheel, ³⁹ Lachish and Bozkath and Eglon, ⁴⁰ and Cabbon and Lahmas and Chitlish, ⁴¹ and Gederoth, Beth-dagon and Naamah and Makkedah; sixteen cities with their villages.

⁴² Libnah and Ether and Ashan, ⁴³ and Iphtah and Ashnah and Nezib, ⁴⁴ and Keilah and Achzib and Mareshah; nine cities with their villages.

⁴⁵ Ekron, with its towns and its villages; ⁴⁶ from Ekron even to the sea, all that were by the side of Ashdod, with their villages.

⁴⁷ Ashdod, its towns and its villages; Gaza, its towns and its villages; as far as the brook of Egypt and the Great Sea, even its coastline.

⁴⁸ In the hill country: Shamir and Jattir and Socoh, ⁴⁹ and Dannah and Kiriath-sannah (that is, Debir), ⁵⁰ and Anab and Eshtemoh and Anim, ⁵¹ and Goshen and Holon and Giloh; eleven cities with their villages.

⁵² Arab and Dumah and Eshan, ⁵³ and Janum and Beth-tappuah and Aphekah, ⁵⁴ and Humtah and Kiriath-arba (that is, Hebron), and Zior; nine cities with their villages.

⁵⁵ Maon, Carmel and Ziph and Juttah, ⁵⁶ and Jezreel and Jokdeam and Zanoah, ⁵⁷ Kain, Gibeah and Timnah; ten cities with their villages.

⁵⁸ Halhul, Beth-zur and Gedor, ⁵⁹ and Maarath and Beth-anoth and Eltekon; six cities with their villages.

⁶⁰ Kiriath-baal (that is, Kiriath-jearim), and Rabbah; two cities with their villages.

⁶¹ In the wilderness: Beth-arabah, Middin and Secacah, ⁶² and Nibshan and the City of Salt and Engedi; six cities with their villages.

⁶³ Now as for the Jebusites, the inhabitants of Jerusalem, the sons of Judah could not drive them out; so the Jebusites live with the sons of Judah at Jerusalem until this day.

JOSHUA 16

Territory of Ephraim

¹ Then the lot for the sons of Joseph went from the Jordan at Jericho to the waters of Jericho on the east into the wilderness, going up from Jericho through the hill country to Bethel. ² It went from Bethel to Luz, and continued to the border of the Archites at Ataroth. ³ It went down westward to the territory of the Japhletites, as far as the territory of lower Beth-horon even to Gezer, and it ended at the sea.

⁴ The sons of Joseph, Manasseh and Ephraim, received their inheritance. ⁵ Now this was the territory of the sons of Ephraim according to their families: the border of their inheritance eastward was Ataroth-addar, as far as upper Beth-horon. ⁶ Then the border went westward at Michmethath on the north, and the border turned about eastward to Taanath-shiloh and continued beyond it to the east of Janoah. ⁷ It went down from Janoah to Ataroth and to Naarah, then reached Jericho and came

out at the Jordan. [8] From Tappuah the border continued westward to the brook of Kanah, and it ended at the sea. This is the inheritance of the tribe of the sons of Ephraim according to their families,

[9] together with the cities which were set apart for the sons of Ephraim in the midst of the inheritance of the sons of Manasseh, all the cities with their villages. [10] But they did not drive out the Canaanites who lived in Gezer, so the Canaanites live in the midst of Ephraim to this day, and they became forced laborers.

JOSHUA 17

Territory of Manasseh

[1] Now this was the lot for the tribe of Manasseh, for he was the firstborn of Joseph. To Machir the firstborn of Manasseh, the father of Gilead, were allotted Gilead and Bashan, because he was a man of war. [2] So the lot was made for the rest of the sons of Manasseh according to their families: for the sons of Abiezer and for the sons of Helek and for the sons of Asriel and for the sons of Shechem and for the sons of Hepher and for the sons of Shemida; these were the male descendants of Manasseh the son of Joseph according to their families.

[3] However, Zelophehad, the son of Hepher, the son of Gilead, the son of Machir, the son of Manasseh, had no sons, only daughters; and these are the names of his daughters: Mahlah and Noah, Hoglah, Milcah and Tirzah. [4] They came near before Eleazar the priest and before Joshua the son of Nun and before the leaders, saying, "The Lord commanded Moses to give us an inheritance among our brothers." So according to the command of the Lord he gave them an inheritance among their father's brothers. [5] Thus there fell ten portions to Manasseh, besides the land of Gilead and Bashan, which is beyond the Jordan, [6] because the daughters of Manasseh received an inheritance among his sons. And the land of Gilead belonged to the rest of the sons of Manasseh.

[7] The border of Manasseh ran from Asher to Michmethath which was east of Shechem; then the border went southward to the inhabitants of En-tappuah. [8] The land of Tappuah belonged to Manasseh, but Tappuah on the border of Manasseh belonged to the sons of Ephraim. [9] The border went down to the brook of Kanah, southward of the brook (these cities belonged to Ephraim among the cities of Manasseh), and the border of Manasseh was on the north side of the brook and it ended at the sea. [10] The

south side belonged to Ephraim and the north side to Manasseh, and the sea was their border; and they reached to Asher on the north and to Issachar on the east. [11] In Issachar and in Asher, Manasseh had Beth-shean and its towns and Ibleam and its towns, and the inhabitants of Dor and its towns, and the inhabitants of En-dor and its towns, and the inhabitants of Taanach and its towns, and the inhabitants of Megiddo and its towns, the third is Napheth. [12] But the sons of Manasseh could not take possession of these cities, because the Canaanites persisted in living in that land. [13] It came about when the sons of Israel became strong, they put the Canaanites to forced labor, but they did not drive them out completely.

[14] Then the sons of Joseph spoke to Joshua, saying, "Why have you given me only one lot and one portion for an inheritance, since I am a numerous people whom the Lord has thus far blessed?" [15] Joshua said to them, "If you are a numerous people, go up to the forest and clear a place for yourself there in the land of the Perizzites and of the Rephaim, since the hill country of Ephraim is too narrow for you." [16] The sons of Joseph said, "The hill country is not enough for us, and all the Canaanites who live in the valley land have chariots of iron, both those who are in Beth-shean and its towns and those who are in the valley of Jezreel." [17] Joshua spoke to the house of Joseph, to Ephraim and Manasseh, saying, "You are a numerous people and have great power; you shall not have one lot only, [18] but the hill country shall be yours. For though it is a forest, you shall clear it, and to its farthest borders it shall be yours; for you shall drive out the Canaanites, even though they have chariots of iron and though they are strong."

Joshua 13-17

Because you have followed the Lord...fully

Those feelings of futility, that sense of impossibility, the settled resignation that you have permanently plateaued – that is not of Heaven but of hell...And Jesus Christ is well prepared and fully equipped to walk you out of that darkness. [1]

~ Dane Ortlund

As we move into this next section of Joshua, the Israelites have conquered the land. From a tactical standpoint, many key battles have been won, adversity and missteps have been overcome, and the land is theirs. However, the Israelites have not yet fully stepped into the destiny God had promised them. God's people need to actually accept, allocate, and occupy the land. In short, while they may be standing in victory, they are not yet where they ought to be.

Perhaps that sounds all too familiar. As a follower of Christ, you are aware of and thankful for your position before God – forgiven and justified – but something is still holding you back. You've not yet fully stepped into what is rightfully yours. Key battles have been won, and you've certainly come through your share of adversity and missteps, but you still feel the tension of the ongoing battle. You feel stuck, aware there is more for you than what you are experiencing.

Among the allocation of land grants in the coming chapters, two men stand out among the ocean of Israelites: Joshua and Caleb. Their lifetime of perseverance reveals that, even if you feel like you still have a long way to go (and we all feel that way), the Lord is with you, ready to walk forward with you. The fact that you're here, digging into God's Word, desiring a closer relationship with Him, proves that God is at work in your life.

In a world ruled by an enemy who wants to steal our affections and hold us back from what is rightfully ours in Christ, the examples of Caleb and Joshua demonstrate the life to be had on the other side of all our straining. They also point to the One who can be trusted to guide us out of our own wilderness, into joy and light.

Friend, despite the discouragement from the enemy and the seemingly insurmountable obstacles before you, fix your eyes and your heart on the thread we have seen woven throughout Joshua: Be strong and follow the Lord. Even on your most difficult day, there is still an inheritance waiting for you.

DAY ONE
Joshua 13

This week, we will cover a lot of ground — literally. At this point, Joshua has led a successful military campaign and the land itself has been conquered. But imagine the multitude of Israelites with looks on their faces that say something to the effect of, "Now what?" We'll get there as we progress through the land allocation this week and next week, but first, take a moment to read over Joshua 13-17 and answer the questions below to get a quick "lay of the land."

Snapshot
of Joshua 13-17

Which two-and-a-half tribes receive their land allotments first? (Joshua 13:7b-8)

As Joshua turns to the allocations west of the Jordan, which tribe receives their inheritance first? (Joshua 15:1)

What important figure in Israel's history emerges for his inheritance in Joshua 14?

What problem seems to persist for the Israelites as they take possession of the land? What do some of the tribes fail to do?

We'll unpack each of these questions as we progress throughout these chapters in this lesson.

Read Joshua 13:1-7.

1. Fill in the blanks for Joshua 13:1 from the text at the beginning of our lesson:

"You are old and advanced in years, and a very large amount of the land remains ____ ____

_____."

It hasn't been that long since Joshua seemed young as he took the reins of leadership from Moses. Now he bears the scars of battle. We don't exactly know Joshua's age at this point, but scholars think he could have been approaching the century mark. After reading Joshua 13:1-7, didn't you feel exhausted for "old and advanced in years" Joshua? All the battles, all the wandering, all the stress – and there is still a very large amount of the land to fight for!

As much as Joshua has accomplished, there is yet more to be done:

- The Philistine territory with its five great cities of Gaza, Ashdod, Ashkelon, Gath, and Ekron have not been conquered. It will be another 300 years before a young King David emerges to finish this task. Until then, the Philistines will be a thorn in Israel's side.
- Jerusalem, along with the hill country toward Mount Herman, has not been taken.
- The coast of Phoenicia (Lebanon) still has not been subdued.
- Some Canaanites still live within areas that have been conquered, which will be an ongoing struggle for Israel.

However, Israel is firmly established in the Promised Land. God has fulfilled His promise to give them the land, and in verse 6 reaffirms that He will "drive out from the sons of Israel" those remaining.

Some Bibles translate the end of Joshua 13:1, "land to be taken over" or "land to be conquered." But as we see in lesson one, the Hebrew word *yaras* used here actually means to possess, occupy, or to inherit.[2] This will be important as we continue to study the possession of the land – and we'll dig into this more soon – but for now, keep in mind this land is Israel's rightful inheritance.

Warren Wiersbe helps us put this into proper perspective:

> The Jews inherited their land. They didn't win their land as spoils of battle or purchase their land as in a business transaction. The Lord, who was the sole owner, leased the land to them. "The land must not be sold permanently," the Lord had instructed them, "because the land is mine and you are but aliens and my tenants" (Leviticus 25:23, NIV). Imagine having God for your landlord! The "rent" God required was simply Israel's obedience to His law.[3]

All that Israel has to do is obey the Lord, accept their inheritance, and move in.

Read Joshua 13:8-14.

As Joshua begins to allocate the land to the various tribes, he starts with land on the other side of the Jordan. You may recall that the tribes of Reuben, Gad, and half of the tribe of Manasseh had previously asked Moses to be able to settle on the east side of the Jordan, outside of the boundaries of Canaan, because the land was suitable for raising livestock.

2. Read Numbers 32:16-27. What condition did Moses attach to granting their request?

These tribes have made good on their end of the agreement, so the time has come to receive their inheritance east of the Promised Land. To these tribes, this land seemed most suitable for their situation. Their cattle could spread out over large amounts of pastureland, and besides, it was right there next to the Promised Land. But I can't help but wonder what they missed out on by not moving into the land God had promised them – the land God found most suitable for them and His people. Wiersbe explains how this decision will affect these tribes in future generations:

> The fact that these two-and-a-half tribes would not be living within God's appointed land didn't seem to worry them. Moses graciously agreed to their choice and let them settle across the Jordan. When we study the twenty-second chapter of Joshua, we'll learn that while their choice may have been good for cattle, it created serious problems for their children. [4]

He goes on to elaborate on the consequences of the choices of the two-and-a-half tribes:

> These tribes became a sort of "buffer zone" between the Jews in Canaan and the heathen nations like Moab and Ammon. Of course, their location made them extremely vulnerable both to military attack and ungodly influence, and both of these liabilities eventually brought about their downfall (1 Chronicles 5:25-26). The boundaries are given for Reuben in the south (Joshua 13:15-23), and the half-tribe of Manasseh in the north (vv. 29-32), with Gad sandwiched between (vv. 24-28). [5]

3. Can you recall a decision you've made that you knew was just short of God's best for you? How did your plans turn out not to be God's best? How were others affected by your decision?

In Joshua 13:13, we see another costly decision by these tribes as they disregard God's command to drive out the foreign nations around them. This is the first account of the tribes' failure to completely expel the inhabitants of the land, but not the last. Sadly, we'll see this over and over as the land is allocated among the tribes.

4. Read Deuteronomy 20:16-18. What was God's command regarding the people of the land, and why did He command it?

Did you know? In Joshua 13:14 and 33, we see that the Levites were "left out" of the land allocation. David Guzik provides a helpful explanation: "Levi, the priestly tribe, was to receive no allotted land as the other tribes received. Instead, the Levites were given certain cities. This was commanded in Numbers 35:1-8 and fulfilled in Joshua 20-21. The Levites had as their inheritance the offerings that Israel would bring to the Lord. Their provision did not come only from the land, but also from the offerings of Israel.... It was important for each tribe to be content with and find joy in what God had allotted to them. This was especially true for the Levites, who had the Lord for their inheritance." [6]

We might read this and think God sounds like a ruthless tyrant. But remember what is at stake. Allowing a pagan nation to live among them will draw the hearts of the people away from the one true God and into horrible, barbaric, and destructive pagan practices. In fact, centuries later, these two-and-a-half Transjordan tribes will be the first to be driven out by the Assyrians as judgment for their worship of pagan gods (1 Chronicles 5:26). **God isn't being callous. He is being protective of His children.**

We'll see more about the Israelites and their interactions with the foreign nations around them as we continue. Unfortunately, it serves as a sort of litmus test regarding the devotion of their hearts and the future of the nation.

Read Joshua 13:14-33.

As the land details and specifications are recorded for these two-and-a-half tribes, we might feel our eyes start to glaze over as we read what feels like the equivalent of an ancient phone book. But there is noticeable repetition in these verses that is key for the rest of our study in Joshua.

5. What word do you see repeated in Joshua 13:7, 8, 14, 15, 23, 24, 28, 29, 32, and 33?

6. Have you ever inherited something? What did you have to do in order to receive this gift?

Taking possession of the land does not come without adversity, but Israel is stepping into what is rightfully theirs — a divine gift from God! Reading through the locations and names included in this section may feel overwhelming (and dare I say boring) at times. But we are filled with awe when we stop and remember that this confirms the fulfillment of God's promise to His people.

7. Read Colossians 1:12 and Ephesians 2:18. What inheritance is described in these passages?

Joshua 13 is only the beginning. As we continue, we'll see the word "inheritance" used over and over. In fact, it's found more than 50 times between Joshua 13-21. [7] Each time you see it, let it remind you of your inheritance in Christ.

He has given us the seal of His promise (Ephesians 1:13). But, every day, we must decide to step into our inheritance – the life that is rightfully ours as daughters of the King.

"No weapon that is formed against you will prosper; and every tongue that accuses you in judgment you will condemn. This is the heritage of the servants of the Lord, and their vindication is from Me," declares the Lord.
Isaiah 54:17

DAY TWO
Joshua 14

Following the allotment of the land east of the Jordan, the land west of the Jordan still needs to be divided among the remaining tribes. This division of land will take us all the way through Chapter 19. At face value, this section may just seem like a deed or land grant as ownership is handed to each tribe. But there is more to discover as we dig below the surface. The *ESV Study Bible* gives us something to look for as we read:

> This section describes the tribal allocations west of the Jordan, and it exhibits literary symmetry.... Chapters 14-19 provide detailed historical information in a carefully structured literary form, and in so doing underscore a fundamental theological truth: those like Caleb or Joshua who wholly follow the Lord (14:8-9, 14) will be able to enjoy their inheritance. [8]

Who knew a historical land grant could pack such a punch? Let's dig in!

Read Joshua 14:1-5.

The mention of Eleazar, the son and successor of Aaron as high priest, indicates that the allotment of land is not just a legal procedure, but is a process of religious significance.

1. What method do Eleazar, Joshua, and the heads of the tribes use to determine the land allotments?

2. Read Proverbs 16:33. Who actually is determining the allotment of land?

We might see this method and question whether or not this was frowned upon by the Lord. Was this a game of chance? Were their methods of divvying out the inheritance a bit crooked? Quite the opposite actually: "That the inheritance was by lot guarantees divine oversight and protects Israel's leaders from any suspicion of favoritism." [9] In Numbers 26:52-56, God had instructed Moses that this was to be the method, and once again, Joshua is careful to do everything according to the Law. We will discover more about how the lots worked out when we get to Chapter 18, but for now, some land needs to be allocated.

Read Joshua 14:6-15.

The next tribe to be settled is Judah. Since Caleb, one of the two faithful spies, is a member of the tribe of Judah, he will receive his inheritance first. In verses 6-10, Caleb reminds his friend and fellow faithful spy, Joshua, of the promise Moses made to them years before. Let's refresh our memories.

3. Read Numbers 14:1-9. How did Joshua and Caleb's view of the task before them differ from that of the people of Israel?

4. Read Deuteronomy 1:34-36. Why has Caleb been promised an inheritance once they finally reach the Promised Land?

What it must have meant to Moses, a weary, lonesome leader, for Caleb to stand up before the entire congregation and testify of God's faithfulness! No one other than Caleb and Joshua believed they could take over the land God had promised to them. And because of the nation's unbelief, they were banished to the wilderness, leaving the land of milk and honey behind them.

5. Compare Joshua 14:7 with 14:10. How much time has passed since Caleb received this promise from Moses?

Forty-five years of waiting have not diminished Caleb's faith in God's ability to come through. He has spent decades in the wilderness with these hard hearted people and fought alongside them as they finally entered the land. All the while, he has never lost heart. Caleb believed then, and he believes now. He knows that God is able.

6. Have you ever been in a season where you were waiting for the Lord to come through? Was your faith shaken or built up during that season?

Caleb persevered in the face of adversity, pain, and frustration. And we can do the same as we follow Caleb's example.

7. According to Joshua 14:8-9, 14, what sets Caleb apart from everyone else?

Robert Smith describes the object of Caleb's faith:

> Caleb followed the Lord without exception. He believed the Lord's promise to keep him alive until he received what he was promised. A believer who remains in the will of God is immortal until God's purpose for his or her life is fulfilled. How long can we wait on the promise of God to be fulfilled in our lives? Time does not matter. Whether it takes four years, forty years, or forty-five years, we must remember: God is not in time. Time is in God. If God said it, He will do it. [10]

Even as an 85-year-old man, Caleb believes God will strengthen him for the task ahead. God will allow Caleb to get his hands dirty as he sees the promise fulfilled. There is something truly beautiful in Caleb physically participating in this invasion. Caleb is ready to finish what he started.

This portion of the land is where the Anakim reside with great fortified cities (Joshua 14:12).

8. Read Numbers 13:28. Who did the spies see that filled ten of them with fear?

Did you know? Hebron, the land that Caleb would inherit, is an area of great significance in the Bible. A number of key events took place here. Hebron is where "God showed Abram the land that would belong to his offspring (Genesis 13:14-17)....It became the city where David ruled over Judah for seven years (2 Samuel 2:1-4)....It's where Abraham buried his wife Sarah (Genesis 23:17-20) and where he was later buried (Genesis 25:10)." [11] It's also likely that Hebron was home to "the valley of Eschol," which is where the original 12 spies found large clusters of grapes — but later ran away in fear, missing out on this bounty.

The Hebrews believed the Anakim to be descendants of the "Nephilim," giant-like warriors. And when they first spied out this land 45 years before, it was the sight of the Anakim that put fear in their hearts. Numbers 13:33 tells us that the Israelites "felt like grasshoppers" compared to the size of these people.

The very land occupied by giants is the land Caleb wants. He has not forgotten the enemy who resides there. But he also has not forgotten his God. He is just as resolved to push out the Anakim now as he was 45 years ago. Speaking in faith, he tells Joshua, "Perhaps the Lord will be with me, and I will drive them out just as the Lord has spoken" (14:12). And "If God is for us, who can be against us?" (Romans 8:31, ESV).

We are all plagued with reminders of past failures, feelings of unworthiness, and all the reasons why we couldn't possibly be a person God desires to use for His purposes. You might think, "I could never be a Caleb." **But there was nothing special about Caleb. He simply collapsed into the arms of his faithful and able God.** Just like Caleb, "we can capture mountains and conquer giants if we wholly follow the Lord." [12]

9. As we close today, call to mind an obstacle the enemy always seems to put in your way. What is the source of discouragement in your life that keeps you from boldly living out God's purpose? Write a prayer below as you resolve to refuse what the enemy says and draw near to God and His strength.

DAY THREE
Joshua 15

The distribution of land continues in Joshua 15, and all 63 verses describe the land given to the tribe of Judah. Let's be careful not to get lost in all the discussion about borders and boundary lines. It is important to keep at the forefront of our minds that God is specifically giving each tribe their inheritance with distinct boundaries to separate them. Smith helps us to understand the importance of these details:

> If you had a home built, it would be of the utmost importance to know the boundary lines of your property so you did not illegally build anything on someone else's property, nor anyone else unlawfully build anything on yours. Land, boundaries, and possessions matter to God. [13]

Judah is the first western land to receive its land grant. Some scholars theorize that this is not a coincidence:

> It has...clear theological purposes...as the kingdom of Judah will endure longer than the remainder of Israel and even form the basis of the people who occupy the land after the Babylonian exile. [14]

The author of Joshua also spends more time on this record than on any of the other tribes' allotments. Why is this? It's a question worth digging into.

1. What are one or two things you already know about the tribe of Judah?

This tribe (and its namesake) has a tumultuous, but rich history. Among many other things that take place among this people group, well-known kings like David and Solomon come from this line. We also learn from Jacob's list of blessings in Genesis 49:10 that "The scepter shall not depart from Judah...." This is a direct prophecy about the coming Messiah – King Jesus.

Judah, indeed, holds great significance.

Read Joshua 15:1-12.

2. In the text at the beginning of the lesson, underline the borders of the land given to the tribe of Judah.

The map on the next page provides a visual of the geographic landscape allotted to each tribe. While this is not a geography class, it's important to remember that these were real places, with real people, accepting a real inheritance granted to them by the Lord. Guzik gives us helpful contextual insight:

> The listing of these specific names, places, and geographic boundaries was of great interest to those who would inherit the land. This collection of places also reminds the reader that

these were real places, not the description of a symbolic or spiritual inheritance. When God promised a land to Abraham and his covenant descendants (Genesis 13:15, 17:8), God meant a real land. [15]

3. Grab some colored pencils and using four different colors, shade in the three-and-a-half tribes we've already learned about in Joshua 14-15.

Read Joshua 15:13-20.

4. What significant event is recorded in Joshua 15:14?

You may remember from Joshua 11 that the Anakim were driven out of the land by Joshua and the armies during the conquest. Some scholars, based on the repetition of the phrase "and the land has rest from war" in Joshua 11:23 and 14:15, believe these two sections describe the same event. It's also possible that Caleb drove out any remaining Anakim who might have survived the earlier conquest or returned. Regardless of the timeline, Caleb and Joshua have made certain that what stood in their way before will never be an obstacle again.

5. Yesterday, we ended the day praying about obstacles that stand in our way of receiving the life God has for us. How's that going today?

Remember, it has taken Caleb 45 years to receive the inheritance. Sometimes we feel like the Christian life is an uphill battle. Often, it's our own sin that causes us to feel like we are spinning our wheels. But you are in the process of being sanctified each day. Dane Ortlund offers beautiful encouragement for those who are tired of the struggle:

> We are complicated sinners. Sometimes, we take two steps forward and three steps back. We need time. Be patient with yourself. A sense of urgency, yes, but not a sense of hurry. Overnight transformations are the exception, not the norm. Slow change is still real change. And it's the normal way God deals with us. Take your time. [16]

In Joshua 15:18-19, we read a fascinating encounter between Caleb and his daughter. Caleb has given his daughter, Achsah, in marriage to a warrior named Othniel who helped him conquer the regions of Kirath-sepher (15:16). Apparently, Caleb's faith and boldness have rubbed off on his daughter.

6. What does Achsah ask Caleb for? (v. 19)

When Othniel and Achsah receive their land inheritance, it is the Negev, a dry area. Knowing the importance of water, Achsah approaches her father and requests a source of water to be given to them as well. In the same loving way that God has blessed him, Caleb generously gives his daughter and son-in-law the upper springs and lower springs so that their land will be productive.

Read Joshua 15:21-63.

In these verses, we see the land of Judah divided up into more specific cities. Despite the success they have experienced, we see a concerning point at the end of the chapter.

7. What does Joshua 15:63 say about the Jebusites?

Did you know? This same Othniel is the one God raised up as a deliverer in Judges 3. By this time, the Israelites had become backslidden and turned to other pagan gods. Typical for the sin cycle they were in at the time, when they reached a breaking point under the hand of God, they would cry out to Him for help. In Judges 3, God sent them Othniel, and in Judges 3:10, we see that "the Spirit of the Lord was upon him." After conquering the king of Mesopotamia under Othniel's leadership, the land rested for 40 years.

This is a different situation from what we saw in Joshua 13:13. There, we learned that the Israelites "did not drive out" (ESV) the Geshurites or the Maacathites. Joshua 15:63 says "the sons of Judah could not drive [the Jebusites] out. The *ESV Study Bible* gives us a sobering insight:

> Against the backdrop of so much success, the notice that the people of Judah could not drive out the Jebusites from Jerusalem...is disconcerting....And it raises a theological question: how is it that the people of Judah "could not" drive out their foes? Surely the god of the Jebusites is not stronger than the God of Judah!....Perhaps statements of what Israel "could not" do are to be read as early evidence of spiritual slippage – of failure to follow the Lord "wholly" – which will become increasingly evident in the book of Judges. [17]

As we wholly follow the Lord, we can and will have victory over the enemy in our lives. But, if we turn our hearts from wholehearted devotion to Christ, the opposite can also be true.

Ask God to examine your heart. Is there any area of "slippage"? No matter how big or small, the enemy's expertise is craftiness directed right at our weak spots. Ask God for wisdom as you guard against the manipulation of the enemy.

DAY FOUR
Joshua 16-17

Read Joshua 16:1-10.

This brief chapter breaks down for us where we get the 12 tribes. If you count the territories divided up among the people, you actually come up with 14 sections of land. (And this is without counting the tribe of Levi, who did not receive a land inheritance.) Two of those sections belong to one tribe, Manasseh. That brings us down to 13 territories. So, how do we get 12 tribes?

1. Based on Joshua 16:4, who makes up the house of Joseph?

2. The first section of land distributed in this chapter is to the tribe of Ephraim. Turn back to our map from yesterday and shade in the area for this tribe with a different color.

Did you know? Here is some helpful insight about the numbering of the tribes: "Technically, there is no tribe of Joseph. Instead, Joseph received a 'double blessing,' and his two sons, Ephraim and Manasseh, each became his own tribe (Genesis 48; Joshua 14:4; Ezekiel 47:13). The Bible does, on occasion, refer to a 'tribe of Joseph' (Numbers 13:11; 36:5; Revelation 7:8). However, in the contexts, the 'tribe of Joseph' seems to be referring to either the tribe of Ephraim or Manasseh, or to the 'house of Joseph,' which included Ephraim and Manasseh." [18] This means that the tribes who received land allocations were Reuben, Simeon, Judah, Dan, Naphtali, Gad, Asher, Issachar, Zebulun, Benjamin, Ephraim, and Manasseh. [19] In the absence of land for the tribe of Levi, Ephraim and Manasseh complete the land allotment for 12 tribes. [20]

We learn in Joshua 16:10 that the problem of failing to drive out the Canaanites has persisted in this tribe as well. Ephraim's solution, since they couldn't drive them out completely, is to conscript the Canaanites into forced labor. Once again, they fail to do things God's way and attempt to make do, leaning into their own understanding (Proverbs 3:5).

We often refer to solutions like this as "sin management." This is when, even though God has told us to flee from temptation and sin (2 Timothy 2:22), we try to manage it ourselves and simply try to hold the sin at bay. And that never works. As my pastor, Steve Gaines, frequently says, "If you don't want to fall down, don't walk in slippery places." [21] In generations to come, allowing the Canaanites to stay in the land will prove to be not only slippery, but deadly.

3. Has there been a time when you've tried to manage your sin rather than repenting and turning to the Lord? What was the result?

Read Joshua 17:1-6.

Now it is time for the tribe of Manasseh, the firstborn son of Joseph, to receive its inheritance of land.

4. Turn back to the map from yesterday and shade in the portion of the land for Manasseh on the west side of the Jordan River. (Use the same color you used for Manasseh's land on the eastern side.)

Joshua 17:3-6 takes an interesting and meaningful detour from the assignments of land. In this narrative, we read about a group of sisters, left without a father or brother to give them covering and land ownership. The Old Testament was written during a time when societies functioned according to a patriarchal structure. Families were governed by the father or oldest living male, with women having little to no voice. As modern scholars have studied this structure, they now believe that because of the complex social and economic system of ancient Israel's culture, it was not as much patriarchal as it was heterachiral. In a heterarchy, any unit can govern or be governed by others depending on the situation, so no one unit is dominant. The cultures of the Bible arranged their heterarchy around the oldest male or father, a structure known as patricentric (father-centered). In a patricentric culture, the father or oldest male is responsible to provide and protect for those under his care. [22]

So, what happens when there is no father or oldest male? As we are about to discover in this account, God has already provided. And this provision will become the law for future generations.

5. Read the story of the daughters of Zelophehad in Numbers 27:1-11. What did God tell Moses about these women in verse 7?

6. Look back at Joshua 17:4 and fill in these blanks:

"The Lord _____ Moses __ _____us an _____ among our brothers."

God, in no uncertain terms, has insisted that these daughters be given a tribal inheritance. But, like Caleb, these five women have waited for about 45 years to see what God promised come to pass. Now, in the Promised Land, Zelophehad's name will continue within the tribe of Manasseh.

Read Joshua 17:7-18.

As we wrap up tomorrow, we'll come back to an important part of this chapter, but for now, skip to verses 14-18.

7. What complaint is raised by some of the descendants of Joseph? (vv. 14-16)

Essentially, the Israelites have reverted back to their old ways. They are complaining about the amount of land apportioned to them because of the size of their tribes. However, it appears the root for their complaint is fear. The hill country and the forest are inhabited by the Canaanites. But Joshua, the incredible leader that he is, challenges them to think higher and better of their God! Wiersbe says,

> Let them do what Caleb did and defeat the giants and claim the mountains! It's worth noting that the people of Ephraim and Manasseh seemed to be given to criticism and pride...It's not your boasting but your believing that gives you the victory and gains you new territory. [23]

Caleb, knowing the Anakim are in Hebron, requests Hebron. He knows His God is able. Manasseh, knowing the Canaanites are in the hill country, requests more land anywhere else. They have already forgotten the power of their God. Thankfully, Joshua won't let them back down so easily.

Close today by reading Joshua 17:18 out loud and personalize it. Remind yourself that God's promise "shall be yours." **Though there are obstacles, you shall clear them. And though your enemy and his weapons are strong, you shall drive him out!**

DAY FIVE
Joshua 13-17 | Because you have followed the Lord...fully

Let's begin today by taking a look back at Joshua 17:7-13.

Notice the wording of Joshua 17:13, "They did not drive them out completely." The ESV says, "They did not utterly drive them out." The original wording tells us that they failed to dispossess the Canaanites from the land entirely. This failure is the antithesis of a different kind of completeness we saw earlier this week.

1. Write down the repeated phrase we read regarding Caleb in Joshua 14:8-9, 14.

This week's warfare principle is:

> **Victory hinges on belief: You must trust that what God has promised will come to pass.**

We must be wholly, utterly devoted to the Lord. That is the only way to completely destroy the enemy's work in our lives. When we devote our hearts to the Lord, like Caleb, we take possession of the goodness God has promised us. When we settle and give Satan even a toehold in our lives, we share what's rightfully ours with an enemy who hates us, hates God, and is plotting our demise while we sit back and watch.

Our problem is that we forget the goodness of our God. He doesn't ask us to turn away from sin to ruin our fun. He hasn't forgotten what our hearts want and need. He doesn't want us to be miserable. **What God wants more than anything is for our hearts to be free and full of joy.** And that's what He wanted for the Israelites. With every battle they won and every people they conquered, His goal was to bring them into His rest.

2. The enemy's tactic is to make us question whether or not God can still accomplish His purpose in our lives. Is there an area where you are currently questioning God's ability to come through for you?

3. What do you do to set your mind on Christ and His ability to save?

Certainly, you're going to read books, listen to podcasts and sermons, or see posts on social media that give you words of encouragement and insight into the things of God. And those can be a helpful means of growing in Christ. But at the end of the day, it simply comes down to belief. Do you trust that God is good and that what He has promised will come to pass?

No matter how far you've fallen or how big your enemy seems, no matter your level of despair as you face what feels like "the hill country and forest," remember your Savior. Ortlund provides this gracious reminder:

> As you despair of yourself – agonizing over the desolation wrought by your failures, your weaknesses, your inadequacies – let that despair take you way down deep into honesty with yourself. For there you will find a friend, the living Lord Jesus himself, who will startle and surprise you with his gentle goodness as you leave self behind, in repentance, and bank on him afresh, in faith. [24]

Our victory hinges on fixing our eyes on Jesus, day in and day out.

Remember, He does not give you strength – He is your strength.
He does not give you victory – He is your victory! [25]
~ Ian Thomas

LESSON EIGHT

They...possessed it and settled in it

JOSHUA 18

Rest of the Land Divided

¹ Then the whole congregation of the sons of Israel assembled themselves at Shiloh, and set up the tent of meeting there; and the land was subdued before them.

² There remained among the sons of Israel seven tribes who had not divided their inheritance. ³ So Joshua said to the sons of Israel, "How long will you put off entering to take possession of the land which the Lord, the God of your fathers, has given you?

⁴ Provide for yourselves three men from each tribe that I may send them, and that they may arise and walk through the land and write a description of it according to their inheritance; then they shall return to me. ⁵ They shall divide it into seven portions; Judah shall stay in its territory on the south, and the house of Joseph shall stay in their territory on the north.

⁶ You shall describe the land in seven divisions, and bring the description here to me. I will cast lots for you here before the Lord our God. ⁷ For the Levites have no portion among you, because the priesthood of the Lord is their inheritance. Gad and Reuben and the half-tribe of Manasseh also have received their inheritance eastward beyond the Jordan, which Moses the servant of the Lord gave them."

⁸ Then the men arose and went, and Joshua commanded those who went to describe the land, saying, "Go and walk through the land and describe it, and return to me; then I will cast lots for you here before the Lord in Shiloh." ⁹ So the men went and passed through the land, and described it by cities in seven divisions in a book; and they came to Joshua to the camp at Shiloh. ¹⁰ And Joshua cast lots for them in Shiloh before the Lord, and there Joshua divided the land to the sons of Israel according to their divisions.

The Territory of Benjamin

¹¹ Now the lot of the tribe of the sons of Benjamin came up according to their families, and the territory of their lot lay between the sons of Judah and the sons of Joseph. ¹² Their border on the north side was from the Jordan, then the border went up to the side of Jericho on the north, and went up through the hill country westward, and it ended at the wilderness of Beth-aven. ¹³ From there the border continued to Luz, to the side of Luz (that is, Bethel) southward; and the border went down

to Ataroth-addar, near the hill which lies on the south of lower Beth-horon. ¹⁴ The border extended from there and turned round on the west side southward, from the hill which lies before Beth-horon southward; and it ended at Kiriath-baal (that is, Kiriath-jearim), a city of the sons of Judah. This was the west side.

¹⁵ Then the south side was from the edge of Kiriath-jearim, and the border went westward and went to the fountain of the waters of Nephtoah. ¹⁶ The border went down to the edge of the hill which is in the valley of Ben-hinnom, which is in the valley of Rephaim northward; and it went down to the valley of Hinnom, to the slope of the Jebusite southward, and went down to En-rogel. ¹⁷ It extended northward and went to En-shemesh and went to Geliloth, which is opposite the ascent of Adummim, and it went down to the stone of Bohan the son of Reuben. ¹⁸ It continued to the side in front of the Arabah northward and went down to the Arabah. ¹⁹ The border continued to the side of Beth-hoglah northward; and the border ended at the north bay of the Salt Sea, at the south end of the Jordan. This was the south border. ²⁰ Moreover, the Jordan was its border on the east side. This was the inheritance of the sons of Benjamin, according to their families and according to its borders all around.

²¹ Now the cities of the tribe of the sons of Benjamin according to their families were Jericho and Beth-hoglah and Emek-keziz, ²² and Beth-arabah and Zemaraim and Bethel, ²³ and Avvim and Parah and Ophrah, ²⁴ and Chephar-ammoni and Ophni and Geba; twelve cities with their villages. ²⁵ Gibeon and Ramah and Beeroth, ²⁶ and Mizpeh and Chephirah and Mozah, ²⁷ and Rekem and Irpeel and Taralah, ²⁸ and Zelah, Haeleph and the Jebusite (that is, Jerusalem), Gibeah, Kiriath; fourteen cities with their families.

JOSHUA 19

Territory of Simeon

¹ Then the second lot fell to Simeon, to the tribe of the sons of Simeon according to their families, and their inheritance was in the midst of the inheritance of the sons of Judah. ² So they had as their inheritance Beersheba or Sheba and Moladah, ³ and Hazar-shual and Balah and Ezem, ⁴ and Eltolad and Bethul and Hormah, ⁵ and Ziklag and Beth-marcaboth and Hazar-susah, ⁶ and Beth-lebaoth and Sharuhen; thirteen cities with their villages;

[7] Ain, Rimmon and Ether and Ashan; four cities with their villages; [8] and all the villages which were around these cities as far as Baalath-beer, Ramah of the Negev. This was the inheritance of the tribe of the sons of Simeon according to their families. [9] The inheritance of the sons of Simeon was taken from the portion of the sons of Judah, for the share of the sons of Judah was too large for them; so the sons of Simeon received an inheritance in the midst of Judah's inheritance.

Territory of Zebulun

[10] Now the third lot came up for the sons of Zebulun according to their families. And the territory of their inheritance was as far as Sarid. [11] Then their border went up to the west and to Maralah, it then touched Dabbesheth and reached to the brook that is before Jokneam.

[12] Then it turned from Sarid to the east toward the sunrise as far as the border of Chisloth-tabor, and it proceeded to Daberath and up to Japhia. [13] From there it continued eastward toward the sunrise to Gath-hepher, to Eth-kazin, and it proceeded to Rimmon which stretches to Neah. [14] The border circled around it on the north to Hannathon, and it ended at the valley of Iphtahel. [15] Included also were Kattah and Nahalal and Shimron and Idalah and Bethlehem; twelve cities with their villages. [16] This was the inheritance of the sons of Zebulun according to their families, these cities with their villages.

Territory of Issachar

[17] The fourth lot fell to Issachar, to the sons of Issachar according to their families. [18] Their territory was to Jezreel and included Chesulloth and Shunem, [19] and Hapharaim and Shion and Anaharath, [20] and Rabbith and Kishion and Ebez, [21] and Remeth and En-gannim and En-haddah and Beth-pazzez. [22] The border reached to Tabor and Shahazumah and Beth-shemesh, and their border ended at the Jordan; sixteen cities with their villages. [23] This was the inheritance of the tribe of the sons of Issachar according to their families, the cities with their villages.

Territory of Asher

[24] Now the fifth lot fell to the tribe of the sons of Asher according to their families. [25] Their territory was Helkath and Hali and Beten and Achshaph, [26] and Allammelech and Amad and Mishal; and it reached to Carmel on the west and to Shihor-libnath. [27] It turned toward the east to Beth-dagon and reached to Zebulun, and to the valley of Iphtahel northward to Beth-emek and Neiel; then it proceeded on north to Cabul, [28] and Ebron and Rehob and Hammon and Kanah, as far as Great Sidon. [29] The border turned to Ramah and to the fortified city of Tyre; then the border turned

to Hosah, and it ended at the sea by the region of Achzib. ³⁰ Included also were Ummah, and Aphek and Rehob; twenty-two cities with their villages. ³¹ This was the inheritance of the tribe of the sons of Asher according to their families, these cities with their villages.

Territory of Naphtali

³² The sixth lot fell to the sons of Naphtali; to the sons of Naphtali according to their families. ³³ Their border was from Heleph, from the oak in Zaanannim and Adami-nekeb and Jabneel, as far as Lakkum, and it ended at the Jordan. ³⁴ Then the border turned westward to Aznoth-tabor and proceeded from there to Hukkok; and it reached to Zebulun on the south and touched Asher on the west, and to Judah at the Jordan toward the east.

³⁵ The fortified cities were Ziddim, Zer and Hammath, Rakkath and Chinnereth, ³⁶ and Adamah and Ramah and Hazor, ³⁷ and Kedesh and Edrei and En-hazor, ³⁸ and Yiron and Migdal-el, Horem and Beth-anath and Beth-shemesh; nineteen cities with their villages.

³⁹ This was the inheritance of the tribe of the sons of Naphtali according to their families, the cities with their villages.

Territory of Dan

⁴⁰ The seventh lot fell to the tribe of the sons of Dan according to their families. ⁴¹ The territory of their inheritance was Zorah and Eshtaol and Ir-shemesh, ⁴² and Shaalabbin and Aijalon and Ithlah, ⁴³ and Elon and Timnah and Ekron, ⁴⁴ and Eltekeh and Gibbethon and Baalath, ⁴⁵ and Jehud and Bene-berak and Gath-rimmon, ⁴⁶ and Me-jarkon and Rakkon, with the territory over against Joppa. ⁴⁷ The territory of the sons of Dan proceeded beyond them; for the sons of Dan went up and fought with Leshem and captured it. Then they struck it with the edge of the sword and **possessed it and settled in it**; and they called Leshem Dan after the name of Dan their father. ⁴⁸ This was the inheritance of the tribe of the sons of Dan according to their families, these cities with their villages.

⁴⁹ When they finished apportioning the land for inheritance by its borders, the sons of Israel gave an inheritance in their midst to Joshua the son of Nun. ⁵⁰ In accordance with the command of the Lord they gave him the city for which he asked, Timnath-serah in the hill country of Ephraim. So he built the city and settled in it.

⁵¹ These are the inheritances which Eleazar the priest, and Joshua the son of Nun, and the heads of the households of the tribes of the sons of Israel distributed by lot

in Shiloh before the Lord at the doorway of the tent of meeting. So they finished dividing the land.

JOSHUA 20

Six Cities of Refuge

[1] Then the Lord spoke to Joshua, saying, [2] "Speak to the sons of Israel, saying, 'Designate the cities of refuge, of which I spoke to you through Moses, [3] that the manslayer who kills any person unintentionally, without premeditation, may flee there, and they shall become your refuge from the avenger of blood. [4] He shall flee to one of these cities, and shall stand at the entrance of the gate of the city and state his case in the hearing of the elders of that city; and they shall take him into the city to them and give him a place, so that he may dwell among them. [5] Now if the avenger of blood pursues him, then they shall not deliver the manslayer into his hand, because he struck his neighbor without premeditation and did not hate him beforehand. [6] He shall dwell in that city until he stands before the congregation for judgment, until the death of the one who is high priest in those days. Then the manslayer shall return to his own city and to his own house, to the city from which he fled.'"

[7] So they set apart Kedesh in Galilee in the hill country of Naphtali and Shechem in the hill country of Ephraim, and Kiriath-arba (that is, Hebron) in the hill country of Judah. [8] Beyond the Jordan east of Jericho, they designated Bezer in the wilderness on the plain from the tribe of Reuben, and Ramoth in Gilead from the tribe of Gad, and Golan in Bashan from the tribe of Manasseh. [9] These were the appointed cities for all the sons of Israel and for the stranger who sojourns among them, that whoever kills any person unintentionally may flee there, and not die by the hand of the avenger of blood until he stands before the congregation.

JOSHUA 21

Forty-eight Cities of the Levites

[1] Then the heads of households of the Levites approached Eleazar the priest, and Joshua the son of Nun, and the heads of households of the tribes of the sons of Israel. [2] They spoke to them at Shiloh in the land of Canaan, saying, "The Lord commanded through Moses to give us cities to live in, with their pasture lands for our cattle." [3] So the sons of Israel gave the Levites from their inheritance these cities with their pasture lands, according to the command of the Lord. [4] Then the lot came

out for the families of the Kohathites. And the sons of Aaron the priest, who were of the Levites, received thirteen cities by lot from the tribe of Judah and from the tribe of the Simeonites and from the tribe of Benjamin.

5 The rest of the sons of Kohath received ten cities by lot from the families of the tribe of Ephraim and from the tribe of Dan and from the half-tribe of Manasseh.

6 The sons of Gershon received thirteen cities by lot from the families of the tribe of Issachar and from the tribe of Asher and from the tribe of Naphtali and from the half-tribe of Manasseh in Bashan.

7 The sons of Merari according to their families received twelve cities from the tribe of Reuben and from the tribe of Gad and from the tribe of Zebulun.

8 Now the sons of Israel gave by lot to the Levites these cities with their pasture lands, as the Lord had commanded through Moses.

9 They gave these cities which are here mentioned by name from the tribe of the sons of Judah and from the tribe of the sons of Simeon; 10 and they were for the sons of Aaron, one of the families of the Kohathites, of the sons of Levi, for the lot was theirs first. 11 Thus they gave them Kiriath-arba, Arba being the father of Anak (that is, Hebron), in the hill country of Judah, with its surrounding pasture lands. 12 But the fields of the city and its villages they gave to Caleb the son of Jephunneh as his possession.

13 So to the sons of Aaron the priest they gave Hebron, the city of refuge for the manslayer, with its pasture lands, and Libnah with its pasture lands, 14 and Jattir with its pasture lands and Eshtemoa with its pasture lands, 15 and Holon with its pasture lands and Debir with its pasture lands, 16 and Ain with its pasture lands and Juttah with its pasture lands and Beth-shemesh with its pasture lands; nine cities from these two tribes. 17 From the tribe of Benjamin, Gibeon with its pasture lands, Geba with its pasture lands, 18 Anathoth with its pasture lands and Almon with its pasture lands; four cities. 19 All the cities of the sons of Aaron, the priests, were thirteen cities with their pasture lands.

20 Then the cities from the tribe of Ephraim were allotted to the families of the sons of Kohath, the Levites, even to the rest of the sons of Kohath. 21 They gave them Shechem, the city of refuge for the manslayer, with its pasture lands, in the hill country of Ephraim, and Gezer with its pasture lands, 22 and Kibzaim with its pasture lands and Beth-horon with its pasture lands; four cities. 23 From the tribe of Dan, Elteke with its pasture lands, Gibbethon with its pasture lands, 24 Aijalon with

its pasture lands, Gath-rimmon with its pasture lands; four cities. 25 From the half-tribe of Manasseh, they allotted Taanach with its pasture lands and Gath-rimmon with its pasture lands; two cities. 26 All the cities with their pasture lands for the families of the rest of the sons of Kohath were ten.

27 To the sons of Gershon, one of the families of the Levites, from the half-tribe of Manasseh, they gave Golan in Bashan, the city of refuge for the manslayer, with its pasture lands, and Be-eshterah with its pasture lands; two cities. 28 From the tribe of Issachar, they gave Kishion with its pasture lands, Daberath with its pasture lands, 29 Jarmuth with its pasture lands, En-gannim with its pasture lands; four cities. 30 From the tribe of Asher, they gave Mishal with its pasture lands, Abdon with its pasture lands, 31 Helkath with its pasture lands and Rehob with its pasture lands; four cities. 32 From the tribe of Naphtali, they gave Kedesh in Galilee, the city of refuge for the manslayer, with its pasture lands and Hammoth-dor with its pasture lands and Kartan with its pasture lands; three cities. 33 All the cities of the Gershonites according to their families were thirteen cities with their pasture lands.

34 To the families of the sons of Merari, the rest of the Levites, they gave from the tribe of Zebulun, Jokneam with its pasture lands and Kartah with its pasture lands. 35 Dimnah with its pasture lands, Nahalal with its pasture lands; four cities. 36 From the tribe of Reuben, they gave Bezer with its pasture lands and Jahaz with its pasture lands, 37 Kedemoth with its pasture lands and Mephaath with its pasture lands; four cities. 38 From the tribe of Gad, they gave Ramoth in Gilead, the city of refuge for the manslayer, with its pasture lands and Mahanaim with its pasture lands, 39 Heshbon with its pasture lands, Jazer with its pasture lands; four cities in all. 40 All these were the cities of the sons of Merari according to their families, the rest of the families of the Levites; and their lot was twelve cities.

41 All the cities of the Levites in the midst of the possession of the sons of Israel were forty-eight cities with their pasture lands. 42 These cities each had its surrounding pasture lands; thus it was with all these cities.

43 So the Lord gave Israel all the land which He had sworn to give to their fathers, and they possessed it and lived in it. 44 And the Lord gave them rest on every side, according to all that He had sworn to their fathers, and no one of all their enemies stood before them; the Lord gave all their enemies into their hand. 45 Not one of the good promises which the Lord had made to the house of Israel failed; all came to pass.

They...possessed it and settled in it

Above and beyond all the battles and struggles
it is His ultimate purpose that we be those who not only take territory
but occupy it to find fruitful lives rich in the abundance of His provision. [1]
~ Phillip Keller

The division of the land among the tribes of Israel takes place in two phases. Up to this point in our study, the tribes of Reuben, Gad, Manasseh, Judah, and Ephraim have received their specific allotments in the Promised Land. It is now time for the remaining seven tribes to take the land granted to them.

As you read about the assignment of land to the remaining tribes, I pray the Holy Spirit will penetrate your heart with the truth of the victory you have in Jesus. I pray His death, burial, and resurrection will serve as a powerful reminder that sin has been conquered, and you have the freedom to take hold of the abundant, Spirit-filled life that Christ Jesus died to give you!

Do not delay! Take possession of the land God has given you!

DAY ONE
Joshua 18:1-3

As you begin your study this week, read Joshua 18-21. This will take a few moments of your time, and honestly, some of the reading may seem a bit underwhelming. But I encourage you to read the text in its entirety. Ask the Lord to open the eyes of your heart to see Him in the pages of His Word.

Let's create a brief snapshot of these chapters to provide a general overview of what you have just read.

Snapshot
of Joshua 18-21

Circle the names of the tribes that have yet to receive their land allotments at the beginning of Joshua 18.
(Hint: Look back at last week's lesson to see who has already received their land.)

Reuben	Simeon	Judah	Issachar	Zebulun	Dan
Naphtali	Gad	Asher	Ephraim	Manasseh	

What is the purpose of the cities of refuge? (Joshua 20)

How do the Levites obtain land and why is it done in this manner? (Joshua 21)

What attribute of God is on display at the end of Joshua 21?

Canaan is now under Israelite control, and the time has come for the remaining land to be divided. The division of land for Judah, Ephraim, and the western half of Manasseh takes place at Gilgal. Before the land allotments for the remaining seven tribes will take place, Joshua moves the people en masse from Gilgal.

Read Joshua 18:1.

1. To what location does Joshua move the center of operations for the Israelites? (v. 1)

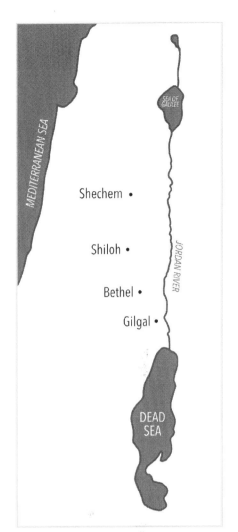

Shiloh is located in the fertile valley within the Ephraimite hills between Bethel and Shechem.

2. What do they do once they gather at Shiloh? (v. 1)

As you can see from the map, Shiloh is centrally located, making it a more convenient location for all the tribes. It will also serve as the location from which the remaining land will be disbursed. Shiloh will be the first permanent site for the Tabernacle (the Tent of Meeting) and will contain the ark of the covenant. For three centuries, the tribes of Israel will "visit [Shiloh] for feasts or peace offerings. From the time Israel entered the land until the time of the prophet Samuel, the ark of the covenant remained in the Tabernacle at Shiloh." [2]

The name Shiloh comes from the Hebrew root word, *shalah*, which means "to be at rest" or "to be tranquil." [3]

> Shiloh is a significant term in the Hebrew Bible, often interpreted as a messianic title or a place name. It is traditionally understood to mean "He whose it is" or "He to whom it belongs," referring to a figure of peace and rest. In Genesis 49:10, it is used in Jacob's blessing over Judah, indicating a future ruler or messianic figure: "The scepter will not depart from Judah, nor the ruler's staff from between his feet, until Shiloh comes, and the allegiance of the nations is his." [4]

I find it most interesting and heartwarming to see the connotations of rest and peace associated with the name Shiloh. As we have traced the journey of the Israelites to the place of settling into the land promised by God, I pray we see the significance and importance in realizing that Jesus, our Messiah, is the only true rest for our souls (more of that coming later in the week). But for now, as you study,

Did you know? Shiloh was the place Hannah went when she visited the Tabernacle to pour out her heart to God, begging Him for a child, whom God gave her – Samuel (1 Samuel 1:1-28; 3:21). [5]

keep in mind that just as the Lord strategically placed and settled His people, He does the same for you and me. He wants us to follow Him without delay and to enjoy His peace and rest. **A life apart from Him will not allow us to "enter in" and rest.**

God's Word amazes me. If you take the time to read it slowly, carefully, and with a desire to know Him, you will see His hand in even the smallest of details. He places the ark of the covenant (the place of His presence) in the center of the tribes, making it easier for His people to attend worship and participate in the yearly festivals – in a place that means rest and tranquility.

If we follow Him, seek His face, and want what He wants more than what we want, He will make a way for us. He will set things in place that are for our good. He will reveal Himself as we seek Him and obey Him. It will not always be smooth sailing, but we will still enjoy His peace and rest as we settle in and take hold of that for which He calls us. We will be able to say, "It is well with my soul."

Read Joshua 18:2-3.

3. What question does Joshua ask of the remaining seven tribes? (v. 3)

Joshua's challenge exposes their slow response in claiming the land. Warren Wiersbe offers insight into their reason for the delay: "These tribes didn't have faith and spiritual zeal. These tribes had helped fight battles and defeat the enemy, but now they hesitated to claim their inheritance and enjoy the land God had given them." [6]

Perhaps it is lack of faith or courage that holds them back. Maybe they have grown accustomed to their nomadic way of life and are not interested in change. We do not know exactly why they put off possessing the land, but this account serves as an encouragement and a challenge to us.

4. What are you promised in Jesus?

- Romans 8:1-2 -

- Ephesians 1:3 -

- Philippians 4:19 -

- 2 Peter 1:3 -

- 1 John 1:3 -

And there is so much more! **As a child of God, your spiritual inheritance is vast, rich, and immeasurable!** Do not miss one single promise of God. If you are in Christ, Satan knows he cannot snatch you from the Father's hand (John 10:28), but he will relentlessly attempt to deceive you into thinking you are unworthy of the abundant, Spirit-filled life.

5. Have you taken possession of what is rightfully yours? If not, what holds you back?

Jesus may be asking you the same question Joshua asked the seven tribes, "How long are you going to wait before taking possession of the remaining land the Lord, the God of your ancestors, has given you?" (Joshua 18:3, NLT).

> *God has been so good to us. Oh, how we can thank Him for His grace,*
> *His love, His goodness, and His mercy. How wonderful He is!*
> *Why don't we move in and possess the land He has given to us?*[7]
> ~ J. Vernon McGee

DAY TWO
Joshua 18:4-19:51

The time has come to finish dividing the land! Joshua will use the customary practice of casting lots (mentioned 70 times in the Old Testament and seven times in the New Testament) [8] to make decisions about distributing the land among the remaining tribes.

Read Joshua 18:4-6.

1. What instructions does Joshua give to the seven tribes? (vv. 4-5)

2. What does Joshua plan to do with the information given to him by the 21 spies sent out to investigate the land? (v. 6)

While casting lots was a frequent practice in decision making during biblical times, it is not a practice we are familiar with in the 21st century. A comparative practice for us would be flipping a coin. Joshua gives the command for the men to go out and survey the land (man's responsibility), and then he will cast lots "in the presence of the Lord our God" (v. 6, NLT) to make the decision (God's responsibility).

Today, we have the complete Word of God at our fingertips (external), and we have the Holy Spirit of God living inside us (internal). We have no need to cast lots or flip a coin to discern what we should do. However, we can follow Joshua's example by doing our part to see what lies before us (surveying the land) and then allow God, through His Word and by the power of the Holy Spirit, to show us the way to go. We do not have to go at it alone, nor should we choose a path flippantly and carelessly.

3. What do the following verses teach us about God's Word (external control) and the Holy Spirit (internal control) as we consider decisions?

   • Psalm 119:105 -

   • John 14:26 -

4. Are you reading God's Word daily and relying on the guidance of the Holy Spirit to direct your paths as you make decisions?

5. What are things that might stand in the way of allowing the Spirit of God to lead us?

To know Jesus intimately, to be acquainted with His voice, to hear Him speak into your heart, nothing compares. I spent so much of my life (even as a Christian) not walking in the power of the Holy Spirit, not leaning on Him for truth and understanding, not yielding to His promptings, and missing out on the Spirit-filled life. I can tell you, by experience, that way of life is such a waste! Jesus did not come just to give you eternal life, but to give you abundant life as you walk this earth waiting to meet Him face-to-face. I do not live with regret or condemnation, but oh, how I would go back and trade my flesh-filled days with Spirit-filled days a thousand times over. **The abundant Spirit-filled life far outweighs the temporal pleasures of the world and self.**

Read Joshua 18:7-10.

In verse 7, Joshua reminds the tribes that the Levites will not receive an allotment of land. The priesthood of the Lord was their inheritance. They lived in the Promised Land, but their blessing "would come from prayer, worship, serving, and helping others." [11]

Then, in verses 8-10, he commands the men to explore the land and come back with a written description. Robert Smith gives us important commentary here,

> Surveying the land was not necessary for God; God already knew what they would find in advance. Rather, it was necessary for the men so they could see the grace of God with their own eyes and the potential the land held for their dwelling and future development.... Spies and investigators were sent out, not to inform God, but to see what God had already promised. God had already promised they would inherit a land flowing with milk and honey. Their position was that of worshipers who would give praise to God prior to the possession of the land. They were to count those things that are not yet as though they already were! [12]

Joshua will then cast sacred lots in the Lord's presence, leaving the decision in the hands of Almighty God. He trusts that God will lead and guide him in the way he should go as he decrees the division of land for the remaining seven tribes.

Revisit Joshua 18:11-19:48.

6. What tribe receives the first lot? (18:11-28)

The *Life Application Study Bible* points out, "The tribe of Benjamin was given a narrow strip of land that served as a buffer zone between Judah and Ephraim, the two tribes that would later dominate the land." [13] This fulfilled the prophecy of Moses in Deuteronomy 33:12, "The beloved of the Lord shall dwell in safety by Him; and the Lord shall cover Him all the day long, and He shall dwell between His shoulders." Wiersbe notes that "Benjamin was going to have a special closeness to the Lord. When the northern tribes later turned away from God, the tribes that stood fast were Judah and Benjamin; so Moses' prophecy was fulfilled." [14]

The tribe of Simeon then receives the second lot (Joshua 19:1-9).

7. Who is Simeon's land taken from and why? (v. 9)

Francis Schaeffer notes, "Simeon did not receive a separate inheritance because, as you remember, Jacob said he was going to be scattered...the Simeonites had no real share of the land (Genesis 49:5-7)." [15]

8. What tribe receives the third lot? (vv. 10-16)

The next three lots go to the tribes of Issachar (vv. 17-23), Asher (vv. 24-31), and Naphtali (vv. 32-39).

9. What tribe receives the seventh (and final) lot and what location do they later add? (vv. 40-48)

God is always in the details. J. Vernon McGee states, "God not only gave them the land of Canaan, He also gave a particular area to a particular tribe. He gave each tribe a certain section of land. God was concerned about each individual and his possession." [16]

He is still the same. He cares about the details of your life. Every one of them. And He has a plan for you – a specific plan, a good plan.

10. Now, turn to the map in last week's lesson (on page 199) and use different colors to fill in the remaining tribal allotments.

Read Joshua 19:49-51.

11. What do we learn about the land given to Joshua?

Joshua chose Timnath-serah in the hill country of Ephraim. "Timhath-Serah means 'My abundant portion' and Mount Ephraim denotes 'Where I shall be doubly fruitful.'" [17]

This brings tears to my eyes as I recount all that has happened up to this point. The failures, the losses, the victories, the mountaintops, and the valleys of this journey. And Joshua stands strong in the face of it all. He knows Who his God is. He knows His power, and he trusts Him. Joshua has made some mistakes along the way, but he has passed through the Refiner's fire and come forth as pure gold. What encouragement this should be to our hearts!

Phillip Keller makes a powerful observation regarding Joshua, "Never, ever, could it be said of Joshua that he was one who lived the double life of duplicity at which the onlooker scoffed and remarked with skepticism, 'Just do what I say, but don't do as I do?'" [18]

Close today by reading Psalm 37:23-25. Reflect on how God orchestrated the details of the land for His people, including Joshua. Consider how He does the same for you.

Christ challenges us to enter new territory, to overcome the enemy, to clear the ground
of our lives from the undergrowth of the world. He stirs us to seek higher ground,
to enter into the rich, abundant life He offers, to find repose and contentment in Him. [19]

~ Phillip Keller

DAY THREE
Joshua 20

...We who have fled to Him for refuge can have great confidence as we hold to the hope that lies before us. This hope is a strong and trustworthy anchor for our souls.
Hebrews 6:18b-19a, NLT

We now come to two of the most captivating chapters in Scripture. Following the division of land among the tribes, God gives Joshua instructions on how the land is to be set up. God had already given this plan to Moses. [20] And now, it is time for Joshua to implement those directives as he establishes two new types of cities, cities that will reveal much about the character of God. We will examine the first of those cities in today's study.

Read Joshua 20:1-3.

1. What instruction does the Lord give to Joshua? (vv. 1-2)

David Guzik explains that these cities are meant "to protect one who killed another, but accidentally or unintentionally. They were to protect someone in the case of manslaughter as opposed to murder." [21] Schaeffer further explains, "If a man was prying out a big rock, and it accidentally fell on somebody coming along the path, this was not murder. It was without preparation and without motive." [22] This new judicial system is being created to ensure fairness and justice in situations not involving premeditated murder. Smith then clarifies, "Just as there was no sacrifice for intentional sin, there was no refuge for intentional homicide." [23]

Read Joshua 20:4-8.

2. List the specifics on how the cities of refuge are to operate. (Pay close attention to verse 6.)

3. Using the chart below, list the cities of refuge in each tribe (vv. 7-8).

Tribe	City of Refuge
Naphtali	
Ephraim	
Judah	
Reuben	
Gad	
Manasseh	

As we see throughout the pages of Scripture (and even just yesterday), God is a God of order and details.

4. Locate and circle the six cities of refuge on this map. Notice how these places are strategically located throughout the land so that a person seeking refuge will never be too far from one. From the pages of Exodus where the plan was first mentioned, God was already making a way for their protection.

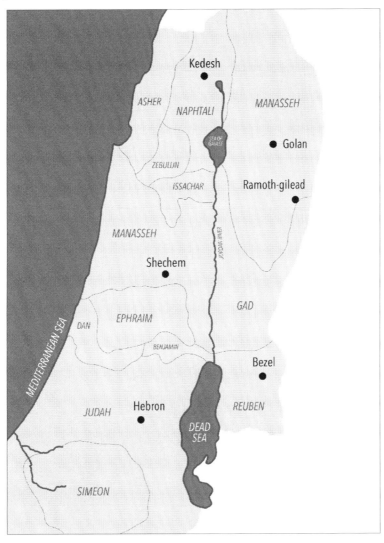

Schaeffer makes this poignant observation, further exposing the heart of our great God:

> God expressly commanded that roads were to be made to these cities (Deuteronomy 19:3). From nonbiblical sources we can add some further detail about the highways. They were carefully repaired every spring after the rains and bad weather of winter. Further, bridges were built where needed so that travelers did not have to run down into a ravine but could go straight across, taking the shortest possible route to the city. At every crossroad were special signs that said, "Refuge!" and pointed in the direction of the city. They had to be large enough so that a person running hard could easily read them. [24]

Not only is God protecting the Israelites, but we also see His unfailing love reaching beyond just this group of people.

Read Joshua 20:9.

5. For whom are these cities set apart?

God's preordained place of refuge is open to all – the Israelite, the foreigner, and the sojourner – "For God so loved the world" (John 3:16).

As I am writing, my heart is overwhelmed at the rich spiritual truth contained in Joshua 20. Not only is God setting up what will ultimately become the due process of law, but He is also pointing forward to the coming of His Son, our Refuge and Redeemer.

Merriam-Webster defines refuge as a "shelter or protection from danger or distress; a place that provides shelter or protection; something to which one has recourse in difficulty." [25]

In the establishment of these cities, we see a foreshadowing of Jesus Christ. The fugitive who is guilty of unintentional murder is required to stay in the city until the death of the high priest. Then, upon the death of the high priest, the fugitive is released and allowed to return home (Joshua 20:6). Jesus, our High Priest, died on the cross and took the punishment for our sins, and in doing so, freed us from the penalty of sin. "So if the Son sets you free, you will be free indeed" (John 8:36, NIV).

God was a Refuge in the days of Joshua. God is a Refuge in the here and now. **God will be a Refuge for all of eternity, for the one who calls on His name for salvation.**

Ponder these stunning comparisons between the cities of refuge and Jesus Christ.

- You can reach Jesus from any place. You are never too far to come running to Him, and He is never so far that He cannot be found. "You will seek Me and find Me when you search for Me with all your heart" (Jeremiah 29:13).

- Jesus is open, available, and ready to receive all. "Everyone who calls on the name of the Lord will be saved" (Romans 10:13, NLT).

- Jesus will never reject those who come to Him (John 6:37).

- If we seek His Kingdom first, He will meet all our needs (Matthew 6:33).

- There is no other way to the Father except through His Son, Jesus Christ...the way, the truth, and the life (John 14:6).

- If we do not believe in Him (our Refuge), we will perish and will spend eternity separated from Him (John 3:16).

What a beautiful and powerful picture of Jesus! We are all guilty of sin (Romans 3:10), intentional and unintentional. But God made a way. From the beginning of time in the Garden of Eden, He made a way for mankind to be redeemed and restored in the promise of the coming Messiah.

There is no "safe" life apart from Him. Nothing this world has to offer will save your soul. Only Jesus.

6. How have you experienced God as your Refuge, both for salvation and as you walk through your daily life?

Close out your time today by soaking in the lyrics from the song, "Refuge" by Shane & Shane. Make this a time of praise and commitment to the One who strengthens, protects, and saves.

Always near the brokenhearted
Always with me through the pain
When my fears are overwhelming
Jesus, You save me

In my sorrow I find comfort
In my weakness I find strength
Every time I reach out for You
Jesus, You save me

You are my refuge, You are my shelter
You are my hiding place forever
I will run to You, I will rest secure
In the presence of my Savior

You are with me every moment
You surround me day and night
Always constant, always faithful
Jesus, You save me

You are my refuge, You are my shelter
You are my hiding place forever
I will run to You, I will rest secure
In the presence of my Savior

I will trust, I will trust in Your promise
I am loved, I am loved, You are with me now
I will rise, I will rise in Your faithful hand
Jesus, You save me

You are my refuge, You are my shelter
You are my hiding place forever
I will run to You, I will rest secure
In the presence of my Savior [26]

DAY FOUR
Joshua 21

We are nearing the end of the journey as it relates to the settling of the Promised Land. Territories have been assigned to each tribe. Cities of refuge have been established. And now, it is time to create a second type of city: a place of spiritual community. Just as there needed to be cities of refuge to offer legal safety, there also need to be cities that will be centers of spiritual activity.

You will remember that as the land was divided, the Levites were not given a specific allotment because their purpose was to minister and serve the people. Being scattered throughout, "they could teach the people the law and influence each of the tribes to be faithful to the Lord." [27]

Read Joshua 21:1-3.

1. What do the leaders of the tribe of Levi remind Joshua and Eleazar about the places they are to be given to live? (v. 2)

2. How do the people of Israel respond? (v. 3)

Although they had not been given a specific region like the other tribes, the Levites need a place to live and raise their livestock, so Levitical cities are placed within the regions given to the other tribes. The *Life Application Study Bible* notes, "Almost no one lived more than a day's journey from a Levitical city." [28] Again, we see the hand of God in the details as He makes these ministers readily available to serve His children.

In Joshua 21:4-40, God calls for the formation of the Levitical cities: "The Kohathites received 13 cities from the tribes of Judah, Benjamin, and Simeon and 10 cities from Ephraim, Manasseh, and Dan. The Gershonites received 13 cities from Issachar, Asher, Naphtali, and Manasseh. The Merarites got 12 cities from Reuben, Gad, and Zebulun." [29]

Guzik says this should remind the reader "that these were real places, not the description of a symbolic or spiritual inheritance. When God promised a land to Abraham and his covenant descendants (Genesis 13:15, 17:8), God meant a real land." [30]

John Huffman elaborates on the importance of the Levitical cities located throughout Israel:

> In a way these cities can be seen as a substitute for the idolatrous high places, shrines, altars, and all of the pagan paraphernalia that was present in the land at the time of the conquest. The Levites were to replace the pagan worship with a saturation presence in the land, a constant reminder of the God who had brought His people out of the bondage of Egypt and the wanderings in the wilderness. These cities were also to be centers of teaching for those such as Rahab who had become part of the covenant people and did not have a historic background in the faith. [31]

Read Joshua 21:41-42.

3. How many towns within the Israelite territory are given to the Levites? (v. 41)

4. What do each of these towns have attached to them to meet a specific need for the Levites? (v. 42)

Jehovah-Jireh, the Lord will provide. We see Him providing for His people as He spreads these ministers of the priesthood immensely throughout the region. We see Him providing for the Levites as all these towns are surrounded by pasturelands, which will enable them to raise their livestock productively. He is a good, good Father.

As we conclude chapter 21, we get to see God's magnificent character on display!

Read Joshua 21:43-45.

5. List the ways you see the faithfulness of God on display in these last verses.

Doesn't your heart cry out, "Praise You, Lord!" He is a Promise Keeper!

6. Referring to your answer on question 5, how have you seen God do the same in your life?

The closing verses of Joshua 21 point to truth that should transform our lives. If we really believe what we say we believe, these verses should affect the way we live, talk, believe, act, react, and interact with the world around us.

Verse 44 says, "And the Lord gave them rest on every side...." Reading this caused me to stop, take a deep breath, and contemplate rest. In a hurried, frantic, non-stop world, we could all use a little extra rest, right? A quiet afternoon snuggled under a blanket (and even a short nap) sounds really nice to me. But this is not the type of rest being referenced here. Guzik explains, "This was the point where Israel stopped commemorating the Passover as if they were equipped to travel (as described in Exodus 12:11). Now they would eat the Passover reclining at rest (as described in John 13:23), because the Lord had given them rest in the land." [32] Don't you just love that?

This is soul rest. Deep-down-inside rest. The kind of rest that leaves your heart and mind settled and at peace. This is part of what comes with the abundant, Spirit-filled life. God has been faithful in His promises, His protection, and His provision. Now the Israelites can rest.

Did you know? The Hebrew verb *nuach* primarily conveys the idea of rest or repose. It is used to describe physical rest, as well as a more abstract sense of peace or tranquility. In ancient Israelite culture, the concept of rest was deeply embedded in religious and social practices. The Sabbath, a day of rest on the seventh day of the week, was a cornerstone of Jewish life, symbolizing not only physical rest but also spiritual renewal and trust in God's provision. The idea of rest extended to the land, with the practice of the Sabbath year, where the land was left to rest every seventh year. This cultural emphasis on rest reflects a broader theological theme of reliance on God and the anticipation of ultimate rest in His presence. [33]

7. Spiritually speaking, are you at rest right now? If yes, describe what that rest is like. If not, what stands in the way?

Has God been faithful to You? Have you experienced His protection, provision, and the truth of His promises? Then rest. Enter the land He has given you: the land of salvation, forgiveness, unfailing love, abundance, and the hope of glory.

As I ponder God being the Levite's inheritance, Lamentations 3:24-25 comes to mind:

> I say to myself, "The Lord is my inheritance; therefore, I will hope in Him!" The Lord is good to those who depend on Him, to those who search for Him (NLT).

8. How can this perspective contribute to experiencing God's rest?

The covenant of God, the power of God, the promises of God – these are the
spiritual resources we can depend on as we claim our inheritance in Jesus Christ. [34]
~ Warren Wiersbe

DAY FIVE
Joshua 18-21 | They...possessed it and settled in it

My heart is overflowing! As I type these words and listen to the rhythm of raindrops on my front porch, my prayer today is that the Holy Spirit will shower you with spiritual treasures from this week's study. We have seen God's character shine brightly as He guides Joshua in the division of land, sets up cities of refuge to protect His people, establishes cities of spiritual activity, fulfills promises, and grants rest. These events should challenge and encourage us to walk *into the promise*, choosing to take hold of and live the abundant, Spirit-filled life we have in Jesus Christ! This week's spiritual warfare principle is:

> **Once you take the land, God wants you to occupy it with abundance.**

In the Old Testament account in Joshua, the people are literally taking the land, taking possession of a physical piece of earth, and going about it with strategy and grand design. God sets forth specific plans, giving direct commands and well-laid instructions. We see tribes listed one by one, cities and towns named with specificity. There is a rhyme and reason to this settlement taking place. And God does it all just as He said He would (Joshua 21:43).

Now, let's apply what we have learned to our own spiritual journey. Think back to when you were saved, the moment you repented of your sins, believed in Jesus, and received His gift of salvation. This is the moment you "took the land" He had given you. You chose to enter into a relationship with Him – a land of salvation, freedom, and victory.

Thinking back through the week's study, use these questions for personal reflection:

- Have you claimed the land, taking all that He has given you by way of salvation?

- Are you following the Holy Spirit's direction as you make decisions?

- Are you seeking and finding refuge in God alone?

- Are you enjoying spiritual rest?

Can I share my story with you?

I was saved as a six-year-old girl. At that time in my life, I did not have a long history of sin and shame from which I was turning. Of course I had sinned (we all have – Romans 3:23), but I did not experience the radical change that many do as they turn away from a life of darkness and depravity into a life of light and freedom. That time came to me many years later.

I grew up in church and was raised in a Christian home, for which I am eternally grateful. I knew the truths of the Bible and believed what it said. As I approached my teenage years, I began to wander away from God and chose to live life my way. Did I lose my salvation? Absolutely not. But I did not fully occupy the ground given to me by God in the way He intended. Satan did not snatch me away from the Father's hand – that is impossible – but, I chose to walk in the flesh rather than the Spirit, giving Satan a foothold in my life. In the words of Jim Logan, I needed to "reclaim surrendered ground." [35]

This is so dear to my heart because understanding and choosing the abundant, Spirit-filled life brought radical change to my life. As much as I knew about the Bible, I really had not learned the truth of what it meant to have life abundant. Nor did I know that the Holy Spirit literally resided in my body and through Him, I was able to do anything and everything the Lord called me to do.

Joshua 18 opens by saying, "Now that the land was under Israelite control...." So, I ask you a simple question: Did they have control? Yes! They did not need to take control of the land. They already had control. Joshua offered some bold chastisement as he asked them, "How long are you going to wait before taking possession?"

In my early 20's, I heard the voice of the Lord ask me a similar question. As I began to study His Word in depth and with intentionality, He began whispering to my heart, "Child of mine, are you going to get serious about following Me? Are you willing to set aside time daily to read My Word and talk to me? Will I reign unchallenged on the throne of your heart? Will you deny yourself and follow Me no matter the cost?"

Did I already have the "land" of salvation? Yes, I did. Was I taking possession of it, and occupying it in abundance? No, I was not. And as a result, I did not have refuge or safety, and I surely did not experience rest. Quite the contrary, as I was opening myself up to danger, to the wiles and evil schemes of the enemy, and I was tossing and turning like a ship on a stormy sea. My heart did not know safety or rest. I was living dangerously, and I was tired.

God's love gift of eternal life cannot be adequately described. In the words of the hymn, "The Love of God":

> *Could we with ink the ocean fill,*
> *And were the skies of parchment made;*
> *Were every stalk on earth a quill,*
> *And every man a scribe by trade;*
> *To write the love of God above*
> *Would drain the ocean dry;*
> *Nor could the scroll contain the whole,*
> *Though stretched from sky to sky.* [36]

But as I learned more than 20 years ago, there is even more.

1. Write out John 10:10b in the space below.

I can have life...and I can have it to the full! Abundant life! I can enter the land by way of salvation, and I can occupy it and live fully as I choose to walk in the abundance He came to give me.

This word "abundant" in the Greek is *perisson,* meaning "exceedingly, very highly, beyond measure, more, superfluous, a quantity so abundant as to be considerably more than what one would expect or anticipate." [37]

2. Jot down your thoughts as you read these verses about the abundant life.

- Luke 6:38 -

- Romans 15:13 -

- 1 Corinthians 2:9 -

- 2 Corinthians 9:8 -

- Ephesians 3:20 -

- Philippians 4:19 -

Look back at John 10:10 and you will see the contrast between the life Jesus desires for you and the life the devil wants for you.

3. Why has the thief (the devil) come?

To steal. To kill. To destroy. This is his plan for your life. Being a child of God does not exempt you from his tactics and schemes. It actually puts a target on your back. The devil knows he cannot take you to hell if you belong to Jesus, but he is determined to take you out of commission. Some of his favorite schemes are doubt, discouragement, fear, anxiety, deception, insecurity, and the list goes on.

We have been given everything we need for life and godliness (2 Peter 1:3), so any thought contrary to that truth is a lie. What do we do with lies? We demolish them by taking every thought captive to make it obedient to Christ (2 Corinthians 10:5). Logan suggests, "When the enemy sends an intruding thought, say 'I give no consent to that,' and move on." [38]

When the devil comes against you, remind him who you are and Whose you are. Feel free to remind him of his future as well. He is a liar and a loser, and he cannot stand the Jesus in you. Logan makes a powerful observation, "I can't even imagine how much power it took to raise Jesus from the dead, can you? That's the power we are to stand in day by day." [39] It far exceeds any power of the enemy, and it is incumbent on you, child of God, to do battle to reclaim any surrendered ground you have allowed the devil to take back.

4. How are you battling against the attacks of the enemy as he seeks to steal, kill, and destroy you?

Take a moment to reflect on this week's study, the definition of the Greek word for "abundance," (mentioned earlier), and the Scriptures you read in question two.

5. Are you living an abundant life? If so, what are the joys and blessings you are experiencing? If not, how can you begin today?

In the light of the Cross, is it not true that the enemy has no right to dwell in the land?
Is it not true that Satan's claim to your life was taken from him at Calvary?
Is it not true that sin has no right to a foothold in the life of the child of God?
Is it not true that Satan has no power in the presence of Omnipotence?
Is it not true that by virtue of His blood and His resurrection,
Jesus Christ is pledged to destroy the enemy utterly?
Is it not true that in the indwelling power of the Holy Spirit there is strength
for every temptation, grace for every trial, power to overcome every difficulty? [40]
~ Alan Redpath

Take the land. Occupy it with abundance. Live *Into the Promise*. Jesus left the glory of Heaven so that you could. Do not delay.

LESSON NINE
Hold fast to Him

JOSHUA 22

Tribes beyond Jordan Return

[1] Then Joshua summoned the Reubenites and the Gadites and the half-tribe of Manasseh, [2] and said to them, "You have kept all that Moses the servant of the Lord commanded you, and have listened to my voice in all that I commanded you. [3] You have not forsaken your brothers these many days to this day, but have kept the charge of the commandment of the Lord your God. [4] And now the Lord your God has given rest to your brothers, as He spoke to them; therefore turn now and go to your tents, to the land of your possession, which Moses the servant of the Lord gave you beyond the Jordan. [5] Only be very careful to observe the commandment and the law which Moses the servant of the Lord commanded you, to love the Lord your God and walk in all His ways and keep His commandments and **hold fast to Him** and serve Him with all your heart and with all your soul." [6] So Joshua blessed them and sent them away, and they went to their tents.

[7] Now to the one half-tribe of Manasseh Moses had given a possession in Bashan, but to the other half Joshua gave a possession among their brothers westward beyond the Jordan. So when Joshua sent them away to their tents, he blessed them, [8] and said to them, "Return to your tents with great riches and with very much livestock, with silver, gold, bronze, iron, and with very many clothes; divide the spoil of your enemies with your brothers." [9] The sons of Reuben and the sons of Gad and the half-tribe of Manasseh returned home and departed from the sons of Israel at Shiloh which is in the land of Canaan, to go to the land of Gilead, to the land of their possession which they had possessed, according to the command of the Lord through Moses.

The Offensive Altar

[10] When they came to the region of the Jordan which is in the land of Canaan, the sons of Reuben and the sons of Gad and the half-tribe of Manasseh built an altar there by the Jordan, a large altar in appearance. [11] And the sons of Israel heard it said, "Behold, the sons of Reuben and the sons of Gad and the half-tribe of Manasseh have built an altar at the frontier of the land of Canaan, in the region of the Jordan, on the side belonging to the sons of Israel." [12] When the sons of Israel heard of it, the whole congregation of the sons of Israel gathered themselves at Shiloh to go up against them in war.

[13] Then the sons of Israel sent to the sons of Reuben and to the sons of Gad and to the half-tribe of Manasseh, into the land of Gilead, Phinehas the son of Eleazar the priest, [14] and with him ten chiefs, one chief for each father's household from each of the

tribes of Israel; and each one of them was the head of his father's household among the thousands of Israel. ¹⁵ They came to the sons of Reuben and to the sons of Gad and to the half-tribe of Manasseh, to the land of Gilead, and they spoke with them saying, ¹⁶ "Thus says the whole congregation of the Lord, 'What is this unfaithful act which you have committed against the God of Israel, turning away from following the Lord this day, by building yourselves an altar, to rebel against the Lord this day? ¹⁷ Is not the iniquity of Peor enough for us, from which we have not cleansed ourselves to this day, although a plague came on the congregation of the Lord, ¹⁸ that you must turn away this day from following the Lord? If you rebel against the Lord today, He will be angry with the whole congregation of Israel tomorrow. ¹⁹ If, however, the land of your possession is unclean, then cross into the land of the possession of the Lord, where the Lord's tabernacle stands, and take possession among us. Only do not rebel against the Lord, or rebel against us by building an altar for yourselves, besides the altar of the Lord our God. ²⁰ Did not Achan the son of Zerah act unfaithfully in the things under the ban, and wrath fall on all the congregation of Israel? And that man did not perish alone in his iniquity.'"

²¹ Then the sons of Reuben and the sons of Gad and the half-tribe of Manasseh answered and spoke to the heads of the families of Israel. ²² "The Mighty One, God, the Lord, the Mighty One, God, the Lord! He knows, and may Israel itself know. If it was in rebellion, or if in an unfaithful act against the Lord do not save us this day! ²³ If we have built us an altar to turn away from following the Lord, or if to offer a burnt offering or grain offering on it, or if to offer sacrifices of peace offerings on it, may the Lord Himself require it. ²⁴ But truly we have done this out of concern, for a reason, saying, 'In time to come your sons may say to our sons, "What have you to do with the Lord, the God of Israel? ²⁵ For the Lord has made the Jordan a border between us and you, you sons of Reuben and sons of Gad; you have no portion in the Lord." So your sons may make our sons stop fearing the Lord.'

²⁶ "Therefore we said, 'Let us build an altar, not for burnt offering or for sacrifice; ²⁷ rather it shall be a witness between us and you and between our generations after us, that we are to perform the service of the Lord before Him with our burnt offerings, and with our sacrifices and with our peace offerings, so that your sons will not say to our sons in time to come, "You have no portion in the Lord."' ²⁸ Therefore we said, 'It shall also come about if they say this to us or to our generations in time to come, then we shall say, "See the copy of the altar of the Lord which our fathers made, not for burnt offering or for sacrifice; rather it is a witness between us and you."' ²⁹ Far be it from us that we should rebel against the Lord and turn away from following the Lord this day, by building an altar for burnt offering, for grain

offering or for sacrifice, besides the altar of the Lord our God which is before His tabernacle."

30 So when Phinehas the priest and the leaders of the congregation, even the heads of the families of Israel who were with him, heard the words which the sons of Reuben and the sons of Gad and the sons of Manasseh spoke, it pleased them. 31 And Phinehas the son of Eleazar the priest said to the sons of Reuben and to the sons of Gad and to the sons of Manasseh, "Today we know that the Lord is in our midst, because you have not committed this unfaithful act against the Lord; now you have delivered the sons of Israel from the hand of the Lord."

32 Then Phinehas the son of Eleazar the priest and the leaders returned from the sons of Reuben and from the sons of Gad, from the land of Gilead to the land of Canaan, to the sons of Israel, and brought back word to them. 33 The word pleased the sons of Israel, and the sons of Israel blessed God; and they did not speak of going up against them in war to destroy the land in which the sons of Reuben and the sons of Gad were living. 34 The sons of Reuben and the sons of Gad called the altar Witness; "For," they said, "it is a witness between us that the Lord is God."

Hold fast to Him

Obedience means marching right on whether we feel like it or not.
Many times we go against our feelings. Faith is one thing; feeling is another. [1]
~ D.L. Moody

Joshua 22 is a story about transitions. Even in the best of circumstances, transitions can be difficult. While change is a natural part of life, it is often accompanied by a mixture of excitement and uncertainty. Whether we're stepping into a new role at work, relocating to a new city, entering a new season of life, or navigating the emotional shifts that come with major life events, transitions force us to leave behind the familiar and embrace the unknown.

And can we just be honest with each other? Adjusting to change – new expectations, roles, routines, and relationships – is hard work. And it almost always takes us longer than we expect to recalibrate amid transition. When life change occurs, it can feel like a time of instability, a moment when we must hold fast to what we know is true, even as everything around us shifts.

This is exactly where we find the Israelites in Joshua 22. We have come to a pivotal point in Israel's history. After spending years battling to take possession of the Promised Land, they are finally ready to settle down and plant roots.

The tribes of Reuben, Gad, and the half-tribe of Manasseh, who had received their inheritance on the eastern side of the Jordan River, are about to transition from their military mission in the Promised Land to settling into their inheritance on the other side of the Jordan River. They have faithfully fought with the army of Israel for what many commentators believe was at least seven years. God has given the Israelites victory, and the land has been conquered. Now, it is time for the two-and-a-half tribes to go back home.

LESSON NINE | 255

I cannot imagine the bittersweet parting of these men who had fought side-by-side for all this time. Francis Schaeffer states it like this:

> If we use a little imagination, we can feel the tremendous emotion involved in the parting of these comrades at arms. We can picture the men going through the camp, finding the friends with whom they had fought side by side, and saying good-bye to some who had even saved their lives. They shook hands and they parted, as worshipers of God, as friends, and as companions in war. [2]

I have felt this way at the end of a mission trip. After praying and preparing for a trip with a group of people, and then spending a couple of weeks in a foreign country, the parting is bittersweet. Over the course of just a few days, you experience spiritual struggles and victories that are difficult to explain to someone who wasn't there. Deep and lasting bonds are formed. The connection that takes place goes beyond mere friendship. This kind of relationship is what binds the hearts of women who join together and pray for their families, or who go to war on behalf of a prodigal.

This is the kind of bond that has formed among the sons of Israel as they have fought together, shoulder to shoulder, for all these years. Although the men from Reuben, Gad, and the half-tribe of Manasseh are anxious to return to their families, they have to feel a sense of loss in leaving their fellow warriors.

As we journey through Joshua 22, we'll see how the Israelites navigate their transition, and how their story speaks to us today.

DAY ONE
Joshua 22:1-5

As has been our practice throughout this study, let's begin by reading the entire chapter of Joshua 22 to get an initial take on what transpires, and then answer the following questions.

Snapshot
of Joshua 22

What are the main events that take place in Joshua 22?

Circle the key words in Joshua 22 and then list them here.

As we get started, let's do a little recap on the background of the tribes of Reuben, Gad, and half-tribe of Manasseh. These Transjordan tribes had made a promise to Moses to remain in the Israelite army until the land was conquered, and they kept their word (Numbers 32, Deuteronomy 3:12-20). After Moses died, they made the same pledge to Joshua as he assumed leadership of Israel (Joshua 1:12-18). Loyalty ran deep in these tribes. They had been loyal to Moses, remained loyal to Joshua, and fought loyally beside their Israelite brothers from the other nine-and-a-half tribes. Warren Wiersbe addresses a question you may be wondering:

> Why had they been so loyal to their leaders and fellow soldiers? Because they were first of all loyal to the Lord their God. It was His mission they were carrying out and His name they were seeking to glorify. In the service of the Lord, far above our devotion to a leader, a cause, or even a nation is our devotion to the Lord. "And whatever you do, do it heartily, as to the Lord and not to men, knowing that from the Lord you will receive the reward of the inheritance; for you serve the Lord Christ" (Colossians 3:23-24, NKJV). [3]

And while we are on the subject of loyalty, have you noticed that there has been greater loyalty and unity among the troops as they were battling for the land than there had been during their 40 years of wandering in the wilderness? H.D.M. Spence makes this observation:

> As long as the Israelitish Church was subduing kingdoms, winning splendid victories, experiencing the encouragement derivable from God's sensible presence and intervention, there was no discontent, discouragement, or wavering. But the trials of the long wandering, as well as those incident to the quiet, unostentatious discharge of duty, were fatal to their faith and patience. [4]

Could it be that we can also begin murmuring and complaining when we are not on mission? The Bible reveals that prosperity is a greater curse than adversity. It is in prosperity that we begin to focus on self and to value comfort above conformity to Christ. But let a crisis strike, and we are digging into God's Word, requesting prayer, fasting, and praying ourselves. It seems that when we are desperate, we are most dependent on and most satisfied in Christ.

Now, let's dig into Joshua 22. It is full of truth that is as relevant today as it was then.

Read Joshua 22:1-4.

Did you know? In Joshua 4:13, we saw that 40,000 men from the tribes of Reuben, Gad, and the half-tribe of Manasseh crossed over the Jordan to help take the Promised Land. These warriors led the charge for all the battles in Canaan. Generations later, during the reign of Saul, the two-and-a-half tribes are tied together again, as they produce an army of 44,760 and defeat the Hagrites "because they trusted in" God (1 Chronicles 5:18-21).

The war years are over, and it is time for all of the fighting men to return to their tents and rejoin their families. Joshua now calls for the troops from the Transjordan tribes to gather so that he can address them before they disperse. As Joshua speaks to the Reubenites, the Gadites, and the half-tribe of Manasseh, he recalls their faithfulness using words that repeat the instructions he gave to them in 1:12-15.

1. List the four commendations Joshua gives to the two-and-a-half tribes in his farewell address. (vv. 2-3)

   •

   •

   •

   •

2. What does Joshua say the Lord has given the tribes in Canaan? (v. 4)

Let's take a moment and think about the concept of rest.

Read Hebrews 4:1-16. The writer of Hebrews is comparing the Israelites who failed to enter the Promised Land due to disobedience with the believers who will miss out on the Promised Life if they do not wholeheartedly obey the Lord.

3. What word does the writer of Hebrews use to describe the entrance into the Promised Land? (vv. 1, 3, 5-6)

4. Read Matthew 11:28-32. How do we experience the rest of the Lord?

Wiersbe explores the application of rest in the life of a believer:

> The spiritual application of this rest for God's people today is made in Hebrews 3 and 4. When we trust Christ as Savior, we enter into rest because we're no longer at war with God (Romans 5:1). When we yield ourselves completely to Him and claim our inheritance by faith, we enter into a deeper rest and enjoy our spiritual riches in Christ. [5]

Can you even imagine the homecoming reception these men will receive after they return home from battle after so many years away? Think of the celebration, the peace, love, and joy that awaits them. Wiersbe goes on to say, "That's just a small picture of what happens when the children of God enter into the rest God gives to those who will yield their all to Him and trust His Word." [6]

Read Joshua 22:5.

After Joshua thanks these tribes for a job well done, he calls on them to continue to obey the Lord.

5. Fill in the left side of the following table with the five actions Joshua instructs the Transjordan tribes to carry out in Joshua 22:5b. (Look for five verbs in 22:5b.)

6. Then, read Deuteronomy 13:4. Complete the second column with the six verbs Moses uses and then notice the similarities in what they say.

Joshua's Action Verbs in Joshua 22:5	Moses's Action Verbs in Deuteronomy 13:4

It is evident by Joshua's leadership and commands that he was mentored well by Moses. Joshua is a faithful leader who challenges those in his charge to honor the Lord. He does not lower the bar, he lifts it high.

How can we raise the bar for ourselves in our walk with Christ?

7. Review the list of verbs in the command in Joshua 22:5. How well are you doing in these five areas?

- Love the Lord –

- Walk in all His ways –

- Keep His commandments –

- Hold fast to Him –

- Serve Him with all your heart and soul –

I love the picture of what it looks like to "hold fast to Him." In Hebrew, the word for "hold fast" is *dabaq*. It means to cling, cleave, adhere, stick, join. [7] *Dabaq* is translated "hold fast" in Joshua 22:5 and "cling to" in Deuteronomy 13:4. The message is the same. We are to follow Christ so closely that we are clinging to Him, sticking to Him like we are literally glued to Him.

Recently, the group of ladies in my Thursday morning discipleship were studying Ruth. We were so moved by Ruth's example in the Old Testament! One of the women pointed out that the text said, "But Ruth clung tightly to Naomi" (Ruth 1:14b, NLT). That began a conversation about other verses that mention clinging.

As we were talking, I had to share about one of my favorite women, Mary Magdalene. Mary would not leave the garden with the empty tomb until she found Jesus. When Jesus revealed Himself to her, Mary must have thrown herself on Him, because the Bible records Him saying,

> "Don't cling to me," Jesus said, "for I haven't yet ascended to the Father. But go find my brothers and tell them, 'I am ascending to my Father and your Father, to my God and your God'" (John 20:17, NLT).

Because Mary would not leave the garden until she found the Lord, He granted her the gift of being the first to see Him in His resurrected form, and sent her as a witness to the disciples. This was outside their cultural norm. Women were not allowed to be witnesses. Christ entrusted her with the news of His resurrection!

I then shared Deuteronomy 13:4, one of my favorite verses. According to the verbs we listed earlier, we are to: follow, fear, obey, listen, serve, and cling. That morning, after talking about the necessity to cling to the Lord so that nothing else captures our heart or attention, our group decided to name our text thread: The Clingers. Just a sweet reminder that "apart from [Him], [we] can do nothing" (John 15:5b).

Are you clinging to Jesus? **Just as a branch draws life from the vine, as we hold fast to Him, we find life, abundant life, that transforms us, shaping our hearts and minds to reflect Him.** Peter tells us that "His divine power has granted to us everything pertaining to life and godliness, through the true knowledge of Him who called us by His own glory and excellence" (2 Peter 1:3).

Spend the next few minutes thanking the Lord for all He has granted us in Christ.

DAY TWO
Joshua 22:6-20

After Joshua instructs the tribes of the Reubenites, the Gadites, and the half-tribe of Manasseh, he then blesses them before sending them back to their homes.

Read Joshua 22:6-9.

1. With what does Joshua bless the two-and-a-half tribes? (v. 8)

In this celebratory moment, Joshua shares with them the spoils of the battle to take back with them. Wiersbe explains:

> It was the custom in Israel that those who stayed home, or who couldn't participate in the battle for some good reason, also shared the spoils (Numbers 31:25-27; 1 Samuel 30:23-25). After all, these people had protected the home cities and kept the machinery of the community going while the men had been out fighting, and it was only fair that they share in the spoils. [8]

Joshua is expressing both the importance of community, and the willingness of those who have received great blessings to share their gains with others who have been part of the endeavor, but whose contributions are less noticed. For the two-and-a-half tribes, this moment is a high point in their transition back home. But transitions can also have low points, and these tribes are about to encounter one of those.

As the Reubenites, the Gadites, and the half-tribe of Manasseh leave Shiloh and march east down the Judean hills, into the Jordan Valley and back up into the hills of Gilead, they pass landmarks that remind them of all that God has done for them over the past several years. Wiersbe expounds on what they must have felt as they reminisced:

> Happy as they were to be going home, it wasn't easy to say good-bye to their brothers and leave behind the nearness of the priesthood and the tabernacle. They were leaving the land that God had promised to bless. Yes, they were going home to the land that they had chosen for themselves, but somehow they began to feel isolated from the nation of Israel. [9]

Unity is a oneness that occurs when people are drawn together by a common task. But when the mission is accomplished and the people disperse, those relationships can begin to unravel. And that is what happens here.

If you go back and read through Numbers 32, you will discover that there is no record of Moses consulting the Lord about granting these tribes land on the eastern side of the Jordan. It seems like more of a negotiation to get the tribes to help in the conquest of the Promised Land. Once again, Wiersbe has astute commentary:

> There's no question that Canaan was God's appointed land for His people; anything short of Canaan wasn't what He wanted for them. The two-and-a-half tribes made their decision, not on the basis of spiritual values, but on the basis of material gain, for the land east of the Jordan was ideal for raising cattle....By making this decision, the people of Reuben, Gad, and Manasseh divided the nation and separated themselves from the blessings of the land of Canaan. They were farther away from the tabernacle and closer to the enemy. They became what I call "borderline believers." You'll recall that Egypt represents the world and Canaan the believer's inheritance in Christ....The two-and-a-half tribes portray believers who have experienced the blessings and battles of Canaan – their inheritance in Christ – but prefer to live on the border, outside God's appointed place of blessing. [10]

The two-and-a-half tribes have a created a problem that they now attempt to solve themselves. But it is a crisis in the making.

Read Joshua 22:10-12.

2. What do the two-and-a-half tribes decide to build on the way home and where do they build it? (v. 10)

3. When the rest of Israel hears what they have done, what do they do? (vv. 11-12)

4. Read Deuteronomy 13:12-16. What were the Israelites to do if any of the tribes worshiped other gods or worshiped God in a way not prescribed by Him?

Read Joshua 22:13-16.

Rather than immediately go to war with the Transjordan tribes, the other tribes form a delegation to send and inquire as to why they would erect an altar without priestly supervision.

5. Who leads the delegation and what is his position among the Israelites? (v. 13)

6. Who does he take with him? (v. 14)

7. What has "the whole congregation of the Lord" concluded about the altar? (v. 16)

Let's pause for a moment here and consider our responsibilities as New Testament believers when a fellow believer or church member is living in sin. Read Matthew 18:15-17:

> If your brother sins, go and show him his fault in private; if he listens to you, you have won your brother. But if he does not listen to you, take one or two more with you, so that by the mouth of two or three witnesses every fact may be confirmed. If he refuses to listen to them, tell it to the church; and if he refuses to listen even to the church, let him be to you as a Gentile and a tax collector.

8. What are the steps to be taken according to Matthew 18?

9. Read Galatians 6:1-3. How are we to respond to a fellow believer who is living in sin?

Why are we commanded to take sin so seriously? We know from the beginning (Genesis 3) that sin separates. It separates us from God and from others. Sin also gives the devil an opportunity or more accurately a "foothold":

> So stop telling lies. Let us tell our neighbors the truth, for we are all parts of the same body. And "don't sin by letting anger control you." Don't let the sun go down while you are still angry, for anger gives a foothold to the devil (Ephesians 4:25-27, NLT).

God desires for us to be united with Him — one heart and mind in Christ Jesus (Acts 4:32). It is what Jesus prayed for us in John 17.

Read Joshua 22:17-20.

As the ruling body of Israel confronts the Transjordan tribes, they remind them of past events which resulted in disastrous consequences.

10. What events does Phinehas refer to in comparison? (vv. 17-20)

11. Read Numbers 25:1-13 and describe what happened at Peor.

12. How did this corporate sin affect all the Israelites?

13. What was the sin of Achan? (Joshua 7)

Spence notes:

> The case of Achan is even more in point than that of Peor. In his case the Israelites had a clear proof that "one man's sin," unless completely and absolutely put away, brought God's displeasure on "all the congregation" (Numbers 16:22). The repulse at Ai, fresh as it must have been in the memory of all, was sufficient evidence of this. [12]

How it must grieve the heart of God that His Bride, the church, in so many ways does not take sin seriously! What we miss of the blessings of the Lord and the outpouring of His Spirit because of "sin in the camp"!

Schaeffer makes this statement:

> These men, who were sick of war, "The holiness of God demands no compromise." I would to God that the church of this century would learn this lesson. The holiness of the God who exists demands that there be no compromise in the area of truth. Tears? I am sure there were tears, but there had to be a battle if there was rebellion against God. [13]

These men are now ready to fight those they once fought side by side with, their own people, to defend the holiness of God. After all they have been through in the wilderness, and then in battle to gain Canaan, they cannot allow this to slide.

Spend some time in prayer today asking the Lord if there is any rebellion in your own heart. Ask the Holy Spirit to reveal any unconfessed and unrepented sin. We will never be perfect, but we can walk blamelessly with the Lord. That means we are living with all revealed sin confessed and repented of, that we might walk in a manner worthy of Him!

Did you know? In the New Testament, the Sanhedrin was the highest ruling court among the Hebrews. Led by the high priest, the Sanhedrin was given limited authority to make decisions in certain civil, religious, and criminal matters by the foreign nations that ruled over Israel at different times in its history. [11]

DAY THREE
Joshua 22:21-30

Hard conversations are never easy to have. Think about how you responded to the last person who had a complaint or offered unsolicited "constructive criticism." Typically, those kinds of words are only perceived as constructive by the one delivering it. Did you respond with grace? Did you internally listen for the voice of the Holy Spirit to reveal if there might be some truth in what was said?

In their book, *Rare Leadership*, Marcus Warner and Jim Wilder point out that "we must always keep the relationship more important than the problem. If we do that, our focus will be on maintaining the relationship while seeking a solution, without having to prove a point." [14]

Yesterday, we saw that when the tribes on the west side of the Jordan confronted the two-and-a-half tribes on the east side, they sent a delegation with questions before assuming their intent and immediately attacking them.

We see in Scripture that the Lord deals with His people in the same way:

> When God showed up in the Garden after Adam and Eve's sin, He expressed curiosity: "Where are you?...Who told you that you were naked?" (Genesis 3:9, 11). Asking questions may have been one way the Lord was seeking to maintain a relationship even as His creatures had been discovered in their sin." [15]

We too need to ask questions, and not jump to conclusions. We should always be working toward peace and restoration. Warner and Wilder write:

> Rare leaders excel at this. They are really good at seeing Jesus in others and waking up that part of the person's heart. Most of us simply see the dysfunction and shortcomings of others. We fail to see who they really are, to see them as God sees them. Until we do, we cannot help them act like themselves. [16]

What does it mean to "act like themselves"? As followers of Christ, we are to act like Him. We are to be imitators of Christ. When we fall short, we don't need condemnation. We need someone to remind us to Whom we belong.

1. Read 2 Timothy 2:22. What are we to pursue?

2. Read Philippians 4:6-8. What brings God's peace?

3. How will obeying Philippians 4:8 impact our thoughts and our peace?

Now, back to the story in Joshua 22.

Read Joshua 22:21-25.

Now it is time for the tribes of Reuben, Gad, and the half-tribe of Manasseh to present their side of the story. After they list a number of wrong reasons for building the altar that would have deserved punishment in verses, they then give the real reason they built the altar.

4. What is the real long-term reason they built the altar? (vv. 24-25)

Read Joshua 22:26-30.

In verses 26-29, the Transjordan tribes explain that their only intention is to prove their connection with the rest of the Israelites. Basically, they do not want future generations to forget "who they are."

5. How do the leaders respond to their explanation? (v. 30)

Here's the thing. The tribes of Reuben, Gad and Manasseh did not need an altar to remind them of their commitment to the Lord and their connection to the people of Canaan. They did not need an altar to remind them who they were. They just needed to obey the charge Joshua had given them in 22:5. Wiersbe comments:

> If the people of Reuben, Gad and Manasseh faithfully attended the feasts in Jerusalem (Exodus 23:17), honored the Lord by obeying His Word, and talked about His Word in their homes (Deuteronomy 6:6-9), they would be able to raise their children to know and serve the Lord. The altar on the Jordan bank, however, was no guarantee of such success. [17]

So, let's bring this forward to us. How do we as followers of Christ not forget who we are?

Jesus is our Rabbi. We are His apprentices. An apprentice would leave their family, village, and trade to train under their rabbi. They were with them all day, every day. The goal of an apprentice is:

1. To be with your rabbi
2. To become like your rabbi
3. To do as your rabbi did [18]

This is the life to which God has called us as apprentices or followers of Christ. Commit to pray this week and ask the Lord to help you focus on His Presence, become like Jesus, and do as He did.

In the words of John Mark Comer:

> Apprenticeship to Jesus – that is, following Jesus – is a whole life process of being with Jesus for the purpose of becoming like Him and carrying on His work in the world. It's a lifelong journey in which we gradually learn to say and do the kinds of things Jesus said and did as we apprentice under Him in every facet of our lives. [19]

Remember who you are!

DAY FOUR
Joshua 22:31-34

A war has been averted because leaders took time to inquire and listen.

Read Joshua 22:31.

Think back on the incident at Peor that we read about in Day 2.

1. What had Phinehas done when the people rebelled at Peor? (Numbers 25:6-9)

But this time, things are different.

2. Who does Phinehas say is among them? (v. 31)

3. What does Phinehas conclude? (v. 31)

Read Joshua 22:32-33.

4. Where do Phinehas and the rest of the delegation return? (v. 32)

Phinehas has proven his loyalty to the Lord by being willing to defend God's Word and demand obedience from His people. It is obvious that the rest of the men of Israel trust his judgment and are satisfied with the answer from the two-and-a-half tribes.

God works through those He puts in leadership. But those He allows to lead must stay humble and dependent upon Him. We have more than enough examples today of those who take their eyes off Jesus and begin to "believe their own press." They begin to think more highly of themselves than they should. I have heard several people say through the years that when pride walks in, God walks out.

We also know that pride goes before a fall (Proverbs 16:18). And the book of James tells us that God opposes ("stiff arms") the proud, but gives grace to the humble (James 4:6). I do not want to be held at arm's length by God because of pride. I want to be held close as I "cling" to Him!

5. Read James 4:4-10. Note how these verses speak to you.

6. Look back at James 4:7. What does it mean to "submit to God"?

To submit is to yield our will to another. I am to desire to will what God wills.

7. Read Proverbs 3:5-6. Write your own paraphrase of these verses.

We must be so dependent upon the Lord that we do not take one step apart from Him. Many of you have probably memorized these verses. If you have not, I would suggest that you write them on a card and commit them to memory.

If I am trusting the Lord with all my heart and not leaning on my own understanding, I am going to be open and able to discern His will.

8. Read Romans 12:1-2. What is a living sacrifice?

9. What do these verses say about God's will?

The enemy is a liar, and he wants us to believe that God is not good. That has been one of his tactics since the beginning. If God is not good, then His will is not good.

All that God created is good. He is good and only does good.

10. Read Psalm 119:68. What does it say about God?

We know that God is good because of Christ. "While we were yet sinners Christ died for us" (Romans 5:8). We don't deserve God's love or forgiveness, but He has freely given it to us in Christ. He alone is good. It is only as I follow Him and cling to Him that I become like Him.

Now, let's see how this story in Joshua ends up.

Read Joshua 22:34.

11. What do the two-and-a-half tribes name the altar? (v. 34)

Did you know? The naming of places and monuments is common in Scripture. For example, Hagar's theophany in Genesis 16:7-14 results in a nearby well being named, Beer-lahai-roi; the well of the God Who sees me. And in Judges 6:24, Gideon names an altar, "The Lord is peace."

Sadly, though, was this pile of stones really a witness? In choosing to live on the east side of the Jordan, they have isolated themselves from community and separated themselves from the land of promise God had given to them.

We close today with these sobering words:

> *Phinehas was pleased, the delegation was pleased, and the children of Israel across the Jordan were pleased; but was the Lord pleased? The delegation rejoiced that the purpose of the altar was for witness and not sacrifice, and this seemed to settle the matter. They rejoiced that God wouldn't send judgment to the land (v. 31) and that there would be no civil war in Israel (v. 33). But the nation was divided, in spite of the "altar of witness." Like Abraham and Lot (Genesis 13), part of the nation had a spiritual outlook while the other part was concerned with material things....*
>
> *The stones may have been a witness, but the people certainly were not. Surrounded by heathen nations and separated from their brothers and sisters across the river, these tribes quickly fell into idolatry and were eventually taken by Assyria*
> *(1 Chronicles 5:25-26).* [20]
> ~ Warren Wiersbe

DAY FIVE
Joshua 22 | Hold Fast to Him

As we have seen in our study, the tribes of Reuben, Gad, and the half-tribe of Manasseh play a significant role in the early history of Israel, particularly in the conquest of the Promised Land, but their ultimate fate and involvement in Israel's later history unfolds in a way that reflects what happens to believers who settle for a borderline life. After the Transjordan tribes return back home, they will remain on the eastern side of the Jordan River, separated geographically from the other tribes in Canaan. Gradually, this isolation, along with the challenges of maintaining religious and national unity with the rest of Israel, results in a decline in influence. When Assyria will conquer Israel in 722 B.C., the northern kingdom will fall, and many of the Israelites will be exiled. The land east of the Jordan, where the two-and-a-half tribes live, is Gilead, an area that will also fall to Assyria:

> In the days of Pekah king of Israel, Tiglath-pileser king of Assyria came and captured Ijon and Abel-beth-maacah and Janoah and Kedesh and Hazor and Gilead and Galilee, all the land of Naphtali; and he carried them captive to Assyria (2 Kings 15:29).

1 Chronicles 5:26 refers to the Transjordan tribes in the context of their exile to Assyria:

> So the God of Israel caused King Pul of Assyria (also known as Tiglath-pileser) to invade the land and take away the people of Reuben, Gad, and the half-tribe of Manasseh as captives. The Assyrians exiled them to Halah, Habor, Hara, and the Gozan River, where they remain to this day (NLT).

By the time of the post-exilic period of Israel, the two-and-a-half tribes will have lost both their distinctiveness and influence, and their prominence in the history of Israel will become greatly diminished.

Early on, these tribes obeyed the commands of God, and He blessed them as they led out in the conquest. But, in the years after they returned home, surrounded by pagan nations and isolated from the other tribes on the west side of the Jordan, they quickly fell into idolatry. This leads us to the warfare principle in this lesson:

> **Obedience is the key to maintaining victory.**

Remember the instructions Joshua gave the two-and-a-half tribes as they were departing? "Only be very careful to observe the commandment and the law which Moses the servant of the Lord commanded you, to love the Lord your God and walk in all His ways and keep His commandments and hold fast to Him and serve Him with all your heart and with all your soul" (Joshua 22:5).

If only they had obeyed the Lord wholeheartedly and entered the land God had promised them. If only they had held fast to Him. If only they had remained faithful. If only.

As we saw in our Lesson Two warfare principle: **Obedience is a prerequisite to victory.** However, obedience is not a one time thing in the life of a believer. It is ongoing. **Obedience is the key to maintaining victory.**

Believers who walk in obedience understand authority. Do you remember the Roman Centurion who sent for Jesus?

Read Matthew 8:5-13.

1. What did the Centurion understand? (v. 9)

2. To what did Jesus equate the Centurion's faith?

I don't think anyone understands and has a respect for authority more those who have served in the military. Why is understanding rank and authority so important? Because without unquestioning obedience in dangerous situations, lives are at risk. Pausing to argue or second guess could mean death.

We know that we are in a spiritual war. The Lord is clear in His Word that He is the ultimate authority. Why do we so often want to question His Word and justify our actions? Any time we do it, it is to our own demise. **We must remember that we have a very real enemy, and he is scheming against us** (Ephesians 6:10-12).

At a conference a few months ago, I heard a man speak who had served in the Army's Delta Force, the elite fighting unit. He explained that serving in the Army was much like being in the army of the Lord. The Warrior Ethos is the commitment the men and women make to the United States and their fellow soldiers. They are the fundamental values by which they live. We would do well to incorporate them as soldiers of the Most High.

Warrior Ethos:
1. I will always place the mission first.
2. I will never accept defeat.
3. I will never quit.
4. I will never leave a fallen comrade.

I was so moved by the spiritual analogy that he drew! Let's think about what the Warrior Ethos means in spiritual terms:

1. I will always put Jesus and His mission first.

2. I will never accept defeat. Christ has already won the war.

3. I will never quit. As long as I have breath, I am in the battle for the advancement of Christ's Kingdom and His glory.

4. I will never leave a fallen comrade. We are commanded to bear one another's burdens and to restore a fallen comrade in a spirit of gentleness (Galatians 6:1-2).

We belong to Christ and are His Bride, the church. We are called to pray for, care for, and restore others for His glory. If we are working together for the advancement of His Kingdom and the spiritual birth of all who do not yet know Christ, we will not have time to focus on self, or fall into strife or jealousy with one another. In fact, contention among believers is a sign that we are living as "mere men" (1 Corinthians 3:3b) and not as spiritual men and women.

We are called to obedience. Every day, in every way, we are to submit to or line up under our King and obey His Word. Sylvia Gunter, the author of *Prayer Portions* and *Living in His Presence*, was a mentor to me when we lived in the Birmingham area. One of the truths Sylvia teaches on is the blessing. In her booklet, *Daily Spirit Blessings*, she includes a blessing for an obedient child. Because we are spirit, soul, and body, she addresses our spirit, where the Holy Spirit dwells.

As you close out your time in God's Word today, reflect on these words and pray them for yourself.

Spirit, I bless you with the joy of obedience
and with obedience being a joy, not a bondage,
I bless you with the unique joy of obeying your Father in great detail
because you are motivated by love.
I bless you with experiencing the rich love of your Father as you obey Him.
I bless you with seeing in the natural the results of your obedience.
I bless your place in the new generation who will blot out the old bondage of legalism,
and the world will see in you the complete merging of obedience and love.
I bless you in the name of the One who was obedient unto death for you. [21]

Hold fast to Him. Cling to Him. Be obedient to His Word. And you will discover that the freedom of the victorious Christian life will be yours!

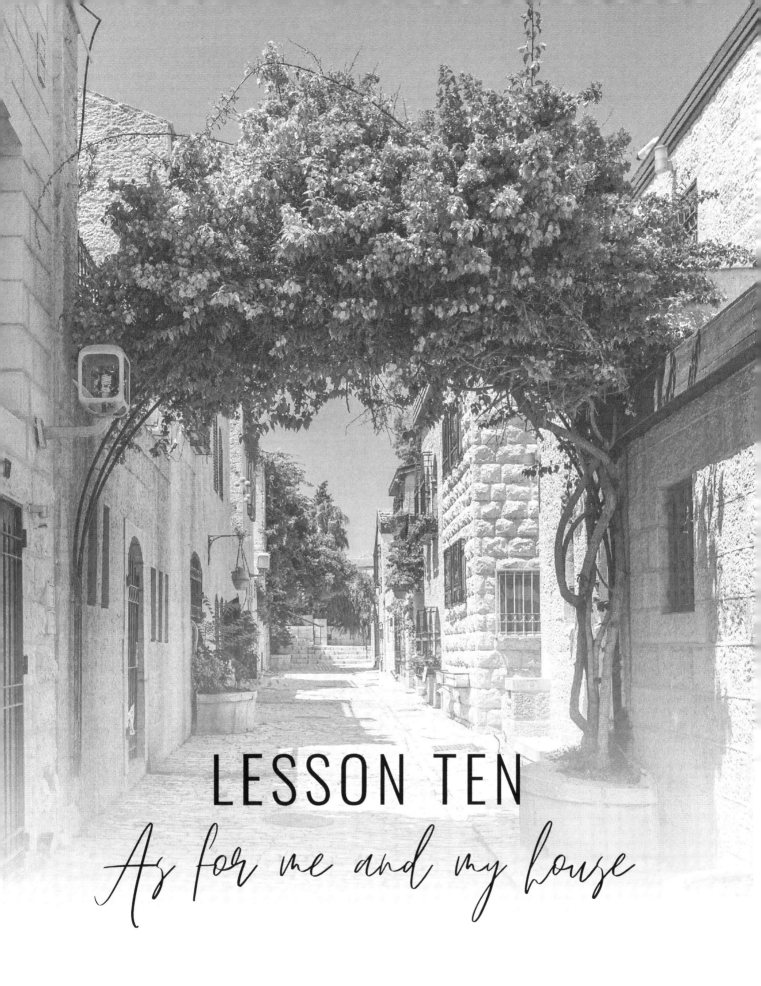

LESSON TEN

As for me and my house

JOSHUA 23

Joshua's Farewell Address

[1] Now it came about after many days, when the Lord had given rest to Israel from all their enemies on every side, and Joshua was old, advanced in years, [2] that Joshua called for all Israel, for their elders and their heads and their judges and their officers, and said to them, "I am old, advanced in years. [3] And you have seen all that the Lord your God has done to all these nations because of you, for the Lord your God is He who has been fighting for you.

[4] See, I have apportioned to you these nations which remain as an inheritance for your tribes, with all the nations which I have cut off, from the Jordan even to the Great Sea toward the setting of the sun. [5] The Lord your God, He will thrust them out from before you and drive them from before you; and you will possess their land, just as the Lord your God promised you. [6] Be very firm, then, to keep and do all that is written in the book of the law of Moses, so that you may not turn aside from it to the right hand or to the left, [7] so that you will not associate with these nations, these which remain among you, or mention the name of their gods, or make anyone swear by them, or serve them, or bow down to them. [8] But you are to cling to the Lord your God, as you have done to this day. [9] For the Lord has driven out great and strong nations from before you; and as for you, no man has stood before you to this day. [10] One of your men puts to flight a thousand, for the Lord your God is He who fights for you, just as He promised you. [11] So take diligent heed to yourselves to love the Lord your God. [12] For if you ever go back and cling to the rest of these nations, these which remain among you, and intermarry with them, so that you associate with them and they with you, [13] know with certainty that the Lord your God will not continue to drive these nations out from before you; but they will be a snare and a trap to you, and a whip on your sides and thorns in your eyes, until you perish from off this good land which the Lord your God has given you.

[14] "Now behold, today I am going the way of all the earth, and you know in all your hearts and in all your souls that not one word of all the good words which the Lord your God spoke concerning you has failed; all have been fulfilled for you, not one of them has failed. [15] It shall come about that just as all the good words which the Lord your God spoke to you have come upon you, so the Lord will bring upon you all the threats, until He has destroyed you from off this good land which the Lord your God has given you. [16] When you transgress the covenant of the Lord your God, which He commanded you, and go and serve other gods and bow down to them, then the anger of the Lord will burn against you, and you will perish quickly from off the good land which He has given you."

JOSHUA 24

Joshua Reviews Israel's History

[1] Then Joshua gathered all the tribes of Israel to Shechem, and called for the elders of Israel and for their heads and their judges and their officers; and they presented themselves before God. [2] Joshua said to all the people, "Thus says the Lord, the God of Israel, 'From ancient times your fathers lived beyond the River, namely, Terah, the father of Abraham and the father of Nahor, and they served other gods. [3] Then I took your father Abraham from beyond the River, and led him through all the land of Canaan, and multiplied his descendants and gave him Isaac. [4] To Isaac I gave Jacob and Esau, and to Esau I gave Mount Seir to possess it; but Jacob and his sons went down to Egypt. [5] Then I sent Moses and Aaron, and I plagued Egypt by what I did in its midst; and afterward I brought you out.

[6] I brought your fathers out of Egypt, and you came to the sea; and Egypt pursued your fathers with chariots and horsemen to the Red Sea. [7] But when they cried out to the Lord, He put darkness between you and the Egyptians, and brought the sea upon them and covered them; and your own eyes saw what I did in Egypt. And you lived in the wilderness for a long time. [8] Then I brought you into the land of the Amorites who lived beyond the Jordan, and they fought with you; and I gave them into your hand, and you took possession of their land when I destroyed them before you. [9] Then Balak the son of Zippor, king of Moab, arose and fought against Israel, and he sent and summoned Balaam the son of Beor to curse you. [10] But I was not willing to listen to Balaam. So he had to bless you, and I delivered you from his hand. [11] You crossed the Jordan and came to Jericho; and the citizens of Jericho fought against you, and the Amorite and the Perizzite and the Canaanite and the Hittite and the Girgashite, the Hivite and the Jebusite. Thus I gave them into your hand. [12] Then I sent the hornet before you and it drove out the two kings of the Amorites from before you, but not by your sword or your bow. [13] I gave you a land on which you had not labored, and cities which you had not built, and you have lived in them; you are eating of vineyards and olive groves which you did not plant.'

"We Will Serve the Lord"

[14] "Now, therefore, fear the Lord and serve Him in sincerity and truth; and put away the gods which your fathers served beyond the River and in Egypt, and serve the Lord. [15] If it is disagreeable in your sight to serve the Lord, choose for yourselves today whom you will serve: whether the gods which your fathers served which were beyond the River, or the gods of the Amorites in whose land you are living; but **as for me and my house**, we will serve the Lord."

[16] The people answered and said, "Far be it from us that we should forsake the Lord to serve other gods; [17] for the Lord our God is He who brought us and our fathers up out of the land of Egypt, from the house of bondage, and who did these great signs in our sight and preserved us through all the way in which we went and among all the peoples through whose midst we passed. [18] The Lord drove out from before us all the peoples, even the Amorites who lived in the land. We also will serve the Lord, for He is our God."

[19] Then Joshua said to the people, "You will not be able to serve the Lord, for He is a holy God. He is a jealous God; He will not forgive your transgression or your sins. [20] If you forsake the Lord and serve foreign gods, then He will turn and do you harm and consume you after He has done good to you." [21] The people said to Joshua, "No, but we will serve the Lord."

[22] Joshua said to the people, "You are witnesses against yourselves that you have chosen for yourselves the Lord, to serve Him." And they said, "We are witnesses." [23] "Now therefore, put away the foreign gods which are in your midst, and incline your hearts to the Lord, the God of Israel." [24] The people said to Joshua, "We will serve the Lord our God and we will obey His voice." [25] So Joshua made a covenant with the people that day, and made for them a statute and an ordinance in Shechem. [26] And Joshua wrote these words in the book of the law of God; and he took a large stone and set it up there under the oak that was by the sanctuary of the Lord. [27] Joshua said to all the people, "Behold, this stone shall be for a witness against us, for it has heard all the words of the Lord which He spoke to us; thus it shall be for a witness against you, so that you do not deny your God." [28] Then Joshua dismissed the people, each to his inheritance.

Joshua's Death and Burial

[29] It came about after these things that Joshua the son of Nun, the servant of the Lord, died, being one hundred and ten years old. [30] And they buried him in the territory of his inheritance in Timnath-serah, which is in the hill country of Ephraim, on the north of Mount Gaash.

[31] Israel served the Lord all the days of Joshua and all the days of the elders who survived Joshua, and had known all the deeds of the Lord which He had done for Israel.

[32] Now they buried the bones of Joseph, which the sons of Israel brought up from Egypt, at Shechem, in the piece of ground which Jacob had bought from the sons of Hamor the father of Shechem for one hundred pieces of money; and they became

the inheritance of Joseph's sons. ³³ And Eleazar the son of Aaron died; and they buried him at Gibeah of Phinehas his son, which was given him in the hill country of Ephraim.

As for me and my house

The Spirit-filled life is not a special, deluxe edition of Christianity. It is part and parcel of the total plan of God for His people. [1]

~ A.W. Tozer

We had no options but to move into a one-car garage/workshop on some land my parents owned. Their plan had been to build on the property in Fayette County and move from their East Memphis home when my dad retired. In the interim, a one-car garage with an attached workshop had been built. Dad was a woodworker and had always dreamed of a dedicated space for his hobby. Electricity was connected and a tiny bathroom was installed in the garage. Gravel was spread to build a road. This small structure allowed my parents to enjoy weekends out on the property, which had a small lake and lots of shade trees. Each visit to the little homestead stoked their dreams for their future. Sadly, an aggressive cancer took my dad before the house could be built, and the land sat neglected for years.

Occasionally, I would drive out to check on the place. The last time I had gone, lizards and mice scattered as I unlocked the door. The air inside was foul, a combination of musty smells and the uninvited critters who had set up housekeeping there. I made a face and immediately backed out, struggling to get some fresh air. Note to self: Avoid going in there at all costs!

Fast forward ten years. A recession in 2008 sent the economy spiraling into a downturn, and consumers held off spending discretionary funds due to the unstable market. Many companies failed, and our family business was one of the casualties. We lost our business, our farm, and our home. The only option we had was to move into the one-car garage with our three pets – two large boxers and one very spoiled Siamese cat. The garage/workshop had been untouched for over thirteen years. And based on what I remembered about the condition of the interior, I gagged at the prospect.

The reality that the garage/workshop was to become our new home was shocking to say the least. As I tried to mentally process how this would work, I asked my husband to drive me out to Moscow to see the soon-to-be-home garage so I could begin to graciously embrace it. As we drove up the gravel drive and saw the little overgrown place, the Lord did something rather amazing in my heart. Instead of dread or disgust, I saw our next home through my Father's eyes! It was no longer a filthy garage, but a fairy-tale cottage, the provision of a loving Father for His beloved children. And this was the verse that came to mind, "I gave you a land on which you had not labored, and cities which you had not built, and you have lived in them; you are eating of vineyards and olive groves which you did not plant" (Joshua 24:13). Indeed, God had given us a land we had not labored for and provided for our needs in a home that was not the work of our hands. That day, I told the Lord I would not dishonor His name by being ungrateful for what He had provided. Like Paul, I determined to live by these words, "More than that, I count all things to be loss in view of the surpassing value of knowing Christ Jesus my Lord, for whom I have suffered the loss of all things and count them but rubbish so that I may gain Christ" (Philippians 3:8-9).

It would take five years to slowly turn the little garage into the Cottage of Grace. Many hands worked on our little place, and financial love gifts allowed us to slowly carve out a home. God gave us grateful hearts for His gift. So often, we fail to recognize God's gifts because they come wrapped in packages we weren't expecting. Think on that for a while!

As we turn to Joshua 23, the leader of Israel is old and nearing the end of his days. I cannot imagine the depth of gratitude Joshua feels as he replays all that the Lord has done for him and for the nation of Israel. As he prepares to give his farewell address, looming large in his mind is concern for the spiritual stability of his people. It was a given for Joshua, who says, "As for me and my house, we will serve the Lord" (Joshua 24:15). But who will the sons of Israel serve? More importantly, who will you serve?

DAY ONE
Joshua 23:1-5

The final two chapters of the book of Joshua contain two addresses from Joshua to the nation of Israel. First, he speaks to the leaders, and then to all the Israelites.

As we prepare to conclude our journey through the book of Joshua, please grab yourself a cup of coffee or tea, go to your study spot, and read Joshua 23-24. As you do, begin thinking on the theme of these two chapters. Circle key repeating words or phrases. This method of mindful reading allows you to build the framework for what we will be studying, drawing us into the text and revealing the heart of the writer. Now, let's formulate an overview of these two chapters by answering the following questions:

Snapshot of Joshua 23-24

In Joshua 23:1-16, Joshua admonishes the people to be faithful to the Lord. What will be the result of their rebellion?

In Joshua 24:1-33, Joshua recaps Israel's history before challenging them to faithfully serve the Lord. The Israelites declare their allegiance to God. What is Joshua's response to their pledge?

What is the theme of Joshua 23-24?

What key words or phrases did you notice?

For today's study, we will be looking specifically at Joshua 23:1-5.

Our text picks up some 20 years or more after the warfare in Canaan has ceased. The years of fighting have taken quite a toll on Joshua and his militia. The fighting men are doubtlessly anxious to be reunited with their families and take up residence in their designated parcels in the Promised Land. I imagine all the wives had long since been ready to pack up their tents, shake the sand out of their belongings, and settle into permanent housing. The children, with their short legs and even shorter attention spans, have become bored and taken to annoying their siblings. It is time to settle down.

The Promised Land not only boasted of a land flowing with milk and honey, it also held the promise of home. Archeologists note that "Israel began as a nomadic people who traveled from place to place and lived in tents, but when they settled down, they built houses usually of stone, wood, and/or bricks made from mud. Often these houses would be grouped together, and extended families would live in these groups with a shared courtyard." [2]

Joshua has settled in Timnath-serah in the hill country of Ephraim (Joshua 19:50). He has not chosen the fertile, fruitful land he had spied out decades before. Instead, he has chosen to build his retirement home where the landscape is marked with deep valleys, and wild, rugged hills. The vistas will be beautiful, but working the land will be arduous. Perhaps Joshua wants one last challenge to conquer.

Did you know? The name Timnath-serah means "city of the sun." It is the same location that will be later be called Timnath-heres (Judges 2:9). [3]

We don't know how Joshua has filled his days in the interim since the wars have ended. In my imagination, I can see him moving among the people, fellowshipping over meals, and swapping war stories with the men who fought beside him. Certainly, he would have been devoted to instructing the people in the things of God and building up their faith. My assumption is based on the fact that Joshua seems to have developed a holy habit of bringing God into nearly every one of his conversations. As he is now quite a bit older than even the oldest Israelites under his leadership, his thoughts would have often turned to his death. How will the people fare after he is gone?

1. As the chapter opens, what is the state of the nation of Israel and who does Joshua credit for it? (v. 1)

Joshua has proven to be a worthy leader, a faithful follower of the God of Israel, and an esteemed military commander. Under his leadership, the Israelites only lost one battle during the entire seven-year military campaign. He has already divided the land and overseen the settling of the 12 tribes. Now, he is about to address the leadership of Israel, whose roles after his death will be supremely important. The final curtain is about to fall.

2. How does Joshua characterize himself? (v. 2)

Phillip Keller paints a graphic description of our hero, Joshua:

> Here he was now, a gnarled and noble veteran of 110 years. He had spent 40 of those years as
> a sweating slave, abused and brutalized by the Egyptians, in the slime pits along the Nile. Then
> he had spent the next 40 years as Moses' lieutenant in the dreadful wilderness wanderings
> where all but his friend, Caleb, and himself died in the desert wastes. Finally, his last 30 years
> had been spent in this glorious land of promised abundance. Here the Almighty Lord of Hosts
> had granted him great victory over the Canaanites and at last peace, prosperity, and rest from
> his foes. [4]

Joshua is well aware the time is near when he will transition from time to eternity. His final act as the
leader of God's people will be to prepare them for his departure. Robert Smith reminds us that aging
is a natural part of life and has some advantages, "Old age can be a blessing if the former years have
been productive and fruitful and if the time has been used constructively and productively. A feeling of
consolation pervades the heart and mind when one can look back and see a life lived in the service of the
Lord and people. This was the case for Joshua." [5]

**Succeeding generations of Israelites will hear the oral history of the exploits of God when He opened the
Jordan and subdued the land. But this generation witnessed it.**

3. What is the value of being eyewitnesses to God's miraculous deliverance? (v. 3)

4. What all has God done for Israel? (vv. 4-5)

The Israelites have seen God fight on their behalf and witnessed His judgment on those who set themselves
as the enemies of God. Having given the pagan nations in Canaan time and space to repent, God used
Israel to exact His vengeance on them. While the fighting men of Israel held the instruments of war, it
was God who fought the battle.

5. There is great power in the firsthand eyewitness account of a movement of God. Can you think of a time when God moved in extraordinary ways on your behalf? Write down the circumstances and spend some time praising the Lord for His faithfulness. Recounting His goodness helps build your faith and steel your courage for the next time you are confronted by the world, the flesh, or the devil.

Joshua understands the vulnerability of a people when a void in leadership occurs. For some 20 or 30 years, the Israelites have looked to him for wisdom and instruction. He is highly regarded and greatly beloved. Grief is beginning to take over as the reality of his impending departure is settling in among the people. His death will be a great loss on many levels. The head of each tribe will step into a greater role of leadership as the Israelites will no longer have a central figure leading them. This marked change is significant and is causing some trepidation among the people. In his remarks, Joshua wisely reminds them of the faithfulness of the God of Israel, who keeps His promises. The people have possessed the land. Now, they must possess the promises of God.

Sweet Jesus, Help me to know Your Word, to stand firm on it, and to obey it.
I know that Your Word is the truth. Forgive me for the times I neglect it.
When my flesh rises up and demands its own way, may the Spirit of God enable me
to refuse the temptations of the world, the flesh, and the devil.
May I be relentless in my desire to possess the promises of God.
"For all the promises of God find their Yes in Him" (2 Corinthians 1:20, ESV).
Help me to cling to you, O Lord. Amen and Amen.

DAY TWO
Joshua 23:6-16

Joshua's farewell addresses to the leaders of the Israelites continue. Joshua has reminded the leaders of what God has done in the past to prepare them to move into the future. God is committed to drive out the enemies remaining in the land, but are the Israelites?

Let's begin digging into our text.

Read Joshua 23:6-13.

Joshua knows there are still many enemies in the land to be conquered. He seems to have observed a growing fascination on the part of Israel with the Canaanite gods around them. Such it is with forbidden fruit. Just ask Adam and Eve. Without the unifying effect of the battlefield where a brotherhood of sorts is born in adversity, complacency is creeping in and leaving God's people vulnerable to the temptations of the Canaanites' way of life.

As we have seen during the seven-year military campaign, all of Israel seemed to be united against a common enemy. With the exception of the battle at Ai, every fight ended in victory for the Israelites. The overt skirmishes are over, but Joshua is mindful the enemy will now take a more subtle approach against God's people.

1. What reminder does Joshua give the leaders of Israel? (v. 6)

Joshua is aware of how easy it is to stray from the path of righteousness. Knowing God's Word and obeying it is the key to avoid poor choices that can lead away from God's intended path. This reminds me of the words of the beloved hymn, "Come, Thou Fount of Every Blessing." The third verse says,

> *O to grace how great a debtor*
> *daily I'm constrained to be!*
> *Let that grace now, like a fetter,*
> *bind my wandering heart to thee.*
> *Prone to wander, Lord, I feel it,*
> *prone to leave the God I love;*
> *Here's my heart; O take and seal it;*
> *seal it for thy courts above.* [6]

2. As Joshua speaks, he is demanding separation from the Canaanites. List the five things he commands them to avoid (v. 7).

- •
- •
- •

         •

         •

3. What one thing does Joshua instruct them to do? (v. 8)

As we saw last week, the Hebrew word for cling means "cleave, keep close." [7]

4. The New Testament truth that corresponds to this Old Testament teaching is found in Ephesians 5:31-32. This verse concludes Paul's teaching on marriage. He quotes Genesis 2:24 and then reveals a great mystery. What is it?

God's people are called to walk in personal holiness and practical righteousness, and to remain separate from heathen nations. Lest this be construed as discrimination, Kenneth Gangel clarifies the purpose for separation from those who worshipped foreign gods:

> These verses do not indicate racial prejudice on God's part. There is no attempt here to keep the purity of the race for other than spiritual reasons. In fact, God allowed for intermarriage when aliens chose to worship him. Again, Rahab is our best example. Spiritual intermingling was the problem and the danger. The people dared not mix their worship of Jehovah with the worship of other gods. They could not serve both. So, Joshua warned the leaders of this danger. [8]

Did you know? The word for cling that Joshua uses is the same word Moses uses in Genesis 2:24, "Therefore shall a man leave his father and his mother and shall *cleave* unto his wife: and they shall be one flesh" (KJV, emphasis mine). As two become one at the marriage altar, so the believer is united with Christ.

As believers, we live in the world, but we are "not of the world" (John 17:14). So, the standard of godly living is God's Word, and this lifestyle requires separation.

Joshua urges them to cling to the Lord, which had been their pattern of behavior thus far. Remember, this generation saw firsthand in the wilderness the consequence of disobedience. If you do the math, over the course of 40 years of wandering, the Israelites probably witnessed around 90 funerals a day!

Joshua once again reminds them of the faithfulness of God.

5. What all has He done on their behalf? (vv. 9-10)

6. In order to avoid being lured into false worship of the Canaanite idols, or adopting the lifestyle of these pagan peoples, what does Joshua command them to do? (v. 11)

Here, Joshua connects love with obedience. A deepening love for the Lord will result in a heart's desire to obey Him as a natural consequence, out of the overflow of devotion. In John 14:15, Jesus says, "If you love Me, you will keep My commandments."

Joshua is seeking to motivate the Israelites to obey God from a grateful heart. But, if that doesn't work, there is always the fear of consequences, and he does not hold back on the seriousness of disobedience. Again, Joshua uses the word "cling" to distinguish between the two options: They can either cling to the Lord (v. 8) or cling to pagan idolatry.

7. If they choose to worship the false gods of the pagan nations, they will make themselves enemies of God with serious ramifications. What will be the dreadful result? (vv. 12-13)

The same God who blessed them so profusely will just as certainly bring destruction on them if they break the covenant. A favorite commentator of mine, Henry Ironside, comments on the dire results of disobedience:

> If, on the other hand, they failed in this and did not cleave to the Lord their God, but turned from His law to walk in the ways of the nations surrounding Palestine or of the remnant of those remaining in the land, then their own God would turn against them and they would learn in bitterness of soul the disobedience to His truth. [9]

Beloved, may we remember God's promise to bless obedience, the serious consequence for disobedience, and make decisions accordingly.

As we saw in Lesson Two, God's promise of blessings for obedience and harsh judgment against disobedience (Deuteronomy 30:15-20) is not a new concept to the Israelites.

Read Joshua 23:13-16.

8. What will happen to the Israelites if they allow themselves to be influenced by the remaining people of Canaan? (vv. 13-16)

In verse 14, Joshua reminds the Israelites that not one Word God has spoken has failed. So, there is no reason to believe He is not willing to carry out judgment on disobedience. Roger Ellsworth perfectly captures Joshua's emphatic warning:

> If they should choose to ignore his warnings and go after the gods and the practices of the remaining Canaanites, they would find that the God who had devoted himself to their good would devote Himself to their judgement. They should not doubt this, because the God who had not failed to keep His promises to bless them (v. 14) would not fail to keep His promise to judge them. [10]

God's hand of blessing is resting on His people in the Promised Land, but His anger will burn against those who transgress His covenant, and they "will perish quickly from off the good land which He has given [them]" (Joshua 23:16). Joshua finishes his address with a warning because he wants them to grasp the serious consequence of turning against the Lord.

In the 21st century, we live in a culture that has little respect for the God we love and serve. Christians are seen as intolerant, and our God considered to be irrelevant. In fact, in many places, believers are hated and persecuted for their faith. Concerning the world, Jesus says, "If the world hates you, you know that it has hated Me before it hated you. If you were of the world, the world would love its own; but because you are not of the world, but I chose you out of the world, because of this the world hates you" (John 15:18-19).

May we be so saturated with His Word, and so perfumed with the aroma of Christ, that we demonstrate the love of God everywhere we go. "We have this treasure in earthen vessels, so that the surpassing greatness of the power will be of God and not from ourselves" (2 Corinthians 4:7). Beloved, God promises that He can use our damaged broken earthen vessels for the glory of His Kingdom!

Dear Lord, Set Yourself on display through my life.
I want others to see Jesus in me!
Amen.

DAY THREE
Joshua 24:1-13

Aware that his days on earth are numbered, Joshua wants to plant lessons deep in the hearts of the Israelites so that they can pass them on to the next generation. He knows that once his leadership role is vacated, the wicked one will intensify his attacks. The Israelites have known tremendous victories, but they must not let down their guard, or the enemy will come in like a flood. Gangel puts this in context for us:

> One of the most important concepts in this book is reiterated by Joshua in this speech: Godly living is not accomplished by winning a single skirmish but by enlisting for lifelong service. For Joshua and Israel, the clashing of swords had stopped, but the need for a faithful, diligent commitment was greater than ever. [11]

Read Joshua 24:1-13.

1. This will be Joshua's final address. Who does he gather at Shechem? (v. 1)

The people "presented themselves before God" (Joshua 24:1). The meaning of this phrase is unclear, but David Guzik weighs in with this insight:

> There are some people who believe that they presented themselves before God means that they did this before the tabernacle, which seems at this time to have been at Shiloh (Joshua 18:1). Either they presented themselves before God without the tabernacle, or the tabernacle was moved to Shechem for this occasion. [12]

Much like Moses before him, Joshua rehearses their history and what God has done for them. Warren Wiersbe writes, "A knowledge of their roots is very important to the Jews because they are God's chosen people with a destiny to fulfill in this world." [13]

Shechem is the ideal location for Joshua's moving farewell address. Remember, it is situated between Mount Ebal and Mount Gerizim, the site where Joshua made a covenant with the people shortly after the Israelites entered the Promised Land (Joshua 8:30-35). What an appropriate place for him to speak to them again about his longing for them to be faithful to the Lord!

Just as the children of Israel have been set apart, Shechem has also been set apart as an important part of Israel's history. This place is indeed holy ground to the people of Israel, and a place of remembrance for Joshua and the Israelites. The selection of Shechem as the location for Joshua's last address is designed to stir memories and build God-stories that were to be handed down by oral tradition to the subsequent generations.

2. Think over your life. Be it a spiritual tradition or a fun family custom, what is your place of remembrance?

As far back as I can remember, I have been a storyteller at heart. Even as a child, I loved to regale my family with funny stories which I loudly proclaimed, often from the top of the family footstool, so that I might control the room and be the center of attention. I have always been considered extra. Extra, as in extra loud, for sure. For all the years that my loud, over-the-top personality has been considered a negative by my family and my teachers, in my Christian life, it has served me well. My husband and I do international ministry, and since we usually serve out in the bush where microphones are unavailable, the ability to project my voice has turned out to be an unexpected blessing!

As I read of Joshua's final address to his people, I can see him projecting his voice in order to be heard. At 110 years old, his back is bent, and his eyesight is dimmed, but his voice thunders out on behalf of the Lord Most High, "Thus says the Lord, the God of Israel" (Joshua 24:2).

God begins by pointing back to Abraham, the father of the Jewish people, but He reminds them that Abraham was not a Jew when God called him. He was an idol worshipper from a long line of pagans. Abraham is not mentioned to remind the people of their supposedly illustrious ancestry. God references him to remind them of their humble, utterly pagan beginnings.

Guzik dispels the notion of any pride that might be developing among God's chosen people with this insight:

> The message was not, "We are all really amazing, so now we must live for God." Instead, it was "We were all a real mess, but God did many amazing things for us and in us. Now, we must live for the God who did such amazing things." The same principle should motivate Christians today. [15]

In our flesh, we tend to view our conversion experience as if the Lord was in great need of us when He brought us into the family of faith. When we do that, we are walking dangerously close to the edge of an over-inflated view of self-importance concerning our place in the kingdom of God. In reality, we:

> ...were dead in [our] trespasses and sins, in which [we] formerly walked according to the course of this world, according to the prince of the power of the air, of the spirit that is now

working in the sons of disobedience. Among them we too all formerly lived in the lusts of our flesh, indulging the desires of our flesh and of the mind, and were by nature children of wrath, even as the rest (Ephesians 2:1-3).

And just in case you need more specific reasons for taking no credit for your salvation, Paul listed out a variety of sins that many believers participated in prior to conversion:

Or do you not know that the unrighteous will not inherit the Kingdom of God? Do not be deceived; neither fornicators, nor idolaters, nor adulterers, nor effeminate, nor homosexuals, nor thieves, nor the covetous, nor drunkards, nor revilers, nor swindlers, will inherit the Kingdom of God. Such were some of you; but you were washed, but you were sanctified, but you were justified in the name of the Lord Jesus Christ and in the Spirit of our God (1 Corinthians 6:9-11).

Good company, right? God sought us, saved us, and sealed us with the Holy Spirit of promise. **Beloved, we are valuable, not because of who we are but because of Whose we are!** "May it never be that I would boast, except in the cross of our Lord Jesus Christ, through which the world has been crucified to me, and I to the world" (Galatians 6:14).

3. Briefly recount the highlights of Israel's timeline from verses 2-13 and enter them in this chart. (The first one is completed for you.)

Scripture	Highlights from Israel's History
vv. 2-3	God took Abraham, an idolator, led him through the land of Canaan, multiplied his descendants, and gave him Isaac.
v. 4	
vv. 6-7	
vv. 8-10	
v. 11	
v. 12	
v. 13	

4. Now, take a few minutes and reflect on your own conversion experience. Make a timeline of how God worked in your life to ultimately bring you to the saving knowledge of Christ. Plot out the events that led up to your conversion. Who influenced your decision? What factors played a part in your conversion experience? Many of us don't know the exact date of when we were saved, but give a general idea of when the event occurred.

When you came to Christ

Or, maybe you are coming to realize you have not yet given your life to Christ. You can see God's hand at work, leading you to this moment, but you haven't taken that step. If that is the case for you, I encourage you to pause now, turn to the "How to Become a Christian" section in this workbook, and spend time with the Lord, committing your heart and life to Him. Then, you can return here, write your date on the timeline, and celebrate this sweet moment of conversion! And just as Joshua will testify of all that God has done on behalf of His people, take a moment this week in your small group (or call a dear friend) and testify of the saving work of Jesus in your life.

5. As you look over the path God took you on, spend a few moments praising the Lord for His goodness in calling you unto Himself.

Back to our passage, unabashed, Joshua continues to recount God's words to His people. God says, "I sent the hornet before you and it drove out the two kings of the Amorites from before you, but not by your sword or your bow" (Joshua 24:12). The hornet may have been a reference to the literal large, stinging insect common in Israel.

Did you know? The Judean town of Zorah, mentioned in Joshua 15:33, literally means place of hornets or wasps, giving us a clue to the abundance of the stinging insects in the land. [16]

God may have sent swarms of stinging hornets to inflict painful bites and create panic in their ranks, or He may be speaking symbolically. Whether the language is literal or figurative, it's clear that the Lord caused the Canaanites to flee before Joshua's army. The victory belongs to the Lord and is not the result of Israel's swords or bows, lest anyone is prone to boast.

Stillness falls over the people of Israel. This is a humbling moment, realizing that the Creator of the Universe has fought for them and given them a land they have not cultivated, with cities they have not built. They are eating out of vineyards and olive groves that they have not planted. As Joshua pauses for impact, the Israelites see themselves stripped of all their pride before God. Keller describes the scene this way: "Joshua speaking with the unction of the Most High upon him stood stark and grand before them. They had never seen him garbed in greater glory. He was at the end of his days but at the pinnacle of power under the hand of God." [17]

Beloved, as we are thinking of Israel's journey to the Promised Land and our own journey with Christ, may we be mindful of the divine kindness of God to redeem us unto Himself. God had promised the land of Canaan to His people. In the same way, He has promised the victorious life of Christ to us. Just as He fought for His people in the Old Testament, He will fight for us and fulfill His promises to us.

DAY FOUR
Joshua 24:14-33

In today's lesson, we will look at the second half of Joshua's farewell address to the people of Israel. Anointed with the presence and power of God's Spirit, Joshua's words are crisp and clear, spoken with passion and precision. Keller uses his sanctified imagination and describes him this way:

> His eyes blazing like lamps lit with celestial fire, the aged veteran lifts up his sun-browned arms and stretches them out across the countryside. His voice thundering like a mighty summer storm he shouts to all of Israel....They have never seen him garbed in greater glory. He was at the end of his days but at the pinnacle of power under the hand of God. [18]

Joshua's recount of Israel's history stirs the people at the deepest level. "Fear the Lord and serve Him in sincerity and truth," Joshua demands (Joshua 24:14). And then he addresses the issue of idols. Idols? Among the people of God? We would assume the Israelites, who have been so richly blessed, would be wholly devoted to the Lord. Of course, we would make the same assumption of us, who have been the beneficiaries of the goodness of God. And yet, are we wholly devoted to the Lord?

Read Joshua 24:14-21.

1. In this section of Scripture, the word serve is found a total of 14 times. Circle each instance in the text provided or in your Bible.

2. Joshua sets two choices before the Israelites. What are they? (v. 15)

    •

    •

Joshua urges the Israelites to get rid of any idols or false gods that their ancestors worshipped beyond the Euphrates or from Egypt. He is calling them to fully commit to the one true God and leave behind any lingering influences of idol worship.

3. Joshua has already made his choice. What is it? (v. 15)

Beloved, we are faced with the same choice. Who will we serve? Will we serve idols, or the one true God? Ellsworth draws an application from the Old Testament book of Joshua to the Christian life:

> Idols have changed over the years. Most of us are not inclined to bow down before images carved from wood or stone. But that does not mean idolatry is dead. All those things which compete with God for our allegiance and our service are idols and must be renounced.

Peter Jeffery shares these insights on Joshua 24:14-15:

Half-hearted, insipid Christianity is an insult to God. Joshua calls for a total commitment based on fear and respect for God, and faithfulness in service. In order to produce this quality of service, there must be a putting away of other gods. Israel was still being influenced by gods of the past, gods their forefathers had worshipped in Egypt. Literally for them Joshua's command meant destroying idols. For us it means putting out of our lives things that challenge the authority of God in our affections and desires.

Jeffery goes on to paraphrase Joshua's words in verse 15 in this way:

If you are not prepared to serve God as he commands, then stop pretending and stop living a lie. Come out openly and say you are going to serve materialism, worldliness, prosperity and all the gods of the modern age. If these are the gods who have the love of your heart, then say so, but you cannot have it both ways. It is either the Lord God or these other gods. [19]

Joshua's hearers seem shocked that he would question their loyalty to Jehovah God.

4. What choice do the people profess to make? (vv. 16-18)

But Joshua senses something insincere in their words and challenges them. He is well acquainted with the Israelites' strengths and weaknesses. He knows human nature, and He knows the character of God.

5. How does Joshua describe God and what will be His response if they forsake Him? (vv. 19-20)

The people then insist, "We will serve the Lord" (Joshua 24:21). Talk is cheap. **A changed heart will produce a transformed life – that is the evidence of a genuine conversion.** How often have we been stirred by a powerful message or a riveting testimony and committed to be more devoted to the Lord, only to lose the passion that fueled our vow as the demands of the world press in?

6. Read Matthew 16:24-26. Here Jesus is teaching His followers to count the cost of following Him. What is required of His disciples?

Read Joshua 24:22-33.

7. What verbal contract does Joshua make with the people of Israel? (vv. 22-25)

8. Who are the witnesses to the contract? (v. 22)

Joshua "made a covenant with the people" (Joshua 24:25). He then "wrote these words in the book of the law of God" (Joshua 24:26) and set up a stone memorial as a reminder of the day's events. He will soon go "the way of all the earth" (Joshua 23:14), but the stone pillar will remain, witness to all that has transpired.

Gangel applies this Old Testament practice into New Testament language:

> We need stones with ears in our lives. We need reminders of who we are and Whose we are. When I see my wife's picture, I am reminded of my commitment to her. When I see my ordination certificate, I am reminded of my commitment to ministry. When I see the American flag, I remember my commitment to my country. And when I sign my income tax forms, I remember my commitment to the laws and financial statutes of our nation.

> Stones with ears. Visual reminders of our commitments to God, His Word, His work, His people. Perhaps in a picture or even a bookmark. Maybe a poster or plaque on the wall. Maybe a special letter in a purse or wallet. We need stones with ears to remind us of our commitments to God as well as His commitments to us. [20]

Stones with ears. Indeed! With that, Joshua dismisses the Israelites. Sometime after that, he dies at the age of 110 years, having been a faithful servant of the Lord: "And Israel served the Lord all the days of Joshua and all the days of the elders who survived Joshua and had known all the deeds of the Lord which He had done for Israel" (Joshua 24:31).

But sadly, the dark days of the time of the Judges are looming ahead for Israel.

9. Read Judges 2:6-10. What happens after the generation who knew Joshua dies?

And it would not be long before "everyone did what was right in their own eyes" (Judges 17:16; 21:25), and God's judgment would fall on the nation of Israel. What a cautionary tale for us, beloved. May we walk in righteousness and truth to the glory of God!

Tucked in the final words of Joshua is a reference to Joseph's bones. Wrapped up in this seemingly insignificant detail, is evidence of God's faithfulness and the fulfillment of His promise, even though it was well over 430 years in the making. Nearing death, Joseph reminds his brothers of God's covenant promise with Abraham to give him and his descendants the land of Canaan (Genesis 15:18-21). God had promised, and He would deliver.

At the time of Joseph's death, he and his family were in Egypt. Joseph would be buried in Egypt, but he made his brothers vow that his bones would be relocated to the Promised Land (Genesis 50:24-26). His descendants would remain in Egypt for 400 years before the Exodus. Generation after generation of Hebrews believed God's promise, and when God led them out of Egypt, Moses took the bones of Joseph with him during the 40 years of wilderness wanderings (Exodus 13:19). Presumably, it is Joshua who carries them into Canaan.

Joseph's faith was resting in the God "who cannot lie" (Titus 1:2). **When faith is rooted in the Word of God, we can stand on it.** And, if necessary, we can wait. We can wait on God's perfect timing for "faithful is He who calls you, and He also will bring it to pass" (1 Thessalonians 5:24).

The book of Joshua ends with three funerals. Joseph, Joshua, and Eleazar are buried. Joseph had saved his family and the Egyptians from starvation by opening the granaries. Joshua had led the Israelites to claim Canaan. And Eleazar, the son of Aaron, served as high priest of God's people. Joseph was a great leader, but he died. Joshua was an anointed leader and military strategist, but he died. Eleazar was a faithful spiritual leader of the people of Israel, but he died. The end of the book of Joshua highlights the temporary nature of human leadership and graciously points to the eternal nature of Christ. Joseph, Joshua, and Eleazar served faithfully, but their roles were limited by time and mortality. This is part of God's design to point us to our need for Christ, who provides what no other human leader ever could. He is our promised Savior and Lord, forever bridging the gap between God and humanity. Hallelujah! What a Savior!

DAY FIVE
Joshua 23-24 | As for me and my house

Beloved, we are engaged in a cosmic conflict with a very real enemy. Satan is referred to "the god of this world" (2 Corinthians 4:4). He has a measure of power here on earth, but only as it serves God's ultimate will. The devil is defeated and is subject to God's authority. Our responsibility is to become acutely aware of Satan's methods, but not become preoccupied by them.

In 2001, we moved to a rural area in Fayette County. Soon after our move, my husband killed a copperhead snake on the driveway. I am terribly afraid of snakes. It doesn't matter if they are poisonous, non-poisonous, big, small, fat, skinny, long, short, whatever! "Kill them. Kill them all," I say.

After my husband dealt a fatal blow to the snake and used a shovel to unceremoniously remove Mr. Snake's head from his body, he suggested I take a good look at it to be able to identify the difference between a poisonous snake and a non-poisonous one. I heard his words, and attempted to move, but my feet felt glued to the linoleum floor in my kitchen where I had taken refuge during the snake killing. Slowly, I willed my feet to move and crept out to view the dead beast. To my horror, even though his head was separated from his body, that snake's head and his body continued to wriggle and thrash about! My mind was convinced the detestable creature was dead, but in the moment, I was not able to overcome a strong emotional response. Adrenaline coursed through my veins, raising my blood pressure, and rendering me paralyzed with fear!

Satan, that slippery serpent, has been defeated by the death and resurrection of Jesus Christ. He is rendered impotent, but he still has the ability to cause us to fear, to shame us, and to torment us with guilt. Intellectually, we know Satan is a defeated foe. However, the academic knowledge is often not strong enough to override the fear his antics evoke in us, at least not at first.

Throughout the book of Joshua, we read of God's miraculous deliverance of His people. Israel's militia consisted of men who were ill-equipped and poorly trained. For about seven years, they went up against vicious warriors entrenched in fortified citadels. Strictly speaking, the odds of victory highly favored the inhabitants of the land of Canaan. Yet, with the exception of the battle of Ai, Israel was victorious in every military campaign. The only explanation is that God fought for His people! This brings us to our final spiritual warfare principle:

> ### The battle belongs to the Lord.

In Joshua's final address, he relays God's words to the people, "You crossed the Jordan and came to Jericho; and the citizens of Jericho fought against you, and the Amorite and the Perizzite and the Canaanite and the Hittite and the Girgashite, the Hivite and the Jebusite. Thus, *I gave them into your hand*...but not by your sword or your bow" (Joshua 24:11-12, emphasis mine). The battle belongs to the Lord.

The book of Joshua challenges us to live *into the promise* of the victorious, Spirit-filled life that Christ made possible through His death and resurrection. God is on our side, and He still fights for His people. His battle cry is, "Be strong and courageous! Do not tremble or be dismayed, for the Lord you God is with you wherever you go" (Joshua 1:9). Just as this promise took the Israelites into the Promised Land, it will allow us to live *into the promise.*

As we consider how this Old Testament story relates to us as New Testament believers, it is important to internalize this truth: We are not fighting for victory – we are fighting from victory. The battle belongs to the Lord, and it has already been won! Since the time sin entered the Garden, the devil has been attempting to destroy the seed of the woman who would crush his head (Genesis 3:15). God's plan of redemption has been in place before the foundation of the world was set in motion. Throughout the Old Testament, we see glimpses of the plan in type or picture. Then, at the end of the Old Testament, God instituted 400 years of silence. Heaven held its breath as redemption in Jesus Christ came to earth in the form of a baby born in Bethlehem (Luke 2:20).

1. Read Philippians 2:5-11. How does Paul describe the ministry of Christ?

At the advent of Christ, Satan's maniacal scheming went into overdrive, as he conspired to derail God's redemption plan by putting Jesus to death. After a number of failed attempts, Satan orchestrated the crucifixion of Christ. What he did not realize was that the cross was God's setup for victory over the devil. The resurrection of Jesus Christ from the dead signaled Satan's defeat. Christ won the victory!

Because Satan was defeated at the cross, he no longer has any authority over the believing saint. His only strategy left is deception: He will do his best to make you believe that the battle is still in play and the winner is undecided.

Satan is defeated – but like the death throes of that copperhead snake – he just doesn't act like it. But here is the truth: He can only weld power over us if we allow him to. John writes, "The Son of God appeared for this purpose, to destroy the works of the devil" (1 John 3:8).

Apart from Christ, all human beings, without exception, are helpless victims of the enemy.

2. Read Colossians 1:13. What did Jesus do when He saved us?

Believing in the promises of God and claiming them is a powerful defense against the devices of Satan. When Joshua led his militia against enemies seemingly stronger and greater than his army, his confidence was rested in God's assurance of the Promised Land. "Be strong and courageous, for you shall give this people possession of the land which I swore to their fathers to give them" (Joshua 1:6). Unbelief will keep you from possessing what is rightfully yours in Christ. **Faith in God's Word unlocks God's power, His presence, and His promises.**

3. Read 1 John 4:4. What does this verse teach us?

I dare not leave the impression that Satan is not a serious threat. The battle is real, the enemy is determined to destroy us, and his weapons are deadly. Like any soldier engaged in war, we stand a chance of suffering wounds at the hands of our enemy. But, the battle belongs to the Lord, and He is our Victor.

4. Paul records a powerful prayer in Ephesians 1:18-23. Read over this passage and make a list of each of Paul's desires for believers. Pray your list back to the Lord and praise Him for all He has done for you.

God raised Jesus from the dead and seated Him at His right hand. And He put all things in subjection under His feet (Ephesians 1:20-22). All things are under His feet, beloved. The battle belongs to the Lord! And that is what allows us to live *into the promise* of the victorious Spirit-led and Spirit-filled life. Now, that really is something to get excited about!

Your, writing team thanks you for joining us on this journey through the book of Joshua. We pray God's blessings on you as you choose to live courageously for the Lord Jesus Christ and lean *Into the Promise.*

Heavenly Father, thank You for Your Word, which instructs us and inspires us to live into the promise of the victorious Christian life. May we heed Your command to be strong and courageous and to possess our possessions.

Enable us to fight for the victorious life which is ours in Christ. Help us to stand against the world, the flesh, and the devil who war against us, trying to draw our affection away from the Lord. Give us eyes to see the deceptions of our enemies, lest we become ensnared and entangled by them.

May we seek You daily: Reading Your Word, meeting You in the secret place of prayer and filling our minds with Your truth. Call us to meditate daily on Your Word and may we be careful to do all that is written in it. Remind us that You bless obedience, and discipline disobedience. May the power of God and the aroma of Christ rest on us, as we trust in the Spirit of God to empower us to live Into the Promise!

Amen and Amen.

"Be strong and courageous! Do not tremble or be dismayed, for the Lord your God is with you wherever you go."
Joshua 1:9

HOW TO BECOME A CHRISTIAN

Dear one, has there ever been a time that you have given your heart to the Lord? Do you have the assurance that if you were to die right now, you would go straight to Heaven to spend all eternity in the presence of the Lord Jesus Christ and all His followers? If not, please let me share with you how you can be saved.

Admit Your Sin

First, you must understand that you are a sinner. The Bible says, "All have sinned and fall short of the glory of God" (Romans 3:23). In Romans 6:23 the Bible says, "For the wages of sin is death." That means that sin has separated us from a Holy God and we are under the sentence of eternal death and separation from God.

Abandon Self-Effort

Second, you must understand that you cannot save yourself by your own efforts. The Bible is very clear that it is "not by works of righteousness which we have done, but according to His mercy He saved us" (Titus 3:5, KJV). Again, in Ephesians 2:8-9 the Bible says, "For by grace you have been saved through faith; and that not of yourselves, it is the gift of God; not as a result of works, so that no one may boast."

Acknowledge Christ's Payment

Third, you must believe that Jesus Christ, the Son of God, died for your sins. The Bible says, "God demonstrates His own love toward us, in that while we were yet sinners, Christ died for us" (Romans 5:8). That means He died a sacrificial death in your place. Your sin debt has been paid by the blood of Jesus Christ, which "cleanses us from all sin" (1 John 1:7).

Accept Him as Savior

Fourth, you must put your faith in Jesus Christ and Him alone for your salvation. The blood of Christ does you no good until you receive Him by faith. The Bible says, "Believe in the Lord Jesus, and you will be saved" (Acts 16:31).

Has there been a time in your life that you have taken this all-important step of faith? If not, I urge you to do it right now. Jesus Christ is the only way to Heaven. He said, "I am the way, the truth, and the life. No one can come to the Father except through Me" (John 14:6, NLT).

Would you like to become a Christian? Would you like to invite Jesus Christ to come into your heart today? Read over this prayer and if it expresses the desire of your heart, you may ask Him into your heart to take away your sin, fill you with His Spirit, and take you to home to Heaven when you die. If this is your intention, pray this prayer.

Oh God, I'm a sinner. I am lost and I need to be saved. I know I cannot save myself,
so right now, once and for all, I trust You to save me. Come into my heart, forgive my sin,
and make me Your child. I give You my life. I will live for You as
You give me Your strength. Amen.

If you will make this your heartfelt prayer, God will hear and save you! Jesus has promised that He will never leave nor forsake anyone who comes to Him in faith. In John 6:37 He said, "The one who comes to Me I will certainly not cast out."

Welcome *Into the Promise*!

END NOTES

Introduction – Into the Promise

1. Tolkien, J.R.R. (2001). *The Lord of the Rings*: *The Two Towers, p. 283*. Kindle edition.

2. Tolkien, J.R.R. (2001). *The Lord of the Rings, The Two Towers*, p. 283. Kindle edition.

3. Vreeland, D. (April 16, 2021). "The Impact of Eugene Peterson: A Conversation with Winn Collier." *Missio Alliance*. Retrieve from https://www.missioalliance.org/the-impact -of-eugene-peterson-a-conversation-with-winn-collier/

4. Turpin, S. (November 9, 2022). "Searching for Sinai." *Answers in Genesis*. Retrieved from https://answersingenesis. org/archaeology/searching-for-sinai/#:~:text=Evaluating%20the%20options%20for%20the%20biblical%20 location%20of%20Mount%20Sinai&text=The%20Bible%20tells%20us%20that,;%20Deuteronomy%20 4:13).&text=This%20new%20interactive%20book%20gives,Get%20your%20copy%20today!&text=Although%20 the%20location%20of%20Mount,himself%20to%20his%20people%2C%20Israel.

5. Wasserman, P. (January 12, 2024). "World Population by Religion: A Global Tapestry of Faith." *Population Education*. Retrieved from https://populationeducation.org/world-population-by-religion-a-global-tapestry-of faith/#:~:text=Christianity%2C%20a%20faith%20that%20began,Oceania%20and%20sub%2DSaharan%20Africa.

Introduction – A Journey Through Joshua

1. McGee, J.V. (1991). *Joshua and Judges*, p. 7. Nashville, TN: Thomas Nelson Publishers.

2. McShane, A. (1994). *Joshua*, p. 7. Kilmarnock, Scotland: John Ritchie Christian Publications.

3. Hess, R. (2008). *Joshua: An Introduction & Commentary*, pp. 33-36. Downers Grove, IL: IVP Academic.

4. Schaeffer, F. (1975). *Joshua and the Flow of Biblical History*, p. 9. Downers Grove, IL: InterVarsity Press.

5. Wiersbe, W. (1996). *Be Strong*, pp. 35-36. New York, NY: Victor Books.

Lesson One

1. Taylor, H. (2009). *Hudson Taylor's Spiritual Secret*, p. 165. Chicago, IL: Moody Bible.

2. Wiersbe, W. (1996). *Be Strong*, p. 17. New York, NY: Victor Books.

3. Keller, P. (1992). *Joshua: Mighty Warrior and Man of Faith*, p. 52. Grand Rapids, MI: Kregal Publications.

4. Wiersbe, W. (1996). *Be Strong*, p. 30. New York, NY: Victor Books.

5. Sanders, O. (1967). *Spiritual Leadership*, p. 132. Chicago, IL: Moody Publishers.

6. Barker, K. (ed). (1985). *NIV Study Bible*, p. 1074. Grand Rapids, MI: Zondervan.

7. Smith, R. (2023). *Exalting Jesus in Joshua*, p. 20. Brentwood, TN: B&H Publishing Group.

8. Smith, R. (2023). *Exalting Jesus in Joshua*, p. 19. Brentwood, TN: B&H Publishing Group.

9. *Yadvashem.org*. (n.d.). Retrieved from https://www.yadvashem.org/blog/the-real-story-exodus.html

10. *Lyrics.com*. (n.d.) "The Exodus Song." Retrieved from https://www.lyrics.com/lyric/8213078/ Exodus+Song+%28This+Land+Is+Mine%29#google_vignette

11. Numbers 20:7-12

12. Smith, R. (2023). *Exalting Jesus in Joshua*, p. 21. Brentwood, TN: B&H Publishing Group.

13. *Blue Letter Bible*. (n.d.). Retrieved from https://www.blueletterbible.org/exicon/h2388/kjv/wlc/0-1/

14. Wiersbe, W. (1996). *Be Strong*, p. 34. New York, NY: Victor Books.

15. Lewis, C.S. (1980). *The Voyage of the Dawn Treader*, p. 186, New York, NY: Harper Collins.

16. Lewis, C.S. (1980). *The Voyage of the Dawn Treader*, p. 186, New York, NY: Harper Collins.

17. Swindoll, C. R. (2009). *Dropping Your Guard*, p. 70. Nashville, TN: Thomas Nelson.

18. Wiersbe, W. (1996). *Be Strong*, p. 35. New York, NY: Victor Books.

19. Kelly, Thomas. (1992). *Testament of Devotion*, pp. 77-78. New York, NY: Harper Collins.

20. Wiersbe, W. (1996). *Be Strong*, p. 37. New York, NY: Victor Books.

21. Wiersbe, W. (1996). *Be Strong*, p. 37. New York, NY: Victor Books.

22. Smith, R. (2023). *Exalting Jesus in Joshua*, p. 33. Brentwood, TN: B&H Publishing Group.

23. Vine, W.E. (1970). *Vine's Complete Expository Dictionary*, p. 182. Nashville, TN: Thomas Nelson.

24. Stedman, R. (n.d.). "Joshua: Guidebook to Victory." *Ray Stedman.org*. Retrieved from https://www.raystedman.org/bible-overview/adventuring/joshua-guidebook-to-victory

25. Stedman, R. (n.d.). "Joshua: Guidebook to Victory." *Ray Stedman.org*. Retrieved from https://www.raystedman.org/bible-overview/adventuring/joshua-guidebook-to-victory

Lesson Two

1. Wiersbe, W. (1982). *Be Strong*, p. 49. Colorado Springs, CO: David C. Cook.

2. *National Park Service*. (n.d.). "An Overview of the Declaration of Independence." Retrieved from https://www.nps.gov/inde/learn/education/classrooms/resources-declarationoverview.htm
   Bomboy, S. (August 2, 2022). "On this day, the Declaration of Independence is officially signed." *National Constitution Center*. Retrieved from https://constitutioncenter.org/blog/on-this-day-the-declaration-of-independence-is-officially- signed#:~:text=August%202%2C%201776%2C%20is%20one,Declaration%20of%20Independence%20in%20Philadelphia

3. Smith, R. (2023). *Exalting Jesus in Joshua (Christ-Centered Exposition Commentary)*, Kindle Edition, p. 41. Brentwood, TN: B&H Publishing.

4. Walton, J., & Mathews, V., & Chavalas, M. (2000). *The IVP Bible Background Commentary: Old Testament,* p. 213. Downers Grove, IL: IVP Academic.

5. Wiersbe, W. (1982). *Be Strong*, p. 47. Colorado Springs, CO: David C. Cook.

6. Jackman, D. (2014). *Joshua: People of God's Purpose,* p. 35. Wheaton, IL: Crossway.

7. Spence, H. D. M. (n.d.). *Joshua: The Pulpit Commentary,* Logos.

8. Hess, R. S. (2008). *Joshua: An Introduction and Commentary*, p. 95. Downers Grove, IL: InterVarsity Press

9. Walton, J., & Mathews, V., & Chavalas, M. (2000). *The IVP Bible Background Commentary: Old Testament,* p. 214. Downers Grove, IL: IVP Academic.

10. Hess, R. S. (2008). *Joshua: An Introduction and Commentary*, p. 96. Downers Grove, IL: InterVarsity Press

11. Henry, M. (n.d.). "Matthew Henry's Commentary on the Whole Bible." *Blue Letter Bible*. Retrieved from: https://www.blueletterbible.org/Comm/mhc/Jos/Jos_002.cfm

12. Carson, D. A., & France, R. R. T., & Motyer, J. A. (2001). *The New Bible Commentary*, Logos.

13. Wiersbe, W. (1982). *Be Strong*, p. 51. Colorado Springs, CO: David C. Cook.

14. Woudstra, M. (1981). *The Book of Joshua*, p. 74. Grand Rapids, MI: Eerdmans Publishing Company.

15. *Blue Letter Bible*. Retrieved from https://www.blueletterbible.org/lexicon/h8615/kjv/wlc/0-1/

16. Keller, W. P. (1983). *Joshua: Mighty Warrior and Man of Faith*, p. 69. Grand Rapids, MI: Kregel Publications.

17. *Biblegateway.com*. (2016). Retrieved from https://www.biblegateway.com/blog/2016/08/the-disciplines-of-the-christian-life-by-eric-liddell/

18. Keller, W. P. (1983). *Joshua: Mighty Warrior and Man of Faith*, p. 68. Grand Rapids, MI: Kregel Publications.

19. Schaeffer, F. (1975). *Joshua and the Flow of Biblical History*, p. 79. Downers Grove, IL: InterVarsity Press.

20. Schaeffer, F. (1975). *Joshua and the Flow of Biblical History*, p. 79. Downers Grove, IL: InterVarsity Press.

Lesson Three

1. Henry, M. (n.d.). "Matthew Henry's Commentary on the Whole Bible." *Blue Letter Bible*. Retrieved from: https://www.blueletterbible.org/Comm/mhc/Exd/Exd_014.cfm

2. Walton, J., & Mathews, V., & Chavalas, M. (2000). *The IVP Bible Background Commentary: Old Testament,* p. 215. Downers Grove, IL: IVP Academic.

3. Guzik, D. *Enduring Word Commentary*. Retrieved from: https://enduringword.com/bible-commentary/joshua-3/

4. *Britannica.com.* (n.d.). Retrieved from https://www.britannica.com/science/cubit

5. Hess, R. S. (2008). *Joshua: An Introduction and Commentary*, p. 109. Downers Grove, IL: InterVarsity Press.

6. "Exalt." (n.d.). *Merriam-Webster Online.* Retrieved from https://www.merriam-webster.com/dictionary/exalt/

7. Wiersbe, W. (1982). *Be Strong*, p. 63. Colorado Springs, CO: David C. Cook.

8. Smith, R. (2023). *Exalting Jesus in Joshua (Christ-Centered Exposition Commentary)*, Kindle Edition, p. 57. Brentwood, TN: B&H Publishing.

9. Hess, R. S. (2008). *Joshua: An Introduction and Commentary*, p. 113. Downers Grove, IL: InterVarsity Press.

10. Smith, R. (2023). *Exalting Jesus in Joshua (Christ-Centered Exposition Commentary)*, Kindle Edition, p. 58. Brentwood, TN: B&H Publishing.

11. Jamieson, R. (1997). *Commentary Critical and Explanatory on the Whole Bible*, vol. 1, p. 144. Oak Harbor, WA: Logos Research Systems, Inc.

12. Thomas, I. (1989). *The Saving Life of Christ*, p. 135. Grand Rapids, MI: Zondervan Publishers.

13. Smith, R. (2023). *Exalting Jesus in Joshua (Christ-Centered Exposition Commentary)*, Kindle Edition, p. 56. Brentwood, TN: B&H Publishing.

14. *The ESV Study Bible* (2008). p. 399. Wheaton, IL: Crossway.

15. Smith, R. (2023). *Exalting Jesus in Joshua (Christ-Centered Exposition Commentary)*, Kindle Edition, p. 60. Brentwood, TN: B&H Publishing.

16. Schaeffer, F. (1975). *Joshua and the Flow of Biblical History*, p. 86. Downers Grove, IL: InterVarsity Press.

17. Hess, R. S. (2008). *Joshua: An Introduction and Commentary*, p. 126. Downers Grove, IL: InterVarsity Press.

18. Morgan, R. (2014). *The Red Sea Rules*, p. 116. Nashville, TN: Thomas Nelson.

19. Smith, R. (2023). *Exalting Jesus in Joshua (Christ-Centered Exposition Commentary)*, Kindle Edition, p. 68. Brentwood, TN: B&H Publishing.

20. Jackman, D. (2014). *Joshua: People of God's Purpose,* p. 54. Wheaton, IL: Crossway.

21. Barna, G. (2023). *Raising Spiritual Champions*, Kindle Edition, p. 57. Glendale, AZ: Arizona Christian University Press.

22. Smith, R. (2023). *Exalting Jesus in Joshua (Christ-Centered Exposition Commentary)*, Kindle Edition, p. 54. Brentwood, TN: B&H Publishing.

Lesson Four

1. Lewis, C.S. (2001). *Screwtape Letters*, p. 46. NewYork, NY: HarperCollins.

2. Hess, R. (1996). *Joshua: An Introduction and Commentary*, p. 129. Downers Grove, IL: InterVarsity Press.

3. *WordPress.com* (2011). Retrieved from: https://jbsandifer.wordpress.com/2011 /10/10/how-long-did-it-take-2-5-million-people-to-cross-the-jordan-joshua-314-17/

4. *Enduring Word*. (n.d.) Retrieved from: https://enduringword.com/bible-commentary/joshua-5/

5. *Prnewswire*. (n.d.) Retrieved from: https://www.prnewswire.com/news-releases/ninety-six-percent-of-americans-are-so-impatient-they-knowingly-consume-hot-food-or-beverages-that-burn-their-mouths-finds-fifth-third-bank-surve-y-300026261.html#:~:text=It commissioned a national survey, 63 percent do so frequently.

6. Gangel, K.O. (2002). *Joshua,* pp. 82-83. B&H Publishing Group.

7. Wiersbe, W. (1996). *Be Strong*, p. 58. Wheaten, IL: Victor Books.

8. Wiersbe, W. W. (1996). *Be Strong*, pp. 60-61. Wheaten, IL: Victor Books.

9. Jackman, D. (2014). *Joshua: People of God's Purpose,* p. 81. Wheaton, IL: Crossway.

10. *Hymnary*. (n.d.) Retrieved from https://www.hymnal.net/en/hymn/h/313

11. Ironside, H.A. (2008). *Joshua*, p. 61. Grand Rapids, MI: Kregel Publications.

12. Keller, P. (1983). *Joshua: Mighty Warrior and Man of Faith*, p. 94. Grand Rapids, MI: Kregel Publications. (Kindle)

13. Tenney, M.C. (1967). *Pictorial Bible Dictionary,* pp. 507-508. Grand Rapids, MI: Zondervan Publishing House.

14. Smith, R. (2023). *Exalting Jesus in Joshua*, p. 92. Brentwood, TN: B&H Publishing Group.

15. Wiersbe, W. (1996). *Be Strong*, p. 88. Wheaten, IL: Victor Books.

16. Smith, R. (2023). *Exalting Jesus in Joshua*, p. 92. Brentwood, TN: B&H Publishing Group.

17. *Got Questions*. (n.d.) Retrieved from https://www.gotquestions.org/Biblical-numerology.html

18. Jackman, D. (2014). *Joshua: People of God's Purpose*, p. 91. Wheaton, IL: Crossway.

19. Wiersbe, W. (1996). *Be Strong*, p. 74. Wheaten, IL: Victor Books.

20. Wiersbe, W. (1996). *Be Strong*, p. 92. Wheaten, IL: Victor Books.

21. Wiersbe, W. (1996). *Be Strong*, p. 94. Wheaten, IL: Victor Books.

22. Jackman, D. (2014). *Joshua: People of God's Purpose*, p. 96. Wheaton, IL: Crossway.

23. *Britannica.org* (n.d.) Retrieved from: https://www.britannica.com/place/walls-of-Jericho

Lesson Five

1. Schaeffer, F. (2004). *Joshua and the Flow of Biblical History*, p. 139. Wheaton, IL: Crossway.

2. Wiersbe, W. (1993). *Be Strong: Putting God's Power to Work in Your Life*, p. 101. Colorado Springs, CO: David C. Cook.

3. Schaeffer, F. (2004). *Joshua and the Flow of Biblical History*, p. 115. Wheaton, IL: Crossway.

4. Wiersbe, W. (1993). *Be Strong: Putting God's Power to Work in Your Life*, p. 102. Colorado Springs, CO: David C. Cook.

5. Hess, R. (2008). *Joshua: An Introduction & Commentary*, p. 159. Downers Grove, IL: IVP Academic.
   Wiersbe, W. (1993). *Be Strong: Putting God's Power to Work in Your Life*, p. 105. Colorado Springs, CO: David C. Cook.

6. Wiersbe, W. (1993). *Be Strong: Putting God's Power to Work in Your Life*, p. 105. Colorado Springs, CO: David C. Cook.

7. Keller, W. P. (1992). *Joshua: Mighty Warrior and Man of Faith*, p. 105. Grand Rapids, MI: Kregel Publications.

8. Keller, W. P. (1992). *Joshua: Mighty Warrior and Man of Faith*, p. 109. Grand Rapids, MI: Kregel Publications.

9. Hess, R. (2008). *Joshua: An Introduction & Commentary*, p. 162. Downers Grove, IL: IVP Academic.

10. Smith, R. (2023). *Christ Centered Exposition Commentary: Exalting Jesus in Joshua*, p. 114. Nashville, TN: B&H Publishing.

11. Wiersbe, W. (1993). *Be Strong: Putting God's Power to Work in Your Life*, p. 107. Colorado Springs, CO: David C. Cook.

12. *Life Application Study Bible, New Living Translation*, p. 430. (2007). Carol Stream, IL: Tyndale House Publishers, Inc.

13. Schaeffer, F. (2004). *Joshua and the Flow of Biblical History*, p. 118. Wheaton, IL: Crossway.

14. Walton, J., Matthews, H., Chavalas, M. (2000). *The IVP Bible Background Commentary*, p. 219. Downers Grove, IL: InterVarsity Press.

15. McGee, J. V. (1982). *Thru the Bible with J. Vernon McGee* (Vol. II), p. 19. Nashville, TN: Thomas Nelson Publishers.

16. Piper, J. (2015). "How Do I Take My Thoughts Captive?" *Desiring God*. Retrieved from https://www.desiringgod.org/interviews/how-do-i-take-my-thoughts-captive.

17. McGee, J. V. (1982). *Thru the Bible with J. Vernon McGee* (Vol. II), p. 19-20. Nashville, TN: Thomas Nelson Publishers.

18. *Life Application Study Bible, New Living Translation*, p. 431. (2007). Carol Stream, IL: Tyndale House Publishers, Inc.

19. Wiersbe, W. (1993). *Be Strong: Putting God's Power to Work in Your Life*, p. 111. Colorado Springs, CO: David C. Cook.

20. Wiersbe, W. (1993). *Be Strong: Putting God's Power to Work in Your Life*, p. 116. Colorado Springs, CO: David C. Cook.

21. *Life Application Study Bible, New Living Translation*, p. 431. (2007). Carol Stream, IL: Tyndale House Publishers, Inc.

22. Wiersbe, W. (1993). *Be Strong: Putting God's Power to Work in Your Life*, p. 116. Colorado Springs, CO: David C. Cook.

23. Keller, W. P. (1992). *Joshua: Mighty Warrior and Man of Faith*, p. 112-113. Grand Rapids, MI: Kregel Publications.

24. Keller, W. P. (1992). *Joshua: Mighty Warrior and Man of Faith*, p. 111. Grand Rapids, MI: Kregel Publications.

25. Keller, W. P. (1992). *Joshua: Mighty Warrior and Man of Faith*, p. 112. Grand Rapids, MI: Kregel Publications.

26. Keller, W. P. (1992). *Joshua: Mighty Warrior and Man of Faith*, p. 112. Grand Rapids, MI: Kregel Publications.

27. Wiersbe, W. (1993). *Be Strong: Putting God's Power to Work in Your Life*, p. 118. Colorado Springs, CO: David C. Cook.

28. Wiersbe, W. (1993). *Be Strong: Putting God's Power to Work in Your Life*, p. 119. Colorado Springs, CO: David C. Cook.

29. Graham, B. (n.d). "Answers." *Billy Graham Evangelistic Association.* Retrieved from https://billygraham.org/answer/does-gods-holy-spirit-live-in-me.

30. Wiersbe, W. (1993). *Be Strong: Putting God's Power to Work in Your Life*, p. 120. Colorado Springs, CO: David C. Cook.

31. Wiersbe, W. (1993). *Be Strong: Putting God's Power to Work in Your Life*, p. 121. Colorado Springs, CO: David C. Cook.

32. Schaeffer, F. (2004). *Joshua and the Flow of Biblical History*, p. 143. Wheaton, IL: Crossway.

33. Keller, W. P. (1992). *Joshua: Mighty Warrior and Man of Faith*, p. 115. Grand Rapids, MI: Kregel Publications.

34. Schaeffer, F. (2004). *Joshua and the Flow of Biblical History*, p. 120. Wheaton, IL: Crossway.

35. Keathley, J. H. (n.d.). "Victory at Ai (Joshua 8:1-35)." *Bible.org.* Retrieved from https://bible.org/seriespage/7-victory-ai-joshua-81-35.

36. Schaeffer, F. (2004). *Joshua and the Flow of Biblical History*, p. 131. Wheaton, IL: Crossway.

37. *Got Questions.* (n.d.). "What were the various sacrifices in the Old Testament?" Retrieved from https://www.gotquestions.org/Old-Testament-sacrifices.html

38. Wiersbe, W. (1993). *Be Strong: Putting God's Power to Work in Your Life*, p. 122.   Colorado Springs, CO: David C. Cook.

39. Schaeffer, F. (2004). *Joshua and the Flow of Biblical History*, p. 128. Wheaton, IL: Crossway.

40. Wiersbe, W. (1993). *Be Strong: Putting God's Power to Work in Your Life*, p. 124, 125. Colorado Springs, CO: David C. Cook.

41. Logan, J. (1995). *Reclaiming Surrendered Ground*, p. 198. Chicago, IL: Moody Publishers.

42. Ingram, C. (2015). *The Invisible War: What Every Believer Needs to Know about Satan, Demons, and Spiritual Warfare*, p. 55. Grand Rapids, MI: Baker Books.

43. Logan, J. (1995). *Reclaiming Surrendered Ground*, p. 13. Chicago, IL: Moody Publishers.

44. Taylor, J. (2013). *Victory Over the Devil*, p. 38. Bedford, TX: Burkhart Books.

45. Gunter, S. (1994). *For the Family*, p. 12. Birmingham, AL: The Father's Business.

46. Taylor, J. (2013). *Victory Over the Devil*, p. 10. Bedford, TX: Burkhart Books.

47. *AZ Lyrics.* (n.d.). "Plead the Blood." Retrieved from https://www.azlyrics.com/lyrics/codycarnes/pleadtheblood.html

Lesson Six

1. Tolkien, J.R.R. (2001). *The Lord of the Rings*: *The Two Towers, p. 251*. Kindle edition.

2. O'Neill, J. H. (March, 24, 2022). "The True Story of the Patton Prayer." *The Imaginative Conservative.* Retrieved from https://theimaginativeconservative.org/2022/03/true-story- patton-prayer-james-hugh-o-neill.htmlCite Neill true story of patton prayer)

3. Walton, J., & Mathews, V., & Chavalas, M. (2000). *The IVP Bible Background Commentary: Old Testament*, p.222 . Downers Grove, IL: IVP Academic.

4. Wiersbe, W. (1996). *Be Strong*, p. 129. New York, NY: Victor Books.

5. Hess, R. (2008). *Joshua: An Introduction & Commentary*, pp. 175-176. Downers Grove, IL: IVP Academic.

6. Keller, P. (1992). *Joshua: Mighty Warrior and Man of Faith*, p. 120. Grand Rapids, MI:Kregal Publications.

7. Getz, G. (1995). *Men of Character: Joshua*, p. 143. Nashville, TN: Broadman & Holman.

8. Wiersbe, W. (1996). *Be Strong*, p. 122. New York, NY: Victor Books.

9. Smith, R. (2023). *Exalting Jesus in Joshua*, p. 130. Brentwood, TN: B&H Publishing Group.

10. Vine, W.E. (1970). *Vine's Complete Expository Dictionary*, p. 50. Nashville, TN: Thomas Nelson.

11. Smith, R. (2023). *Exalting Jesus in Joshua*, p. 131. Brentwood, TN: B&H Publishing Group.

12. Santayana, G. (1998). *Life of Reason*, p. 5. Amherst, NY: Prometheus.

13. Wiersbe, W. (1996). *Be Strong*, p. 134. New York, NY: Victor Books.

14. Wiersbe, W. (1996). *Be Strong*, p. 134. New York, NY: Victor Books.

15. Wiersbe, W. (1996). *Be Strong*, p. 134. New York, NY: Victor Books.

16. Hess, R. (2008). *Joshua: An Introduction & Commentary*, p. 57. Downers Grove, IL: IVP Academic.

17. Wiersbe, W. (1996). *Be Strong*, p. 130. New York, NY: Victor Books.

18. Jackman, D. (2014). *Joshua*, p. 110. Wheaton, IL: Crossway.

19. Wiersbe, W. (1996). *Be Strong*, p. 135. New York, NY: Victor Books.

20. Hess, R. (2008). *Joshua: An Introduction & Commentary*, p. 207. Downers Grove, IL: IVP Academic.

21. Jackman, D. (2014). *Joshua*, p. 115. Wheaton, IL: Crossway.

22. Hess, R. (2008). *Joshua: An Introduction & Commentary*, p. 205. Downers Grove, IL: IVP Academic.

23. Thorp, K. (1988). *Joshua,* p. 109. Colorado Springs, CO:NavPress.

24. *Got Questions*. (n.d.). "Book of Jasher." Retrieved from https://www.gotquestions.org/book-of-Jasher.html

25. Wiersbe, W. (1996). *Be Strong*, p. 139. New York, NY: Victor Books.

26. Wiersbe, W. (1996). *Be Strong*, p.139. New York, NY: Victor Books.

27. Jackman, D. (2014). *Joshua*, p. 125. Wheaton, IL: Crossway.

28. Keller, P. (1992). *Joshua: Mighty Warrior and Man of Faith*, p. 132-133. Grand Rapids, MI: Kregal Publications.

29. Thorp, K. (1988). *Joshua,* p. 111. Colorado Springs, CO:NavPress.

30. Wiersbe, W. (1996). *Be Strong*, p. 144. New York, NY: Victor Books.

31. Woudstra, M. (1981). *The Book of Joshua*, p. 196. Grand Rapids, MI: Eerdmans Publishing Company.

32. Wiersbe, W. (1996). *Be Strong*, p. 144. New York, NY: Victor Books.

33. Refers to scenes from *The Lord of the Rings* movies directed by Peter Jackson.

34. Jackman, D. (2014). *Joshua*, p. 104. Wheaton, IL: Crossway.

35. Quote is commonly credited to Leon Trotsky.

36. Guzik, D. (2024). *Enduring Word Commentary*, Retrieved from

37. Ingram, C. (2006). *The Invisible War*, p. 140. Grand Rapids, MI: Baker Books.

38. Vine, W.E. (1970). *Vine's Complete Expository Dictionary,* p. 683. Nashville, TN: Thomas Nelson.

39. Ingram, C. (2006). *The Invisible War*, p. 141. Grand Rapids, MI: Baker Books.

Lesson Seven

1. Ortlund, D. (2021). *Deeper: Real Change for Real Sinners*, p. 160. Wheaton, IL: Crossway.

2. Vine, W.E. (1970). *Vine's Complete Expository Dictionary,* p. 182. Nashville, TN: Thomas Nelson.

3. Wiersbe, W. (1982). *Be Strong*, pp. 144-145. Colorado Springs, CO: David C. Cook.

4. Wiersbe, W. (1982). *Be Strong*, p. 146. Colorado Springs, CO: David C. Cook.

5. Wiersbe, W. (1982). *Be Strong*, p. 147. Colorado Springs, CO: David C. Cook.

6. Guzik, D. *Enduring Word Commentary*. Retrieved from https://enduringword.com/bible-commentary/joshua-13/

7. Wiersbe, W. (1982). *Be Strong*, p. 146. Colorado Springs, CO: David C. Cook.

8. *ESV Study Bible*. (2008). p. 417. Wheaton, IL: Crossway.

9. *ESV Study Bible*. (2008). p. 417. Wheaton, IL: Crossway.

10. Smith, R. (2023). *Exalting Jesus in Joshua (Christ-Centered Exposition Commentary)*, Kindle Edition, pp. 169-170. Brentwood, TN: B&H Publishing.

11. *Gotquestions.org*. (n.d.). Retrieved from https://www.gotquestions.org/Hebron-in-the-Bible.html

12. Wiersbe, W. (1982). *Be Strong*, p. 148. Colorado Springs, CO: David C. Cook.

13. Smith, R. (2023). *Exalting Jesus in Joshua (Christ-Centered Exposition Commentary)*, Kindle Edition, p. 179. Brentwood, TN: B&H Publishing.

14. McConville, J. G. (2013). *Joshua: Crossing Divides*, p. 69. Sheffield: Sheffield Phoenix.

15. Guzik, D. *Enduring Word Commentary*. Retrieved from https://enduringword.com/bible-commentary/joshua-15

16. Ortlund, D. (2021). *Deeper: Real Change for Real Sinners*, p. 18. Wheaton, IL: Crossway.

17. *ESV Study Bible*. (2008). pp. 419-420. Wheaton, IL: Crossway.

18. *Gotquestions.org* (n.d.) Retrieved from https://www.gotquestions.org/tribe-of-Joseph.html

19. Gotquestions.org (n.d.) Retrieved from https://www.gotquestions.org/twelve-tribes-Israel.html

20. Wiersbe, W. (1982). *Be Strong*, p. 150. Colorado Springs: David C. Cook.

21. Pastor of Bellevue Baptist, Steve Gaines, often uses this phrase in sermons.

22. From lecture by Katie McCoy, "Old Testament Cultural Backgrounds." *Lifeway Women's Academy*.

23. Wiersbe, W. (1982). *Be Strong*, p. 150. Colorado Springs, CO: David C. Cook.

24. Ortlund, D. (2021). *Deeper: Real Change for Real Sinners*, p. 49. Wheaton, IL: Crossway.

25. Thomas, I. (1989). *The Saving Life of Christ*, p. 136. Grand Rapids, MI: Zondervan Publishers.

Lesson Eight

1. Keller, W. P. (1992). *Joshua: Mighty Warrior and Man of Faith*, p. 152. Grand Rapids, MI: Kregel Publications.

2. Riggleman, H. (2021). "What Christians Should Know about Shiloh in the Bible." *Crosswalk*. https://www.crosswalk.com/faith/bible-study/what-christians-should-know-about-shiloh-in-the-bible.html.

3. *Bible Hub*. (n.d.). "Strong's Concordance." Retrieved from https://biblehub.com/hebrew/7951.htm

4. *Bible Hub*. (n.d.). "Strong's Concordance." Retrieved from https://biblehub.com/hebrew/7886.htm

5. Riggleman, H. (2021). "What Christians Should Know about Shiloh in the Bible." *Crosswalk*. https://www.crosswalk.com/faith/bible-study/what-christians-should-know-about-shiloh-in-the-bible.html.

6. Wiersbe, W. (1993). *Be Strong: Putting God's Power to Work in Your Life*, p. 152. Colorado Springs, CO: David C. Cook.

7. McGee, J. V. (1982). *Thru the Bible with J. Vernon McGee* (Vol. II), p. 33. Nashville, TN: Thomas Nelson Publishers.

8. *Got Questions*. (n.d.). "What was the practice of casting lots?" Retrieved from https://www.gotquestions.org/casting-lots.html

9. *Life Application Study Bible, New Living Translation*, p. 223. (2007). Carol Stream, IL: Tyndale House Publishers, Inc.

10. *Life Application Study Bible, New Living Translation*, p. 452. (2007). Carol Stream, IL: Tyndale House Publishers, Inc.

11. *Inspired Scripture*. (n.d.). "Joshua 18: Lessons from the Inheritance of the Last Seven Tribes and Benjamin." Retrieved from https://inspiredscripture.com/bible-studies/joshua-18#gsc.tab=0

12. Smith, R. (2023). *Christ Centered Exposition Commentary: Exalting Jesus in Joshua*, p. 196. Nashville, TN: B&H Publishing.

13. *Life Application Study Bible, New Living Translation*, p. 452. (2007). Carol Stream, IL: Tyndale House Publishers, Inc.

14. Wiersbe, W. (1993). *Be Strong: Putting God's Power to Work in Your Life*, p. 180. Colorado Springs, CO: David C. Cook.

15. Schaeffer, F. (2004). *Joshua and the Flow of Biblical History*, p. 180, 181. Wheaton, IL: Crossway.

16. McGee, J. V. (1982*). Thru the Bible with J. Vernon McGee* (Vol. II), p. 34. Nashville, TN: Thomas Nelson Publishers.

17. Keller, W. P. (1992). *Joshua: Mighty Warrior and Man of Faith*, p. 151. Grand Rapids, MI: Kregel Publications.

18. Keller, W. P. (1992). *Joshua: Mighty Warrior and Man of Faith*, p. 152. Grand Rapids, MI: Kregel Publications.

19. Keller, W. P. (1992). *Joshua: Mighty Warrior and Man of Faith*, p. 153, 154. Grand Rapids, MI: Kregel Publications.

20. You may want to take a few moments and look back to Exodus 21:12-14, Numbers 35, and Deuteronomy 4:41-43, 19:1-13. In these passages, you will see where this plan was first mentioned, and then explicit directions laid out on how to establish these cities.

21. Guzik, D. (n.d.). "Joshua 20." *Enduring Word*. Retrieved from https://enduringword.com/bible-commentary/joshua-20/

22. Schaeffer, F. (2004). *Joshua and the Flow of Biblical History*, p. 200. Wheaton, IL: Crossway.

23. Smith, R. (2023). *Christ Centered Exposition Commentary: Exalting Jesus in Joshua*, p. 203. Nashville, TN: B&H Publishing.

24. Schaeffer, F. (2004). *Joshua and the Flow of Biblical History*, p. 204, 205. Wheaton, IL: Crossway.

25. "Refuge." (n.d.). *Merriam-Webster*. Retrieved from https://www.merriam-webster.com/dictionary/refuge

26. *AZ Lyrics*. (n.d.). "Refuge." Retrieved from https://www.azlyrics.com/lyrics/shaneshane/refuge.html

27. Wiersbe, W. (1993). *Be Strong: Putting God's Power to Work in Your Life*, p. 156. Colorado Springs, CO: David C. Cook.

28. *Life Application Study Bible, New Living Translation*, p. 457. (2007). Carol Stream, IL: Tyndale House Publishers, Inc.

29. *Got Questions*. (n.d.). "Who were the Kohathites, Gershonites, and Merarites?" Retrieved from https://www.gotquestions.org/Kohathites-Gershonites-Merarites.html

30. Guzik, D. (n.d.). "Joshua 21." *Enduring Word. Retrieved from* https://enduringword.com/bible-commentary/joshua-21/

31. Huffman, J. (2002). *Joshua: The Preacher's Commentary (Vol. 6), p. 228*. Nashville, TN: Thomas Nelson Publishers.

32. Guzik, D. (n.d.). "Joshua 21." *Enduring Word. Retrieved from* https://enduringword.com/bible-commentary/joshua-21/

33. *Bible Hub*. (n.d.). "Strong's Concordance." Retrieved from https://biblehub.com/hebrew/5117.htm

34. Wiersbe, W. (1993). *Be Strong: Putting God's Power to Work in Your Life*, p. 157. Colorado Springs, CO: David C. Cook.

35. Logan, J. (1995). *Reclaiming Surrendered Ground*. Chicago, IL: Moody Publishers.

36. *Hymnal.net*. (n.d.). "The Love of God." Retrieved from https://www.hymnal.net/en/hymn/h/28

37. *Got Questions*. (n.d.). "What did Jesus mean when He promised an abundant life?" Retrieved from https://www.gotquestions.org/abundant-life.html

38. Logan, J. (1995). *Reclaiming Surrendered Ground*, p. 42. Chicago, IL: Moody Publishers.

39. Logan, J. (1995). *Reclaiming Surrendered Ground*, p. 159. Chicago, IL: Moody Publishers.

40. Redpath, A. quoted in Guzik, D. (n.d.). "Joshua 21." *Enduring Word. Retrieved from* https://enduringword.com/bible-commentary/joshua-21/

Lesson Nine

1. Moody, D.L. (n.d.). *The Home Work of D.L. Moody*. Retrieved from http://www.swartzentrover.com/cotor/E-Books/holiness/Moody/HomeWork/THW_04.htm

2. Schaeffer, F. (2004). Joshua and the Flow of Biblical History, p. 182. Wheaton, IL: Crossway.

3. Wiersbe, W. (1993). *Be Strong: Putting God's Power to Work in Your Life*, p. 162. Colorado Springs, CO: David C. Cook.

4. Spence, H.D.M. (1950). *The Pulpit Commentary, Vol. 3: Deuteronomy, Joshua, and Judges*, p. 315. New York, NY: Funk and Wagnalls Company.

5. Wiersbe, W. (1993). *Be Strong: Putting God's Power to Work in Your Life*, p. 163. Colorado Springs, CO: David C. Cook.

6. Wiersbe, W. (1993). *Be Strong: Putting God's Power to Work in Your Life*, p. 163. Colorado Springs, CO: David C. Cook.

7. Vine, W.E. (1970). *Vine's Complete Expository Dictionary,* p. 37. Nashville, TN: Thomas Nelson.

8. Wiersbe, W. (1993). *Be Strong: Putting God's Power to Work in Your Life*, p. 164. Colorado Springs, CO: David C. Cook.

9. Wiersbe, W. (1993). *Be Strong: Putting God's Power to Work in Your Life*, p. 164. Colorado Springs, CO: David C. Cook.

10. Wiersbe, W. (1993). *Be Strong: Putting God's Power to Work in Your Life*, p. 165. Colorado Springs, CO: David C. Cook.

11. Tenney, M.C. (1967). *Pictorial Bible Dictionary,* p. 752. Grand Rapids, MI: Zondervan Publishing House.

12. Spence, H.D.M. (1950). *The Pulpit Commentary, Vol. 3: Deuteronomy, Joshua, and Judges*, p. 319. New York, NY: Funk and Wagnalls Company.

13. Schaeffer, F. (2004). *Joshua and the Flow of Biblical History*, p. 183. Wheaton, IL: Crossway.

14. Warner, M. and J. Wilder. (2016). *Rare Leadership*. Chicago, IL: Moody Publishers.

15. Warner, M. and J. Wilder. (2016). *Rare Leadership*, p. 130. Chicago, IL: Moody Publishers.

16. Warner, M. and J. Wilder. (2016). *Rare Leadership*, p. 142. Chicago, IL: Moody Publishers.

17. Wiersbe, W. (1993). *Be Strong: Putting God's Power to Work in Your Life*, p. 165. Colorado Springs, CO: David C. Cook.

18. Comer, J. (2004). *Practicing the Way*, p. 26. Colorado Springs, CO, Waterbrook.

19. Comer, J. (2004). *Practicing the Way*, p. 27. Colorado Spring, CO: Waterbrook.

20. Wiersbe, W. (1993). *Be Strong: Putting God's Power to Work in Your Life*, p. 169. Colorado Springs, CO: David C. Cook.

21. Gunter, S. (2023). *Daily Spirit Blessings*. Kindle.

Lesson Ten

1. Tozer, A.W. (2016). *How to Be Filled with the Holy Spirit*, p. 41. Chicago, IL: Moody Bible.

2. *Britannica.com.* (n.d.). Retrieved from: https://www.google.com/search?client =safari&rls=en&q=what+was+life+like+for+the+Israelites+agter+they+had+conquered+Canaan&ie=UTF-8&oe=UTF-8"Timnath-serah." (2008). *Zondervan Bible Dictionary*, p. 855. Grand Rapids, MI: Zondervan.

3. Simpson, A.B. (n.d.). *Christ in the Book of Joshua*. Retrieved from https://worthychristianbooks.com/ab-simpson/christ-in-the-book-of-joshua/chapter-10-timnath-serah-or-the-city-of-the-sun/#:~:text=Its%20name%20is%20suggestive %20of,of%20our%20own%20Christian%20life

4. Keller, P. (1992). *Joshua: Mighty Warrior and Man of Faith*, p. 166. Grand Rapids, MI: Kregal Publications.

5. Smith, R. (2023). *Exalting Jesus in Joshua*, p. 229. Brentwood, TN: B&H Publishing Group.

6. *Hymnary.org.* (n.d.). "Come thou Fount of Every Blessing." Retrieved from https://hymnary.org/text/come_thou_fount_of_every_blessing

7. *Blueletterbible.org* (n.d.). Retrieved from https://www.blueletterbible.org /lexicon/h1692/nasb95/wlc/0-1/

8. Gangel, K.O. (2002). *Joshua*, p. 298. Nashville, TN: B&H Publishing Group.

9. Ironside, H. (2008). *Joshua*, p. 137. Grand Rapids, MI: Kregel Publications.

10. Ellsworth, R. (2008). *Opening up Joshua*, p. 112. Carlise, PA: Day One Publications.

11. Anders, M; Gangel, K. (2002). *Joshua*, p. 301. Brentwood, TN: B&H Publishing Group.

12. *Enduringword.com* (n.d.). Retrieved from https://enduringword.com/bible-commentary/joshua-24/#:~:text=There are some people who,ii

13. Wiersbe, W. (1996). *Be Strong*, p. 150. New York, NY: Victor Books.

14. Keller, P. (1992). *Joshua: Mighty Warrior and Man of Faith*, p. 167. Grand Rapids, MI: Kregal Publications.

15. *Enduringword.com* (n.d.). Retrieved from: https://enduringword.com/bible-commentary/joshua-24/)

16. *BlueletterBible.org*, Easton's Bible Dictionary (n.d.). Retrieved from https://www.biblestudytools.com/dictionary/zorah/

17. Keller, P. (1992). *Joshua: Mighty Warrior and Man of Faith*, p. 168. Grand Rapids, MI: Kregal Publications.

18. Keller, P. (1992). *Joshua: Mighty Warrior and Man of Faith*, p. 168. Grand Rapids, MI: Kregal Publications.

19. Ellsworth, R. (2008). *Opening up Joshua*, pp. 119-120. Carlisle, PA: Day One Publications.

20. Gangel, K.O. (2002). *Joshua*, p. 317. Nashville, TN: B&H Publishing Group.

Made in the USA
Columbia, SC
13 January 2025